FAMILY DESIGN

FAMILY DESIGN

Marital sexuality, family size, and contraception

LEE RAINWATER

ALDINE PUBLISHING COMPANY | CHICAGO

HQ 10
R 15

Acknowledgments

THIS STUDY was sponsored by the Planned Parenthood Federation of America, Inc. — World Population Emergency Campaign. I am grateful to Planned Parenthood for its continued support of research begun in an earlier pilot study. The findings and interpretations reported here are, however, the sole responsibility of the author and should not be taken as reflecting the policies or points of view of Planned Parenthood, or of individuals who have given me the benefit of their critical advice.

The Social Science Committee of Planned Parenthood, under its Chairman, Edward Solomon, provided helpful criticism and encouragement in the initial planning stages of the study, as did Ronald Freedman and the late P. K. Whelpton. Arthur A. Campbell, Steven Polgar, Margaret Snyder, Christopher Tietze and Charles Westoff were kind enough to read various portions of the manuscript and give me their critical comments. I have been helped by these comments, as well as by the example of their own work on family planning and limitation.

The data for the study were collected by Social Research Services, Inc. I am grateful to Mrs. Leone Phillips, its President, and to her associates, Hannah Bratman and Cynthia Fennander, for supervising the field work. Needless to add, I owe a great debt to the interviewers, whose persistence and resourcefulness in handling a difficult assignment contributed immeasurably to the study. There are too many of them to mention by name, but to all of them, my thanks.

Finally, I wish to thank my wife, Carol Kampel Rainwater, for her work in preparing the index, and for other wifely facilitations during the writing of this book.

Lee Rainwater

Contents

FAMILY DESIGN

1

Introduction

THE QUESTION of the number of children they will have is a vital, complex, deeply involving one for American couples. Though some couples maintain an attitude of fatalism and vague hopefulness about the size their families may eventually reach, most give a good deal of active consideration to the number of children they really want and can afford (psychologically, socially, economically) and to ways of achieving this goal. In doing so couples deal with many kinds of conflicts — conflicts between their own views and those they feel society offers as appropriate, conflicts between themselves, mixed feelings within themselves. These conflicts can apply to both the question of the family size preferred and to the means for seeing that preference becomes a reality. Some couples experience all of this in a context of not being able to have all of the children they want, but most are concerned with the problem of not having more children than they want.

With respect to family size preferences, a couple's problem is essentially that of coming to some successful resolution of (1) each individual's desires with those of his partner, and (2) their joint desires with their perception of the society's norms about family size. The technology for accomplishing these goals, contraception, does not make the task easy — no method now on the market is regarded as really perfect, each makes demands on the user, each has certain difficulties people would like to avoid, and all have the disadvantage of reminding one of the unfortunate necessity to limit and coerce nature, and of the necessity for being rational about such private and disturbing aspects of the human state as sexual relations and the genitals. Almost all of the methods are known to be imperfect in their effectiveness, which introduces a very disturbing note of uncertainly into what is already an emotionally complex situation. In sum, the individual husband or wife is confronted with

1. a demanding social task of integrating personal, marital, and cultural demands about an appropriate number of children
2. by means which require conscious attention to usually avoided sexual aspects of marital living
3. and by means which, furthermore, are believed to have an alarming potential to fall short of 100 per cent effectiveness.

All of this becomes important when considering problems of encouraging effective family planning because each of the difficulties and challenges enumerated above can repercuss on the use and choice of contraceptive methods. Attitudes having to do with feelings about how many children one should have can affect contraceptive behavior, as when a couple resolves differences between them in desired family size by having "accidents" which are then blamed on the method, or chooses a highly reliable method only after having enough children to feel above social criticism and thus keep peace in the family. Similarly, couples who choose a method they regard as not 100 per cent effective may end up practicing the method rather carelessly on the ground that "it's not much good anyway" (this often happens with rhythm). And attitudes and feelings about sexual relations and the genitals can condition both the choice of contraceptive method and the care in practicing it.

Most of these themes can be seen in the following discussion by a woman in her early thirties who has four children.

> I have a daughter who was born in 1949, and a son born in 1951, and then in 1953 we had another daughter and finally we had our youngest, a boy, in 1955. [Do you want more?] Heavens, no! I'm 34 and my husband is getting close to 40. I like to be young with my children and enjoy them, and since we got married so darned young I want time alone later. My husband's in complete agreement with me. With the high cost of education and the necessity of having a child go to college we would be foolish to have more. I used a diaphragm before and after our children were born until I started using the pill (about three years ago). I hated the diaphragm and so did my husband—it was messy and miserable. I'm so glad we have the pill. We both have complete faith in it. It is such a convenient thing to pop a pill in your mouth every morning. I'm completely sold on it.

An interest in children and a concern with parenthood seem universals of the human condition. Most men and women in all cultures are concerned with themselves as parents and with how their children fare. Parenthood is thus a deeply significant biological, psychological, and social fact of life. As such, the dynamics of parenthood and child training have been central concerns of all of the behavioral sciences from their inceptions; a great deal of the total research effort of psychology, sociology, and anthropology in recent decades has been concerned in one way or another with having and rearing children, whether the particular concern be child rearing practices, socialization to adult roles, intellectual or personality or moral development, mental health problems, processes of identification, or any of a number of other possible specifications of the general question of parent-child relations and the development of children into adult members of their society.

It is all the more curious then, that, aside from demographers, social scientists have shown only a casual interest in how couples come to have the particular number of chil-

dren they have, and in the consequences of having a particular number of children. While the ethnographer may note
in passing the value a group places on having many children,
or the child-training specialist may comment upon the importance of older siblings in socializing the child, there has been
little concentrated attention devoted to *number* as an important variable in how parents and children live their lives.
(There has been somewhat more concern among psychologists
with *order* of birth as this affects life experiences.)

In the last few years social realities at home and abroad
have focused increasing attention on this question of number
of children. As the death rate has declined in underdeveloped
parts of the world, the absence of a similar decline in birth
rates has meant that family size and population have grown
rapidly, effectively slowing the rate of economic growth at
the same time that appetites for a higher standard of living
and greater national strength have burgeoned. Concern over
these facts has led to a recent increase in research efforts to
understand the dynamics of family size, and to practical programs intended to encourage couples in underdeveloped lands
to limit their families. It seems clear that both research and
practical programs will be greatly increased in the next few
years as fear of the "population explosion" mounts.

Meanwhile, in the United States, the dramatic postwar
"baby boom" focused interest on the factors behind the
apparent change toward large families. More recently, an
increasing awareness of the problem of "residual" and apparently ineradicable poverty, coupled with the knowledge
that poor couples are those most likely to have more children than they can support or want, has directed interest to
this group's family size norms and family planning behavior.
While there is now in this country little sense of great urgency
about domestic population problems, there is nevertheless a
growing awareness that a prosperous economy is not immune
to the problems of having to support too many people.

It is a mistake, however, to regard research on these subjects as simply an exercise in the application of social science

to a practical problem. Much can be learned about families that is of basic social psychological interest from an examination of the ways husbands and wives cope with the biological facts of procreation, the processes of goal formation and decision making concerning family size, the motives that operate to condition family size goals and the choice of methods to achieve these goals. The choices couples make in their efforts to control conception have a fatefulness for their lives together that few other choices in marriage have. The ways they make these choices, just as much as the choices themselves, focus a strong light on the inner working of the family as a social system, and on the individual personalities of its heads. Studies of family planning and limitation offer promise as a testing ground for theories about family functioning, and as a fertile field for discovering insights into the forces and processes which operate as men and women design and build families.

This study has two main focuses: First, what are the factors that lie behind the goals of family size that people set for themselves and what are the social norms they apply in evaluating their own and other people's family sizes; second, what factors affect the effectiveness with which couples apply family limitation methods, if any, to achieve their own family size goals. With respect to the latter, this study tests some of the hypotheses advenced in an earlier study (Rainwater, 1960). With respect to the first goal, we have sought to develop an understanding of family size norms and goals without clearly formulated prior hypotheses.

As will be apparent in the discussion of method and sample that follows, this study must be regarded as exploratory, though based on a somewhat larger sample than the earlier study mentioned above, and following a more structured approach to the analysis of data. Some of the findings reported here are similar to those developed by other researchers; others have not been observed before, or have been observed only to be discarded as unsupported by adequate data. In any case, although we have avoided a reiteration of tentativeness in what follows. the findings reported here should be understood as suggestive and subject to revision after more intensive study and more extensive sampling. The questions are complex enough, however, for this to be inevitable for any single study; more secure knowledge about family size and family limitation can come only from a multiplicity of research efforts.

The study sample

The research is based on interviews with 409 individuals — 95 of these interviews were also used in an earlier study (Rainwater, 1960). One hundred and fifty-two couples, and 50 men and 55 women not married to each other were interviewed. Thus, 257 families are represented. The interviews averaged $2\frac{1}{4}$ hours in length for each respondent. Of the couples interviewed, in 53 per cent of the cases the husband and wife were interviewed at the same time. This allowed some check on the extent to which interviews with husbands and wives at different times created a bias in the later interview because of prior discussions between the spouses. We found no evidence in our analysis that the responses of those couples not interviewed simultaneously differed in any systematic way from those of couples interviewed at the same time. (This does not mean, however, that a study which seeks more precise quantitative measures of the variables under study could safely ignore the desirability of simultaneous interviews.) Of the total number of families included in the sample (257), the majority (185) lived in Chicago, forth-five lived in Cincinnati, and 32 in Oklahoma City.

The interviews were selected by a purposive sampling method organized around quotas for class and religion groupings. We sought approximately equal numbers of interviews from whites of the upper-middle, lower-middle, upper-lower, and lower-lower classes, and from Negroes of the upper-lower and lower-lower classes (budget limitations prevented our interviewing middle class Negroes). Within each of the white class groups, we established quotas for Catholics and non-Catholics. In order to assure some correspondence in family stage of the couples in each of these groups, quotas were set for each in terms of the age and duration of marriage.

Class, race, and religion, then, represent the three main variables in which we are interested. By limiting the sample to couples in which the wife was under forty years of age and by achieving a fairly matched balance in terms of stages of the family cycle within each of these groups, we sought to highlight whatever influence these factors, and the characteristics of the marital relationship related to them, have on family size preferences and family planning behavior.

Table 1 – 1 indicates some of the social and familial characteristics of our sample in each of the four social class groups for whites and two social class groups for Negroes. From the table it is apparent that these class-race groups are fairly comparable in terms of number of years of marriage except in the case of lower-lower class Negroes. The biasing effect of this latter group's having been married longer is offset somewhat, however, by the fact that separations are more common in the group; the difference in median number of years of cohabitation with a husband would be less than the difference shown in the table.

The four social classes that concern us in this study may be briefly characterized as follows:

The upper-middle class is composed of the families of professionals, executives, and business proprietors who are established in their occupations, who exercise important authority in their professional and business organizations, and who generally earn well above average incomes from these activities. The incomes of some of the professionals average quite a bit below those of the business executives and proprietors, but they are accorded similar prestige because of the value placed on their advanced training, autonomy, and learned activities. Upper-middle class families live in resi-

TABLE 1-1:
CHARACTERISTICS OF THE STUDY SAMPLE

		Whites				Negroes	
		Upper-Middle	Lower-Middle	Upper-Lower	Lower-Lower	Upper-Lower	Lower-Lower
		(34)*	(35)*	(61)*	(73)*	(24)*	(39)*
Type of Interview							
Couple	(N=)	26	28	22	24	24	28
Husband only	(N=)	4	4	16	26	–	–
Wife only	(N=)	4	3	23	23	1	1
Total							
individuals	(N=)	60	63	83	97	49	57
Religion							
Protestant		53%	48%	42%	53%	88%	97%
Catholic		23	49	46	33	12	3
Jewish		9	3	3	–	–	–
Mixed, wife							
Catholic		12	–	7	7	–	–
Mixed, husband							
Catholic		3	–	2	7	–	–
Husband's Education							
College graduate		71%	43%	–	–	8%	–
Some college		9	23	7	–	20	–
High school							
graduate		9	20	30	–	28	3
Some high school		–	9	39	30	32	35
Grade school							
graduate		3	–	7	26	8	3
Some grade school		–	–	8	37	–	55
No information		8	5	9	7	4	4
Wife's Education							
College graduate		41%	23%	2%	–	–	–
Some college		35	17	5	–	12	–
High school							
graduate		15	46	36	6	44	17
Some high school		–	9	43	40	32	48
Grade school							
graduate		–	–	3	29	4	17
Some grade school		–	–	8	22	4	17
No information		9	5	3	3	4	–
Median Income		$13,300	$8,900	$5,100	$4,700	$5,900	$3,900
Husband's Median Age		32.0	31.8	32.3	32.1	31.7	35.5
Wife's Median Age		28.0	30.1	25.8	27.4	27.7	29.1
Median Years Married		6.8	6.8	5.4	8.0	8.6	12.2
Mean No. of Children		1.3	1.8	1.6	2.7	2.8	3.5
Four or more children		15%	20%	21%	40%	40%	58%

*Number of families – not individuals – represented in the sample.

dential areas that are well above average in reputation and regard themselves as the better educated and more sophisticated group in their communities. They take it for granted that their children (both sons and daughters) will complete college, and that the sons will probably continue into graduate or professional schools. They tend to be quite active in voluntary associations, and to provide the leadership for these groups. A majority of the upper-middle class men in our sample are under 33 years of age, so it should be noted that they are just beginning their careers, are on the way toward mature responsibility at upper-middle class occupational levels, and see before them at least twenty years of career advancement and hard work to achieve it. (This is in strong contrast to most of the lower class respondents who, at the same age level, see their own work futures as not dramatically different from their present activities and responsibilities.) About 12 per cent of the population in a city like Chicago can be classified as belonging to this class.

The lower-middle class is composed of the families of white-collar workers who do not exercise important managerial or autonomous professional authority, and of the families of skilled workers and foremen who, though engaged in "blue-collar" work, live in a way that conforms to the model set by the white-collar portion of the group. Most of these men and women graduated from high school, and quite a few of the men completed college. Their education, however was not directed to the higher managerial or professional activities of the upper-middle class. They are engaged, instead, in more routinized occupations, as accountants, engineers, supervisors of clerical workers, etc. Lower-middle class families live in good, average neighborhoods in houses or apartments which they strive to maintain in attractive and respectable ways, but they do not place emphasis on sophistication and organized good taste. Their organizational activity is not as extensive as that of the upper-middle class and they participate more as followers than as leaders (except in organizations that do not include upper-middle class members). About 29 per cent of Chicago's population falls in this group.

The upper and lower portions of the working class include the majority of the population in most urban areas.

The upper-lower class includes the larger portion of the group (46 per cent) of Chicago's total population) and is characterized by greater prosperity and stability than the lower-lower class. Upper-lower class workers generally are in semi-skilled and medium-skilled work; they are in manual occupations or in responsible but not highly regarded service jobs such as policemen, firemen, or bus drivers. They have generally had at least some high school education. Their families live in reasonably comfortable housing, in neighborhoods composed mainly of other manual and lower-level service workers. Although people in this group tend today to regard themselves as living the good life of average Americans, they are still aware that they do not have as much social status or prestige as the middle class white-collar worker or the highly-skilled technician and factory foreman.

The lower-lower class represents approximately one-quarter of the working class and about 13 per cent of the population of a city like Chicago. The people in this group are very much aware that they do not participate fully in the good life of the average American; they feel at the "bottom of the heap" and consider themselves at a disadvantage in seeking the goods that the society has to offer. They generally work at unskilled jobs, and often they work only intermittently or are chronically unemployed. Few people in this group have graduated from high school, and a great many have gone no further than grammar school. They live in slum and near-slum neighborhoods, and their housing tends to be cramped and deteriorated. Although many earn fairly good wages when they work ($75 to $100 per week is not uncommon), the seasonal or intermittent nature of their jobs and their relatively impulsive spending habits often prevent them from maintaining what most Americans regard as a "decent" standard of living.

Method of analysis

As Davis and Blake (1956) have noted, fertility in modern Western society has come to be very much a function of contraceptive practice, and the factors that operate in other societies to lower fertility are no longer relevant. Thus, although in the nineteenth century, postponement of marriage was important in keeping family size within tolerable limits (Banks, 1954), even this custom seems to have become superfluous in our time. Of all of the possible voluntary influences on fertility, only contraception seems really important in our own society, and variations in fertility from time to time or group to group can be understood as in large part due to the practice or non-practice of contraceptive methods. This practice, in turn, is a function both of a desire for children and of an ability to practice contraception effectively. We are concerned in this study with both these aspects of family limitation, voluntary abstention from contraception because pregnancy is desired, and abstention from or ineffective practice of contraception that arises from factors other than desired family size. Of the many different factors that can directly affect the fertility of a couple, our interviews and analysis focus sharply on only one, contraception, and consider two intervening variables most closely connected with it: the desire for more children, and the ability to engage in contraceptive practice in ways that maximize the chance of realizing these desires.

The interviews collected were open-ended and conversational in nature, rather than structured (see Appendix B). Respondents were encouraged to express themselves freely and fully on a series of topics raised by the interviewer. These ranged during the interview from one general area to the next in the following order; number of children born to wife, general discussion of the marriage, of the responsibilities, and personal qualities of husband and wife, and of problems the couple had met in the marriage; discussion of family size ideals, the couple's own desires in terms of number of children, ideas about why couples want large and small families; contraceptive experiences and attitudes and feelings about medical resources for contraceptive advice; and, finally, discussion of sexual relations in the marriage.

The interviews from the previous study covered essentially these same topics, and in the same order, except that information on family size norms and values were not collected in detail (we only asked how many children the individual considered ideal, and how many he himself wanted). Thus, the sample base for the tabular material in the following chapters varies depending on whether the data were available for the total sample or only for the interviews collected as part of our second study. (In addition, there are minor variations from table to table due to the fact that in this kind of unstructured interviewing the interviewers do not always elicit answers to each question.)

The method of analysis followed in this study is basically qualitative and interpretive in the sense that we sought patterns in the interview data from reading rather than from statistical manipulation. However, we have tried to code the more important factual material and interpretations, and to present the findings in tabular form as well as in qualitative discussion. In the coding process, the interviews were taken apart and each of their major segments (the topics outlined above) were coded separately; all of the information for one segment was coded for all interviews, then the next segment was coded, and so on. Since this process took several months, and since the researcher could not possibly remember a respondent's answers to one set of items by the time he coded the same respondent on the next set, it is unlikely that the interpretation of material on one topic affected the interpretation of other materials. After the coding process was completed, the interviews were read on a case basis, so that a qualitative analysis of the interrelations among areas was also possible. It is important to note that the investigator's coded interpretations of individual cases are only his own individual interpretation of the data; had our budget allowed, it would, of course, have been desirable to work with one or more researchers who would follow the same coding process and thus allow for a reliability check.

In the tables presented in the following chapters, two statistical measures have been used where appropriate to call attention to questions of statistical significance and degree of association. One is the "chi-square test" (corrected for continuity), which indicates the probability of the existence of an association between the variables being tested; the other is Tschuprow's "T coefficient," which indicates the degree of association between two variables (Hagood, 1941). This latter measure varies from zero to one, from no association to perfect association, and is standardized for sample size and degrees of freedom. In a few cases where the sample sizes are too small for the chi-square test to be calculated, Fisher's "exact test" has been used to test for significance of association (Pearson and Hartley, 1958).

2
Social class and
conjugal role-relationships

CONJUGAL LIFE is a highly variegated and complex experience, and each of its aspects can be examined in great detail; only a careful evaluation of the many aspects of family interaction can present a really full and valid picture of family life. Noting that "the general functional problems facing the family are analogous to those facing the society as a whole," Bell and Vogel (1960:19ff.) delineate four broad functional problems of activity within the nuclear family: (1) task performance, (2) family leadership, (3) integration and solidarity, and (4) pattern maintainence. Hess and Handel (1959:4) outline five overlapping major processes that "give shape to the flux of family life": (1) establishing a pattern of separateness and connectedness, (2) establishing a satisfactory congruence of images through the exchange of suitable testimony, (3) evolving modes of interaction into central family concerns or theses, (4) establishing the boundaries of the family's world of experience, and (5) dealing with significant biosocial issues of family life. Studying total families with these kinds of questions in mind is obviously a large order and beyond the scope and practical requirements of the present study.

Conjugal role-relationships

However, one central characteristic of families which differentiates them from each other and has important consequences for their actions lies in the nature of the role-relationship between husband and wife — their typical ways of organizing the performance of tasks, their reciprocal expectations, their characteristic ways of communicating, and the kind of solidarity that exists between them. We will take the concept of conjugal role-relationship as central in our characterization of the family life of the couples studied. We will use it to organize our presentation in this chapter of variations in marital relations from class to class, and in later chapters to shed light on the psychosocial background of large and small family preferences, effective and ineffective contraceptive practice, and choice of contraceptive method.

Following Bott (1957:3), we mean by a conjugal role-relationship those aspects of the relationship between husband and wife that consist of reciprocal role expectations and the activities of each spouse in relation to the other. Thus, a characterization of the conjugal role-relationship of a particular couple would involve many of the dimensions cited by Bell and Vogel and by Hess and Handel. Patterns of task performance and expectations about it are involved, as are the kinds of family leadership, the solidarity characteristic of couples, and the value systems used to legitimate marital role execution. Separateness and connectedness (one aspect of family solidarity) is an important theme in characterizing the role-relationship, as are the central family concerns and the way the couple establishes boundaries for its world. Consensus (congruence of images) between the partners is significantly conditioned by the acceptance each partner gives to the role-relationship as it has developed in the marriage.

Bott (1957:53 – 55) sees conjugal role-relationships as ranging along a continuum from the "jointly organized" to the "highly segregated." Following her conceptual approach, three

three types of conjugal role-relationships have been used in characterizing the couples in this study:

1) *Joint conjugal role-relationship* refers to relationships in which the predominant pattern of marital life involves activities carried out by husband and wife together (shared) or the same activity carried out by either partner at different times (interchangeable). In these relationships, husband and wife undertake many activities (including recreation as well as task performances) "together with a minimum of task differentiation and separation of interest. They not only plan the affairs of the family together but also exchange many household tasks and spend much of their leisure time together." In discussing family life they stress the value — and not just the functional efficacy — of sharing and the mutual interpenetration of the concern, understanding and interest of each in what the other does. Thus, even where there is a division of labor in task performance — husband as breadwinner and wife as housekeeper — each is expected to be interested in and sympathetic to the other in his assigned duty.

2) *Segregated conjugal role-relationship* refers to relationships in which the predominant pattern of marital life involves activities of husband and wife that are separate and different but fitted together to form a functioning unit or that are carried out separately by husband and wife with a minimum of day-to-day articulation of the activity of each to the other. Among such couples,

> "husband and wife have a clear differentiation of tasks and a considerable number of separate interests and activities. They have a clearly defined division of labour into male tasks and female tasks. They expect to have different leisure pursuits, and the husband has his friends outside the home and the wife has hers (Bott, 1957)."

Such couples tend to emphasize a formal division of labor in the family rather than a solidarity based on interchangeability of role activities, or the indentification and empathy of each with the other's activities and concerns. While too much separateness can be disruptive to the family's stability, such couples do not see the positive value in "togetherness" shown by couples with less segregated conjugal roles.

3) *Intermediate conjugal role-relationship* refers to relationships that are not sharply polarized in either the jointly organized or highly segregated direction. Such couples value sharing and interchangeability of task performance but they do not carry this as far as do the couples with joint relationships. They preserve more of the skeleton of formally organized division of labor, particularly in connection with household tasks other than child rearing (fathers in this group want to be more occupied with the parental role than fathers in more segregated relationships). Among these couples, the statuses "father" or "husband", "mother" or "wife," are still very central to the functioning of the family rather than the somewhat more *pro forma* designations they represent for couples who emphasize joint organization. Among jointly organized couples of the latter type there is instead much more emphasis on husband and wife relating as persons, as individuals, and less as actors of normatively-specified and encompassing roles (cf. Goffman, 1961:150–52). For couples with intermediate relationships, separate leisure time pursuits (particularly evening activities) may be frowned upon and held to a minimum, but this does not carry with it the emphasis on active sharing of such interests that is characteristic of couples with joint relationships. In many ways the paradigm of the intermediate relationship is that of leisure time pursuits dominated by watching TV or reading magazines; the husband and wife amuse themselves alone, do not talk with each other about what they see or read, but still feel that such activities reflect their "togetherness." The integrity of the family is maintained in this way without requiring the couple to meet the emotional demands of joint relating.

The couples in the study sample were categorized in one

of these three types on the basis of their responses to several general questions. They were asked first to tell something about their family life and about the important things that happened during their marriage. Then they were asked how decisions were made in the family, about the main duties of husband and wife, about the interests and activities of each, and each respondent was asked to evaluate how his spouse felt about him. From all of this material a judgment was made as to which of the above three types the couple most closely approximated. Clearly no couple is a pure type; each represents a mixture of joint and segregated relationships, and the classification of a couple indicates simply the preponderant direction of role performances in the family and of the values emphasized by husband and wife in talking about their life together.

A more concrete idea of what these terms denote can be gained from an examination of what couples of each type say about their married life. First, however, an examination of Table 2 – 1 will indicate the variations in the distribution within our sample of conjugal role-relationship types by social class. Joint relationships are characteristic of 88 per cent of the

TABLE 2–1:
SOCIAL CLASS AND CONJUGAL ROLE-RELATIONSHIPS

| | | Role-Relationships | | |
		Joint	Intermediate	Segregated
Upper-middle class	(32)	88%	12%	—
Lower-middle class	(31)	42	58	—
Upper-lower class*				
Whites	(26)	19	58	23%
Negroes	(25)	12	52	36
Lower-lower class*				
Whites	(25)	4	24	72
Negroes	(29)	—	28	72

*Whites and Negroes at each class level combined for test.
$X^2 = 100.34$ df = 6 P < .0005 T = .50

upper-middle class couples, and segregated relationships of 72 per cent of the lower class couples. The two classes between have a more mixed distribution of the types. A majority of the lower-middle class couples have intermediate relationships, but 42 per cent of them share the joint role-relationship pattern that characterizes the upper-middle class. A majority of the upper-lower class couples also have intermediate relationships, but very few have joint relationships, and about one-third of them have highly segregated relationships.

At this broad level of characterization, marital relationships show sharp class differences, particularly in the distinctiveness of upper-middle and lower-lower class patterns. The former overwhelmingly emphasize sharing and joint participation in married life; the latter almost equally strongly emphasize separateness and isolation of the marital partners from each other. As we shall see, this latter pattern is comfortable for some couples and a source of friction for others (usually it is the wife who is unhappy with the segregated state of affairs). The intermediate pattern characterizes the majority of the middle group.*

To exemplify how couples characterized in these three ways speak of their married life we have chosen three couples at the same (upper-lower) class level in order to minimize class differences and highlight differences in the role-relationship.*† The first case is that of a thirty-four year old man and twenty-eight year old woman who have been married a little over a year. They have three children by her former marriage

*Herbert J. Gans, in a recently published study of an Italian-American working class group, notes these same class differences, and in surveying the findings of other studies of working and lower class subcultures he notes that most research on such groups comes to similar conclusions (1962: 50–53, 229 ff.).

†In the balance of this chapter we discuss role-relationships as complex patterns of role expectations and enactments; in Appendix A the reader will find a more detailed discussion of role concepts and of problems in marriage as these vary by social class and role-relationship type.

and she is pregnant. He has had some training as a commercial artist but has worked most recently as a dance instructor. Now they both work part-time while he studies to be a hairdresser. They live in a small apartment which the interviewer describes as bare but nicely maintained. Here is how they speak of their marriage:

The husband:

The most important thing is that there must be a great deal of love and mutual understanding. One other thing is that the husband and wife should have some common interests in activities outside the home. They should have some future goal that they are working for. We are both working now so I can go to school and become a hairdresser. This will give us security which is very important in marriage; insecurity in money matters is probably what people fight over most. A satisfactory adjustment sexually is also important. I don't believe in one person making a decision. I believe that the people involved should have some say in the decision. I would say this is true of us in most areas. My main duty is to be the bread winner; you should make it a duty to do all you can for your family. I've never balked at doing the dishes. Even if the husband is tired he should help. . . . My wife is very nice. She's interested in dancing. She's very generous, understanding in certain areas. She's not as understanding in certain areas like finances but she's certainly not a spendthrift. . . . I'm very artistically inclined and I enjoy all types of sports. I believe I am very understanding and considerate. Sometimes I'm too emotional, with a tendency to drown my sorrows in a couple of beers. Being impulsive is my worst fault. . . . My wife thinks I'm pretty good with the kids. Actually I'm too easy with them, we both are.

The wife:

I guess we're both looking for a future together, and making each other happy. My husband enjoys family life; there was no family life in my first marriage. My first husband made good money but he was never around. . . . My husband gives me his check and I pay the bills. With the children, except when they're very naughty and he tells them to stand in the corner and sees that they stay there, which ever one of us is nearest corrects them. We decide together if we want to go to the beach or go out. We relax together mostly. . . . He's very considerate. He hasn't got many bad points; he can't hurt people even with words. When he gets a bottle of beer he likes to talk. He's the type that anyone can get along with. He's independent, too. . . . I'm impatient and I'm independent. . . . We've had some financial problems but nothing much else. We haven't been married long so he wants lots of attention. He's the type of person who sits down and talks things out when there's a problem before it grows.

Both husband and wife emphasize the twin theme of interchangeability of duties in the home and the importance of sharing interests and gratifications together. The husband is pleased that his wife is interested in dancing, as he is; the wife emphasizes that they want to "make each other happy," unlike the situation in her first marriage. There is probably more conflict between them about their economic situation than either hints at, but both seem to value mutual understanding and working together toward a solution to this problem. It is important to them that they spend time together, either by themselves or with the children. That they have not been married long perhaps encourages the joint relationship ("We haven't been married long so he wants a lot of attention"), but there are other couples in essentially the same situation in which the husband moves into a going household of mother and children and assumes either a segregated male role (often the case among lower-lower class Negroes) or an intermediate role in which little need is felt by either partner for an extended honeymoon period.

A second upper-lower class couple illustrates a segregated relationship. The husband and wife are twenty-three years old, have been married three years and have two children. The husband works as a machinist's helper. Both attended but did not finish high school. They live in a four-room basement apartment that the interviewer found rather dilapidated.

The husband:
I pay the bills and help with the kids when the wife needs help. I fix things around the house. She has to take care of the kids, clean the house, do the wash and like that. She keeps pretty busy. She usually gets the shopping done by herself OK. She's a good mother to the kids. She's a good cook, mostly she does cooking. . . . She's always lending things out which she generally never gets back; she's too good-hearted, people take advantage of her. . . . I like hunting, fishing, swimming. I try to take care of my family. . . . My bad points are going out sometimes and not coming home until late. I don't overdo it I guess, but sometimes I goof up. . . . We've had mother-in-law troubles, that's the main one. I guess you could say we've had money problems, too. We're pretty much over the mother-in-law problem now; she hasn't bothered us too much lately.

The wife:
I worry about the children, the house, the shopping, meals and laundry. . . . My duties are to cook his meals, that's about all. . . . He helps with the kids, babysits for me, supports us, chauffeurs me around until I get a license. I hope to work when I get the opportunity. Oh, he takes out the garbage, that's a big thing around here. He's hard to talk to. He tries to be understanding. He likes fishing, hunting, cartoons on TV. He was so kind and nice when I met him and so courteous. [Why "was",] He's changed; he's not courteous at all; he's moody now. Bills bother him; he jumps when the bills are piling up. I'm always nagging at him because he throws his clothes around, and he's always late for everything. I like to take trips, even with the kids. I like to drink. I like to go shopping *with money enough to spend.* I like to cook; that is, bake. I don't like to clean or wash or scrub. I try to have supper ready when my husband comes home and I *try* to keep the house clean. Sometimes I'm moody and can't get up in the morning and I forget to do things —like I'll do part of the ironing and forget the rest. I don't keep up with things. . . . We've had it rough from the start; two months after we were married we separated because of in-law trouble. He was always going over to his mother's. [Here followed an extended discussion of their problems at that time.]

But we got back together. We've had bill problems. [When did that start?] About an hour after we were married. When we had children it got worse.

This couple present a sharp division of labor for task performances in the family, and not much sense of common interests and activities. The husband works, pays the bills, does maintainence work around the house and drives the car since the wife does not have a license. Occasionally he helps with the children as babysitter or when the wife is loaded down. The wife does the housework and looks after the children; she also does most of the shopping (he "chauffeurs" her but neither says that they shop together). She thinks of her responsibility toward him mainly in terms of providing his meals. He likes masculine recreation—hunting, fishing, going out by himself. She probably would like to go out with him but they do not seem to do this very often. Apparently segregation has characterized their marital relationship from the beginning; only after a separation did he stop depending on his own family for companionship. And apparently he feels that she also is sometimes too loyal to others, since he criticizes her for lending things out and letting people take advantage of her.

As time goes on the husband may spend more time at home, and the sharp segregation which now marks their marriage may moderate. Older lower class couples often describe their marital history in terms of a gradual settling down of the husband and greater willingness on his part to give up separate leisure pursuits. Sometimes this is accompanied by a greater willingness to share activities with the family, but sometimes the husband seems rather to shift his isolated life from outside to inside the home—perhaps tinkering with his car in the back alley on weekends and watching TV programs of interest only to him (westerns and sports) in the evening.

A third upper-lower class couple, illustrating an intermediate degree of conjugal role-organization, have been married for seven years and have two children; the husband is thirty-seven and the wife twenty-seven years old. He works as a baggage room clerk. They live in a five-room, modestly furnished apartment in a building owned by his mother.

The husband:

I want to make my kids happy; I want a good education for them. I want a little money saved up; insurance policies paid up. I want to see the kids go to college to get a good education. It will give them more sense, more facts of life. It will give them a job easier; a good office job. . . . We make decisions together; we talk about them. Her and me make the decisions on money. I leave my check on the desk for her; we don't have no trouble over it. [Who makes decisions regarding the children?] On certain things I do, on others she does. I make decisions on how long they should stay up and what TV programs they watch. I keep us in bread, keep the bills paid always. My wife sees that the kids go to school; she feeds them. We both do the shopping; if she can't, I do it. I clean the walls in the house and I do the painting. I don't help with the house cleaning or the dishes. . . . Well, she was raised by nuns in a Catholic boarding school. She's real swell. She likes to go to movies; I don't. She gets a little hot-headed. . . . I don't get hot like she does; She does the arguing, I keep quiet. I like fishing. I work; even when I'm sick I go to work. . . . I go to the corner saloon once in a while. I don't take my wife out enough.

The wife:

I have a good marriage. My husband is a little more than ten years older than I am but sometimes I feel I'm older than he is. My husband is so calm he never gets angry. We make most decisions together. . . . We agree on the children. If I punish them he don't say anything and if he punishes them I don't say anything. He gives me the money and I pay the bills. We go on picnics to the park with the kids. I take care of the kids and I wash and iron and take care of the house. Between the kids and the dog and the fish and the birds I keep pretty busy. My husband helps me with the children; he washes them and puts them to bed. He is a great person; I don't have no complaints about him. He had a pretty bad temper when we got married but he's calmed down. He loves sports and he loves to tinker with his car. He's handy, he put up all my cabinets and he's putting up shelves for me in the basement so I can can peaches and tomatoes. . . . I'm hot-headed for one thing. I enjoy taking care of the family. . . . I like making those plastic models like rockets; I have the X – 15 and the Redstone. I sew and make clothes for the girls. I knit, too. [How does your husband feel about you?] My husband never complains about me.

This couple seems to have a fairly elaborate division of labor and rather clear-cut notions of what are husband-tasks and what are wife-tasks. On the other hand, there is a good deal of sharing of child care, and making decisions together seems important to them. They share leisure activities in which the children participate but they do not seem to attach much importance to shared recreation in which only adults participate (he goes out by himself, does not take her out enough). Much of their activity at home is closely articulated and would require a good deal of joint planning; on the other hand, both seem to value a sense of separate roles and probably would not respond positively to the emphasis couples in joint relationships put on interchangeability. If this couple had a more complete division of labor we would classify them as in a segregated relationship; their emphasis on joint decisions and the value they place on whole family activity suggest that the intermediate category is more accurate. It is possible that this couple's relationship is becoming less segregated as time goes on—the wife's reference to the husband's bad temper earlier in marriage may be an allusion to his greater independence and lack of attention to his family responsibilities; he probably goes to the corner saloon less often than he used to. His children have become for him a new focus of interest which probably makes it easier for him to give up the saloon-car-sports way of life: "Kids keep families together;

I enjoy taking the kids on picnics, swimming, and to the forest preserves. I take them up North for vacations, too."

As was apparent in Table 2 – 1, each of the role-relationship types is characteristic of particular social classes — the joint relationship is most characteristic of the upper-middle class, the segregated relationship of the lower-lower class, and the intermediate type of the lower-middle and upper-lower class. The role-relationship typical of a class is an integral part of the life style of members of that class and is closely articulated with the self-concepts and concepts of spouse that reflect these life styles (discussed in detail in Appendix A). Let us look in a little more detail, then, at the role-relationship patterns characteristic of each class.

The upper-middle class

An emphasis on equality and joint participation by husband and wife has been a mark of persons with higher class status for many years. It is quite possible that this emphasis has trickled down over the years to lower and lower class levels; now we find upper-lower class men and women speaking of a "togetherness" that would have been quite foreign to their forebears (Handel and Rainwater, 1964). Nevertheless, it seems that joint relationships still appear on a class gradient. The description by Davis, Gardner, and Gardner (1941:90) of the husband-wife relationship among upper class Southerners in the early nineteen-thirties applies equally to that of the present day upper-middle class in our sample, but not to other classes:

> In their overt behavior upper-class husbands and wives have, roughly, a relationship of equivalence. There is no clear-cut division of labor between them, as in other classes. Most upper-class husbands, however, rule the economic sphere of home life, earn the living, and hold the purse strings. Most wives concern themselves with the direction and supervision of the

care of the house and children. . . . The general equivalence in the husband-wife relation in the upper class is also indicated by their joint social participation. Whereas men and women in the middle and lower classes tend to have a separate recreational life, informal participation in the upper class is generally by couples together. Although there is some social activity, during the daytime, of the sexes separately, this entertainment is not considered so interesting, nor does it occur so frequently, as mixed evening gatherings.

Even the sharpness of the husband's "rule of the economic sphere in the home" described by these authors is not apparent in our data, in that many upper-middle class couples seem to deal with economic matters as a unit, although it is probably true that the husband is more involved here than in the lower classes where the wife more often handles the finances on her own (Rainwater, Coleman, and Handel, 1959:82−85).*

These themes of equivalence, sharing, and joint participation are emphasized over and over by upper-middle class men and women, as in the following excerpts from interviews with a twenty-seven year old man and his twenty-two year old wife. The husband now earns $12,000 a year working in a business owned by his father and in another business in which he is a partner. They have been married four years, have a two-year-old child and a newborn and hope to have a third child in several years.

The husband:
    Well, we spent our honeymoon in Germany −2½ years of it. We have been back in the States about a year. This gave us a chance to get away from the kin folks, and being away from our

*Cf. Blood and Wolfe (1960:30−34) who find that the husband's voice in family decisions increases directly with increasing social status. In the light of our findings this could be interpreted as a result of the shift from segregated to joint relationships as status increases, having the effect that matters regarded as the wife's business in lower status groups are increasingly regarded in higher status groups as *also* the husband's.

parents gave us a chance to adjust. It was nice in Germany. The people there were all in the service and all about our age. That's probably the main thing that happened in our marriage so far. Our first girl was born there, and then we brought her back to the states. Also we were completely on our own, and this gave us a chance to adjust away from the family. It was a nice honeymoon with Uncle Sam paying the bill. [How do you make decisions?] We discuss them. We just decide together on things. I don't make all the decisions, but neither does the wife. I probably have a little more weight than she does. [Can you give an example?] Well, I built this house, and there are a million decisions that have to be made. Sometimes my wife would come up with ideas, and if I thought they weren't right, I'd tell her. There are lots of decisions to be made in building a house. If it is something unusual, we usually discuss it. Little items she buys. I don't pass any judgment on it—but on large items we talk it over. . . . The children are so young, no real decisions need to be made about which school to send them, etc. There are just the normal routine decisions. It's hard to answer that. I like the wife to take care of the kids. Mostly, she never asks me. . . . Well, I have the duty of bringing home the bacon. She doesn't work. Well, I really don't know where to start. [Pause.] I take care of most of the physical things. I do most of the things in the yard. She is busy with the baby. I do the heavy work and she does the light work. She takes care of the babies, but when I come home I help her with the babies in the feeding. She feeds one and I feed the other. Just kind of go along naturally. [What does your wife do?] She makes the beds, takes care of the washing—we send most of the shirts out now—but we do have a washing machine. She keeps the house clean and things like that. Those are the normal things for housewives. [What is your wife like?] She is very congenial. She is the type that trusts me completely. We don't have any worry that the other one is unfaithful. She is very sweet—I would marry her again. She is a good worker, not lazy. She makes an ideal housewife and wife. She likes to entertain, enjoys being with people—let's see what else. She is real good with the children—plays a lot with them. She is taking a correspondence course from the University on child rearing practices. She just has one year at college and this summer she is going to summer school at [a nearby college]. She attends from 7 to 8 in the morning, and then comes back and I go to work. She likes bridge. She is a radio amateur. She has a license. She got the license so she could talk to me in the field. She likes to go to the movies, dances, and go to parties. She likes the new house, and she likes to work with children. [What are her bad points.?] [Long pause.] I know she must have some. Let's see. [thinking—laughs.] I just can't think of any. I am sure there are some, there must be some things that get me, but I just can't think of any. This is probably unusual, but I just can't think of any. [How about you?] I am a radio amateur, a pilot, like to hunt and fish. I don't particularly like to play bridge, but I do play because my wife wants me to. I did a lot of skin diving, at one time, and took lots of underwater color film. I am friendly. I don't try to cheat anybody and I am pretty easy to get along with. My wife and I have few arguments—it's more of a teasing thing. We didn't have more than half-a-dozen arguments the first year. I don't argue much with anyone. I try to avoid arguments. I am good at staying out of arguments—that's why I get along. I avoid arguments. One of my bad points is I hate to study—to sit down and study anything. I am not as accurate as I should be. I have to double and triple check my work. Mainly math is what I am referring to. I am a little slower to learn than a lot of people. It takes me a little longer to learn, but usually when I learn it I am ahead of the other people. By the time I learn it I really have it. I am basing this on my service experience. I also have a tendency to leave clothes lying around, but my wife has broken that. [What does she think of you?] I think she is contented. I haven't heard any gripes otherwise. I have a tendency to be lazy and she has to prod me into doing it. She will have to ask me several times. I don't jump right up but eventually I do it. [What do the children think of you?] The older one seems to like me. She's always running to her Da-Da. It is kind of a typical case. She doesn't shy away from me. If she is scared of something she will run and talk to me. The younger one is only three months old, so I really can't tell about her.

The wife:

Do you want our family history since we got married? We were married that summer after I had spent one year at the

university, and he had gone through the four years and graduated. He was being sent to Germany and we got married and
that was our honeymoon. We had thought about it as a career
then. We had a good time, we enjoyed the whole tour. They were
all young couples like we were and we enjoyed the whole time
there. We took two trips too. One to Italy and one to Paris. Our
oldest child was born in Germany. I guess we got the wander-
lust out of our systems and came back ready to settle down and
raise our family. [How do you make decisions?] We always try
to compromise. We always give our opinions on all the dec-
sions and then try to come to a compromise. If we both agree on
something we do it, if not, we don't. [What are your responsibilities?] Oh, planning meals so as to be nutritious, doing
laundry, keeping house clean. Playing with the children, trying
to steer them in the right way. Doing the marketing. Keeping
my own appearance up and keeping his clothes in order, taking
them to cleaners, etc. I think I should read and keep up with
things. He, of course, has to work and he likes his work. I think
it is very important for a man to like his work, he needs to be
doing something he likes to do. He is devoted to his children, he
needs to help care for them, to learn to play with them as well
as to know how to discipline them. [What's he like?] He likes to
barbecue, so he prepares the dinner for me this way, and if I'm
in a real bind he might occasionally fix breakfast. I attend a
class at the college and he takes care of the children and encourages me to go. He likes to swim and hunt and fish. He is
working on a new hobby now. He is trying to get his private
pilot's license. [What are his bad points?] Well, let's see, he
hasn't got money! He wants a boy real bad and didn't conceal
his disappointment with the last little girl. He talked about a boy
all the time. But he hasn't given up on getting his boy and wants
to keep trying. [And you?] Oh, let's see, I like to do all the things
he does. I like to skin dive with him. I like to fish and I like to
read. I am determined someway to get my college degree. I
manage someway to get to my seven o'clock class in History,
but sometimes I think I won't make it. I like to sew, I like to
play the piano. [What are your bad points?] I've noticed I get
impatient with our oldest too easy. Sometimes I'm so impatient
with her that I'm really ashamed of myself. [What does your
husband think of you?] Oh, I think he likes me as well as loves
me and I think he respects me.

This is a very busy couple. The husband works hard at two businesses (he also belong to "The Tippers Club," which he describes as "a breakfast club in which we pass around tips to get more business"), he has a number of hobbies and interests, most of which his wife shares, and he has been involved in building (and now furnishing) a new house. His wife is equally busy as wife, mother, and student, and as participant in the outdoor sports which they both enjoy. They apparently enjoy an active social life. The sense of involvement of each in the other is communicated as much in the way each talks about the activities he does not share with the other as in their discussion of the things they do together — she comments that "it is very important for a man to like his work, he needs to be doing something he likes to do," and the husband seems helpful about and interested in his wife's efforts to finish the college education she interrupted when he went into service.

Like many middle class husbands this man wants to feel that he is in control of the major decisions made about money and the household, but both their comments suggest that this is done in a context of full consultation and receptivity to what the wife wishes. Information in other interviews suggests that this is a common pattern when the wife is young; some husbands seem to feel that their wives need guidance in learning to manage a complex household and its economy, though it is not clear why young husbands feel they are competent to provide such guidance.* Also, the husband's desire to have a say about what goes on in his home has to do with his conception of the home as not simply a woman's place. That is, upper-middle class men see their homes as expressions of themselves to a much greater extent than working class men; for them the home and the activities that go on in it are expressions of their personalities and of their social status. Working class men are much more likely to perceive the home as a place women maintain to take care of their

---

*Cf. Blood and Wolfe who report that the husband's voice in family decision-making is greatest when the wife is in her twenties and decreases steadily as wives get older. (1960: 27, 42–44)

children, and to provide bed, board, and a TV set for their husbands. Lower-middle class men, often share the conceptions described for upper-middle class men, but they also are more likely to see the home as a kind of refuge maintained for them by their wives with much less emphasis on the home as an expression of their own selves (other than of their ability to contribute financially and participate in money decisions about what should be done).

Upper-middle class wives, in turn, expect both to penetrate the world of their husband's careers with interest, understanding, and positive contributions and to have their husbands participate in the building of the world that centers on the home, a home which (as will be discussed in appendix A) serves not simply as a place apart from work but as a focus for a network of social relations which combine career and social activities. (One would expect, for example, that some of the members of the Tippers Club and their wives are occasional guests in the home of the couple discussed above.) Upper-middle class wives do not regard it as appropriate that their husbands should keep strictly to themselves what goes on at work, or that the husband should refuse to contribute to the development of a style of living distinctive to the couple.

Although our data provide no direct index of the amount of joint social participation by husbands and wives, some findings by Blood and Wolfe (1960:167–72) are appropriate here. They find that wives of higher social class indicate substantial joint participation with their husbands in organizational membership, in friendships, in discussing what goes on at the husband's job, and in socializing with his work colleagues. These women are also generally satisfied with the amount of companionship they share with their husbands.

The nature of the social network in which the couples with joint role-relationships are embedded is outlined by Bott (1957:94–95). It is her hypothesis that a joint relationship is functional where the husband and wife are not bound up in close-knit relationships with people on whom they can depend for help and advice about how to conduct their lives and fulfill their responsibilities. Upper-middle class people, especially in larger communities, tend not to be participants in this kind of network. They keep their relatives at a distance and try not to depend on them (see, for example, the first remarks of the husband quoted above). They are involved in a complex network of relationships with friends and acquaintances whom they know for different reasons and who seldom know each other or make up a tightly organized primary group. As Bott summarizes:

"In other words, their external relationships are relatively discontinuous both in time and space. Such continuity as they possess lies in their relationship to each other rather than in their external relationships. In facing the external world they draw on each other, for their strongest emotional investment is made where there is continuity. Hence their high standards of conjugal compatibility, their stress on shared interests, on joint organization, on equality between husband and wife. They must get along well together, they must help one another in carrying out familial tasks, for there is no sure source of material or emotional help. . . . They are unable to rely on consistent external support. Through their joint external relationships they present a united front to the world and they reaffirm their joint relationship with each other. Joint relationships with friends give both husband and wife a source of emotional satisfaction outside the family without threatening their relationship to each other.

The joint role-relationship pattern which characterizes the upper-middle class couple, then, is seen as functional for them. It provides emotional support and greater organizational resources for coping with the complex interpersonal world of this class, a world in which the spheres of career and home life are not sharply separated and in which extensive social participation, both formal and informal, are requisites for membership in the status group. As always, a value system, emphasizing equal rights of the sexes and the importance of mutual give-and-take and understanding, legitimates this method of coping with the realities of the social situation.

The lower-middle class

In the lower-middle class the relations of husband and wife are focused more sharply than in the upper-middle class on familial functioning, and there tends to be more emphasis on the family as a whole than on their personal relationship. While in the upper-middle class the husband-wife relationship stands somewhat apart from their common relationship to their children, in the lower-middle class the emphasis tends to be on the total family, and the way in which husbands and wives talk about their life together suggests that children enter much more completely into their thinking about their life together. Discussions of marital relations, therefore, focus much more on the combined roles of husband/father and wife/mother than is true in the upper-middle class; lower-middle class men and women seem to think of themselves as acting in these roles more of the time, and simply as persons less of the time, than is the case with upper-middle class men and women. This emphasis on family statuses and on the division of labor in role performances which tends to go with it means that there is less concern with joint participation between husband and wife and more with complementary functioning. Lower-middle class husbands and wives expect to be together much of the time and there is little of the separate social participation common in the lower class, but they are together as *husband* and *wife,* often as *father* and *mother,* rather than simply as *persons* who share and value their life together. Thus there is a subtle element of social distance between spouses that most upper-middle class couples seek to overcome with their emphasis on joint interests and participation.

At the same time, as suggested above, lower-middle class husbands and wives see the home as the center of their lives, as a haven for relaxation, recuperation and informality for the husband when he leaves his job. Husbands retreat to the home; they do not show the same interest in excursions that characterizes upper-middle men (who expect to be accompanied by their wives) or lower class men (who want to be off by themselves in a man's world). Their wives tend to value this attitude since they, too, feel more secure at home, although they may occasionally complain that their husbands do not want to go out at all.

These themes are illustrated by the following couple. In many ways what this couple says is quite similar to the statements of the upper-middle class couple presented above, but there are important differences in the underlying conception they have of marital life and in the way they go about performing the tasks necessary to their life together. The husband in this case is twenty-eight years old; he attended college in the evening for two years while working in his father's small business. He continues there and is active in business associations, a luncheon group and two religious organizations. He and his wife have been married for two years and hope to have a child soon. She is twenty-four years old, completed high school, and worked as a secretary until shortly after marriage. She has moved up from an upper lower class background (which helps explain her deference to her husband's more successful family)

The husband:
   We both want to succeed economically. We want the prestige of success—financially and in the community. We want a long happy life with children. [What about the children?] Well, children is the reason we bought this home. Apartment living does not lend itself to children. In apartments they are noisy and families fighting. Our apartment was in a good neighborhood. [What are the important things in married life?] I want a calm tranquil marriage—no headaches. When I come home from work, I want to relax and unwind from the job. . . . I make the financial decisions. I handle all the money and what is purchased. I made this clear before we were married. I make all deposits and purchases,

and disbursements. I balance the checkbook. I pay for utilities, and all auto repairs. All checks are OK'd by me. It's cheaper to live when you're married than when I was single and dating. I'm also home more now than when I was single. My wife makes all the decisions in the house, except for upkeep. . . . We make joint decisions on entertainment. My wife is the decision-maker on social life at home such as guests, and she makes decisions on visiting or socializing with friends. . . . My wife is more cost conscious on this than me. I make the living. I told my wife that she was not to work at the start of marriage. The lawn is my domain and area of responsibility. I give my wife a house and food allowance of twenty-five dollars a week plus ten dollars a week for her own personal use. [What about in the house?] I help with the dishes only when my wife is sick or under the weather. Other times, I don't help her in the house — I'm too busy. I go read my paper or I'm busy with paperwork from the office. [Do you do anything in the house?] No, all light work is a woman's job. My wife helps me with my book work from the job, acts as my secretary at home when needed. She helps with accounts. [Did your wife go to college?] No, she's a high school graduate. I feel the man should be the smarter of the two. But my wife keeps up with current events, she reads the same magazines and publications I do. She keeps up with discussions. [What is your wife like?] She's an excellent housekeeper and cook. She's very meticulous and neat. She even follows me around and picks up after me. [How is she as a person?] She's sweet and understanding. But she has a mind of her own. She's stubborn at times. [What are her interests?] Well, sewing drapes. She loves to cook. She likes good plays and books. [Her good points?] Well, she can put up with me, I'm pretty grouchy at times. She is level-headed and even-tempered. [Her bad points?] Sometimes she's stubborn, and she won't listen, sometimes. She also dislikes to be corrected. [And you?] I'm ambitious. I want and like to do things my own way. I'm stubborn. Psychologically I get upset easily. I'm worrisome. I sometimes let off steam when driving. However, most of the time I turn my tensions inside. Many times I work myself up over nothing. However, I want to be liked. [Your other bad points?] Well, as I said I'm stubborn, and I also dislike to be corrected. [What about good points?] I enjoy being with people.

I don't like to stay at home. I will talk to anyone. I'm an extrovert rather than an introvert. One instance, well, I behave very well, but I have a temper. I have a habit of bringing home tensions from the office. But, my wife knows of my inward directed tensions. . . . She was told of this by me before our marriage. [How do you behave with family?] My wife feels I behave less warm to her parents than to my family.

The wife:

Our daily habits are important. I guess buying our home here was the most important. It was our biggest decision. [What else is important?] Getting used to the mannerisms of each other and creating a peaceful and happy home. [Other important things?] That's about all. We've only been married for a few years. [Who makes the decisions?] My husband makes them. [What kinds?] He makes all of them. [Such as?] Who spends the money and on what. Whether or not we should buy a home. [Recreation, etc.?] We both do. If we are going on a vacation we discuss where we would like to go and then we both decide. The housekeeping, the cooking and the shopping and washing are my responsibilities. He is the earner of the money, and balances out the checkbook that I usually mess up. [Explain?] I usually add something wrong and he has to correct it. [What is your husband like?] He is very sensitive, honest, and a very loving person, and needs a lot of attention. [Anything else?] He is interested in a lot of groups, he likes to be a leader. [In what types of groups?] Business groups like Junior Chamber of Commerce and just social groups and religious groups like the Knights of Columbus. He enjoys debating over political and social problems. [What are his good points?] He is a good husband and trys to please. He is a very close family man, even very close to his mother and father. He does everything he is able to do to please them. [His bad points?] He has a bad temper and likes to swear which I am trying to stop him from doing. [And you?] I like to go out but not carry it to far. [Explain?] I mean once or twice a week, not every night. I, too, like to join social groups, that's about all. [Your good points?] I try to please my husband and our families. I try hard to please them. [Is this intentional?] No, I like people and like to feel close to them. I don't like unpleasantness. I try to be kind and pleasing, I try to think of what would please them. [And your bad points?] I'm impatient and selfish, that's all. [How does your husband feel about you?] He is very happy with our relationship.

This young man is ambitious, anxious to prove himself and to demonstrate his ability to carry on the family business and build it. In these respects he is in a very similar position to that of the upper-middle class man discussed above, and, like him, he expects to be dominant in his relations with his wife. But marital relationships appear quite differently in the two couples. This couple expects and accepts a sharper line of demarcation between the husband's and the wife's role-functioning. The husband seems to take his wife less into account. The wife, while a little wistful about her inferior status in both the nuclear and extended family, does not seem really to expect much more in the way of sharing and consulation, but rather wishes only that her husband recognized her status and allowed her a little more autonomy. A good deal of the couple's social participation seems to be joint, although the wife makes it clear that her husband is a more active participant than she, and it seems likely that he does maintain some relationships of importance to him in which she has little part. Nevertheless, both seem to value the idea of functioning as a unit (composed of rather separate roles), and there is little of the acceptance of separate worlds for husband and wife that is characteristic of those in segregated role-relationships. Both expect the wife to make efforts to keep up (but *not* to catch up) with her husband intellectually and socially so that they can have a sense of sharing perspectives and ways of thinking, but none of this communicates the sense of interpenetrating interests and activities seen in the upper-middle class couple previously discussed.

The pattern of husband-dominance which this couple illustrates is in no sense as representative of the lower-middle class as is their intermediate role-segregation. From our interviews judgments about dominance or equality (that is, whether one partner dominates decisions in the family, or whether there is a concerted effort to balance out voices in decisions—either by division of responsibility or through consultation) yield the distribution given in Table 2–2. It is apparent that the main pattern in the middle class involves an effort to achieve some kind of equality in decision-making, or at least to conduct the family business in such a way that there is a show of equality and each partner's "face" is protected. Where this is not the case, the direction of authority tends to be toward the husband (especially in the upper-middle class where the ratio of husbands to wives exercising dominance is almost three to one). In the lower classes there is less effort to maintain equality of authority,. and in the lower-lower class there is a strong trend toward maternal dominance (often by husbandly default more than wifely design). This is particularly true of the Negro lower-lower class, as will be discussed more fully below.

In most lower-middle class couples, then, husband and wife both have important voices in what the family does, but their voices are those of persons acting in familial roles, and reference to familial values is strong in what they decide. More than in the upper-middle class, the home is the woman's place, but the husband is expected to be interested in it and helpful to his wife in doing the things a man can do better. He is also expected to help the wife at her duties

TABLE 2–2:
DOMINANCE OR EQUALITY IN FAMILY DECISION-MAKING

Social Class		Husband judged to have greater voice	Equal voice	Wife judged to have greater voice
Middle class	(61)	25%	62%	13%
Upper-lower whites and Negroes	(51)	39	35	26
Lower-lower whites	(24)	38	16	46
Lower-lower Negroes	(29)	21	21	58

$X^2 = 28.31$ df = 6   T = .26   P < .0005

when she is overburdened. We will see in chapter vi that this greater separateness between husband and wife, more common in the lower-middle class then in the upper-middle class, has an effect on the family size desires that wives express.

The upper-lower class

In general, upper-lower class couples display less joint participation in their relationships than do lower-middle class couple; they tend toward a somewhat more segregated relationships, in which the husband spends time with his own friends and the wife with hers. The couple described on pp. 38–39 are illustrative. The husband retains some of his separate friends from earlier days, and he does not really think it important that he spend time with his wife except when the whole family goes on outings. In contrast, the lower-middle class husband quoted immediately above thinks it socially important and appropriate to have his wife join in much of his social life. The fact that a significantly fewer upper-lower class families have patterns of equal voice in decision-making also reflects a greater tendency toward segregation.

It is interesting in this respect that the relation between conjugal role segregation and equal authority versus dominance by one partner is different in the middle and in the lower class. In the middle class, the tendency for one partner to dominate is independent of whether the couple has a joint or intermediate role-relationship; in each case about 60 per cent of the couples show equal authority. Even where one partner has a stronger voice in what goes on in the family, his influence tends to be spread equally over all the activities of concern to the family and is not part of a sharp division of labor. In the lower class this is not true, as is apparent from Table 2–3; here, of the majority of couples in segregated or intermediate role-relationships, one or the other partner is

TABLE 2-3:
RELATION OF DOMINANCE IN FAMILY DECISION-MAKING TO
CONJUGAL ROLE-ORGANIZATION: LOWER CLASS COUPLES

Conjugal Role-Organization		One Partner Dominant	Relatively Equal Influence
Joint	(9)	33%	67%
Intermediate	(40)	62	38
Segregated	(55)	87	13

$X^2 = 12.13$ df = 2   T = .29   P < .005

seen as dominant. In the lower class, the proportion of couples
with joint relationships who see each partner as having equal
influence on family decisions is the same as for the middle
class as a whole, but in each of the other role-organization
types the proportion drops significantly.

In the upper-lower class, this often means that even the
couples in intermediate relationships do not take each other
into account as much as lower-middle class couples do.
Though husband and wife may not go their separate ways as
much as in the lower-lower class, they tend to adhere to a
sharper division of labor than is true in the lower-middle
class, and though they may participate together in many
family activities, this seems to be more the result of default
(they are thrown together in the same small home) or of a
desire to keep away from unwelcome involvements outside
the home than to be dictated by the values of equality and
togetherness that dominate the thinking of lower-middle class
men and women.

The lower-lower class

The pattern of role-segregation characteristic of the lower-lower class has been implied at various points above in
contrast with the role-organization patterns of the other
classes. The upper-lower class interview excerpted on page

36 could be duplicated many times from the lower-lower class sample. These couples carry the separation of conjugal activities even further, in that the husband participates minimally and in specialized ways around the home, the wife carries the responsibility for the home and children largely by herself, and she seldom participates with her husband in outside activities.

The following lower-lower class Negro couple illustrates most of the themes which characterize this pattern of highly segregated role-relationships. The husband is thirty-nine years old, completed the eleventh grade of high school, and works as a general laborer for a construction firm ("I like it well enough to stick with it for nine years"). His wife is thirty-two years old, completed the eighth grade, and does not have a job. They have been married for fourteen years, have five children, and do not want more. They have, everything considered, a fairly stable marriage, and are by no means among the more disorganized lower-lower class families in the sample (which includes several unstable consensual unions and a number of marriages in which the conflict between husband and wife is greater).

The husband:
   Well, I didn't finish school before I got married, I went in the Army and got married when I come out. I likes it all right. [What do you like about it?] I like my family life, it gives me something to devote my time to. I really like kids and I'm trying to raise them so that they will take advantage of an education. My oldest boy wants to go to college and I want to send him. . . . Well, I gets the wife's ideas; but I think that I should make the final decisions. [Who decides on children's discipline?] That's her job entirely. [What do you do for recreation?] I haven't had much time for recreation, I'm so tired so often when I get home. But I let the boys decide on what sports they want to attend. [Your duties?] Well, I really do think that the husband's duty is to be the main provider for the family. She runs the house. I guess it's like I make the money and she spends it. [chuckles] I usually wash windows but there's one thing I won't do, I won't wash

dishes! I do other little maintenance jobs around the house. [What's your wife like?] [Laughs] Oh she's — well, to really say it right she's nice. But she has a bit of temper. [How much of a "bit"?] Oh, a big bit. [About what?] Oh, she gets very angry because I don't spend more time at home. She says I'm on the go too much. [What are her good points?] She is civic-minded, interested a lot in the kids. [Her hobbies?] She loves to sew. All in all, I think she is a very nice person. [And you?] I'm an easy going person. I don't make much noise. As the old saying goes — action speaks louder than words. I try to keep busy at any work. I try to get the kids what they need, same goes for the wife. I might yap about it, but I usually give them what they want. I would rather give somebody something than take something from them. [Your bad points?] I used to gamble heavy; but I had to overcome that habit. The same goes for drinking, I don't bother around with drinking much at all now. My wife says I won't listen. She may be dissatisfied about my temper — not that I do anything to her. I just walk out on an argument. [How does she feel about you?] Well, now, I guess she feels fairly well about it. She used to think I acted bad. But I can control my temper better and my money isn't going in the wrong direction on gambling and whiskey. [And how do the children feel about you?] They do whatever I tell them. I don't believe in regularly beating them. When I do something nice for the oldest boy he will tell me and others how he likes it.

The wife:

I think the most important thing as far as the family is concerned is that I have five healthy kids, and I am healthy and he is healthy so far. Well, I do think they're pretty wonderful. They're under pretty good control. And my husband is pretty good. [What do you mean?] Well, he used to drink quite a bit but now he don't and he's home more and the kids need a mother and father now. It's much different now, it was like walking a chalk line then 'cause maybe, because I hadn't any experience or something. It was sort of rough in the beginning. [Kinda rough?] I had my mind set one way and he had his another. He wasn't adult, and I wanted him to be more adult. [More adult — how was he?] Just in and out running around as he did before he married, but he's settled down now. . . . There's not too many decisions to be made unless I just say what's to be done and what's not to be done. If something had to be done so far as disciplining the kids, telling them what to do and what not to do, I have to do it. The only decision he thinks of is the money, and all the time he doesn't know what to do with it either. [How is that?] Well, I do all decisions about the children and he the money, but I help. Otherwise, there's no togetherness — except as far as the kids. I goes one way and he goes another, we never go together any-place, not enough to put your finger on. I think of two places this year — we went shopping together once, the second time we took one of the boys to the doctor. [What are your main duties?] Everything — from — whew! I cover the whole thing, from taking care of the kids to figuring out what's to be done and what's not. [What about your main duties as a wife?] Well, I guess they're well taken care of, for my part about it. [How do you mean that?] Well, I try to satisfy and all the time it's not satisfactory to him, so I'm afraid to say whether I know exactly what it should be. [What do you consider to be your husband's main duties to you as a wife?] I think if a man can see that you want to go all the way or half-way, he should go at least half-way, but some people don't. They never show love and respect. [Is your husband like this?] Uh-huh, he don't meet me not even part of the way. [What's he like?] Um . . . Good or bad? [Both.] I don't know . . . [laughter] [Describe him as a person?] Well, let me see, how could I put that and sound sensible. Um-huh — any kind of monstrosity with two legs. Well, no side, front or back. He just look like a lot of monstrosity — and he don't look like nothing to me in the form of a human being. He don't seem like much of nothing to me, except trouble or bother. [After a very long, de-pressed pause — What sort of things is he interested in?] Himself. He just interested mostly in himself, then his car, and his people. No, I take that part back, not his people either. [What are his good points?] I don't think there's no good points, on some he does pretty good, well, on sleeping and eating. He don't like to buy nothing but he always want to eat. [What other good points has he?] I haven't really thought about it — there aren't any. He works, but if I did he wouldn't. [And you?] It's harder to describe myself than it is anyone else. Well, I think I can take care of the home and cooking, or at least, I know I do those things. [What are you like, what are you interested in, what do you do?] Well,

I help out at the Boys' Club, PTA or Mother's meeting or whatever they have at school. And I'm concerned and get along with friends and neighbors. [What are you like as a person?] I think I'm pretty irritable sometimes—I know so, when I get tired and nerve-wracked. Screaming is one of my bad points—at the children and sometimes at the old man. [What does he think of you?] I really wouldn't know. He never talk about nothing. If he would talk then you know. But he's home and asleep or he's gone, so I really don't know, pretty bad I think. [Even though he doesn't say, how does he impress you as feeling?] Well, I really don't know, I don't think he thinks any more, 'cause the only way you know how a person feels is by their telling you. [And the children how do they feel about you?] Oh, well, so far as them letting me know, they think nothing wouldn't go on if I was gone, so. Their father works, but so far as any discipline or anything they need, they come to me. They call him daddy, but that's about it; cause he never disciplines them, never gives them a penny and he just don't talk, that's one thing.

This husband is notable for his frankness; he makes it clear that he does not take an active part in what goes on at home, although he does like to spend time with his sons. In many other lower-lower class interviews the husband speaks of his family role in a general way that indicates more involvement than his wife validates. This suggests that lower-lower class husbands do not feel too comfortable about the extent of their separation from family matters, and that their actual behavior does not match the view they prefer to offer the outside world. As the wife talks, she makes it increasingly clear that she feels she has the total responsibility for the family, that her husband simply provides the money on which it runs.

The lower-lower class husband, then, tends to be tangential to family functioning; often his wife prefers it that way. That is, in spite of the worrying she may do about the possibility of her husband straying away from home and thus depriving the family of its source of support and measure of respectability, the lower-lower class wife seems to find handling the family on her own to her liking, or at least consistent with what she has learned to expect from living in her particular social world. Her objections to her husband's separateness, as we will see in the next chapter, are likely to have more to do with dissatisfaction over money or socially demeaning behavior than over his failure to contribute interpersonal resources and skills to coping with the internal tasks of the family.

3

Sexual and marital relations

SEXUAL BEHAVIOR in marriage can be viewed as both an expression of and a conditioner of the general character of the marital relationship. Again and again, couples speak of sexual relations as the central fact and expression of marriage, as the base from which grows most of what is important about marriage and family. Thus, we will examine sexual attitudes and behavior first to develop a clearer understanding of the conjugal relationship as a whole, and secondly, because of the intimate bearing sexual relations have on family planning and contraceptive behavior.

This chapter is concerned with several aspects of the sexual experience of the husbands and wives studied. Most central is the question of the levels of sexual interest and enjoyment that characterize different men and women with the related question of frequency of sexual intercourse. We also need to understand the attitudes each partner has toward the other as these express and influence the kind of enjoyment each takes in sexual acts. Finally, there is the question of what functions people feel sex serves in marriage and the contribution it makes to the marital relationship.

In an earlier study (Rainwater, 1960: 92 – 93) we cautioned that "Individual feelings about sexual relations are extremely complex and often contradictory. Interview data of the kind collected in our study cannot be expected to capture the full complexity of the way respondents feel and behave sexually." This caution applies to this study as well, although we will explore sexual behavior somewhat more broadly and systematically here. A careful examination of what follows, however, will impress the reader, as the author has been impressed, with the extent to which the findings reported are more indicative than certain. Much more systematic research must be done if the study of sexual behavior is to be dynamically related to other marital behavior, as both take place in the context of family life lived by individuals who do not take their problems to psychologists and psychiatrists and who cannot be portrayed adequately by the simplistic approach of the pioneer Kinsey studies.

Level of enjoyment of sexual relations

The discussion by each husband and wife of their sexual relations can lead to a judgment of their degree of interest in, enjoyment of, and commitment to sexual relations as a part of marriage. Individuals range in the value they place on sexual relations from enthusiastic participation ("If God made anything better he kept it to himself") to strong rejection ("I would be happy if I never had to do that again").

In our evaluations we placed each individual (except in the few cases where the data were very sparse) into one of four gross categories: very positive, accepting but not enthusiastic, somewhat negative, and very negative. Into the first category go those men and women who regard sex as one of the most important parts of marriage and who say they gain important gratifications from sexual relations (though they may vary in the type of gratification they consider important). In the second category are those who are positive about sexual relations and find them gratifying, but who in one way or another (by comparisons with other "more important" things, or by moderating adjectives and lack of superlatives) indicate that they are less enthusiastic than the first group. In the third category are those women who find sexual relations unpleasant or say they are indifferent but without indicating sharp displeasure (only 6 per cent of the men say they have little interest in or dislike sexual relations). In the fourth category go those women who not only dislike sexual relations but actively reject sexuality and are strongly displeased, disgusted, or disturbed by the necessity to have intercourse with their husbands.

What is postulated here is a continuum from strong positive involvement with marital sexuality to strong rejection. The preceding categories are gross, but will serve for the comparisons necessary as a background for our exploration of attitudes toward family size and family planning. These categories do not take into account most of the subtleties which are of interest to psychologists of sex. For example, two women may be placed in the "very positive" category although one may find it easy to achieve orgasm during intercourse and the other finds it difficult; the latter, who is essentially frigid in terms of orgasm, may nevertheless be placed in our positive category because she values the closeness and non-orgastic physical contact that intercourse provides.* Our data, though in many ways quite full, are admittedly not very precise for the exploration of subtleties. However, for our purposes, judgments about the general value assigned sexual relations in marriage are more important than the psychic ease or difficulty of achieving these values.

In general, the variability of response about sex was much

*Women, and their husbands, were asked specifically about whether and how often the wife achieved orgasm (or "came" or reached a "climax" or some other synonym). Most of the respondents understood the question and were able to give a response that sounded reasonable. However, over a third of the women answered in ways that left the analyst unsure of whether they actually referred to orgasm. For this reason, no effort was made to tabulate these data, and not much systematic reliance has been placed on answers to this question, although in individual cases the answer can be quite enlightening. Instead, judgments about gratification in sexual relations were based on the total discussion in response to all questions on this subject.

greater among wives than among husbands. The majority of men indicated strong interest (often in ways suggesting that they regarded such an interest as central to the definition of a man), and only 6 per cent said that they found no pleasure in sexual relations. In the discussion which follows we will examine the variations in the wife's sexual enjoyment, in the husband's interest in sexual relations with his wife, and the degree to which husbands and wives have similar or dissimilar degrees of enjoyment of sex. In all of these instances we will look first at the variability among different class groups and then at the difference between lower class couples in intermediate or highly segregated conjugal relations (there are no differences in the middle class between those in joint and in intermediate relations).

Women differ considerably from class to class in the extent to which they take pleasure in sexual relations (Table 3–1). On the positive side, middle and upper-lower class women say they find sexual relations highly gratifying more than twice as often as lower-lower class women; fully half of both the former groups are in the positive category, compared to only 20 per cent of the latter. On the negative side, there is a steady increase from middle to lower-lower class in the proportion of women who are indifferent to or reject sexual relations. Strong rejection appears frequently only among the lower-lower class women. In our data there are no differences at all in the sexual gratification indicated by women of the upper- and lower-middle classes, although social observers have believed that "Victorianism" lingers more in

TABLE 3–1:
WIFE'S GRATIFICATION IN SEXUAL RELATIONS

		Very Positive	Positive	Slightly Negative*	Rejecting*
Middle Class	(58)	50%	36%	11%	3%
Upper-Lower Class	(68)	53	16	27	4
Lower-Lower Class	(69)	20	26	34	20

*Combined for test. $X^2 = 29.85$ $df = 4$ $T = .28$ $P < .0005$

the lower-middle class. Perhaps in some areas this is true, but apparently not with respect to the wife's overall feeling about her sexual relationship with her husband; as we will see, sex takes a valued place in the family-oriented context of lower-middle class life.

Within the lower class, conjugal role-organization seems to be more strongly related to the wife's sexual enjoyment than is the division between upper-lower and lower-lower class (see Table 3–2). Although the Negro-white differences at each class level were small enough to allow the two groups to be combined in Table 3–1, the differences between the races when role-organization is considered are larger, and results are presented separately for the two groups. Very positive attitudes toward sexual relations are characteristic of almost two-thirds of Negroes and whites in intermediate relationships, but of only a small minority of those in segregated relationships. On the other hand, strong rejection is essentially a phenomenon of the lower-lower class in segregated relationships. Each of the in-between categories are somewhat more frequent among those in segregated relationships.

TABLE 3–2:
CONJUGAL-ROLE SEGREGATION AND WIFE'S ENJOYMENT OF SEXUAL RELATIONS: THE LOWER CLASS

		Very Positive	Positive	Slightly Negative*	Rejecting*
White					
Intermediate segregation	(25)	64%	4%	32%	—
Highly segregated	(22)	18	14	36	32%
Negro					
Intermediate segregation	(22)	64%	14%	18%	4%
Highly segregated	(25)	8	40	32	20

*Combined for test.
Whites: $X^2 = 8.41$ T = .42 P < .005
Negroes: $X^2 = 9.21$ T = .44 P < .005
Combined: $X^2 = 23.82$ T = .50 P < .0005

The main difference between Negroes and whites is that among Negroes with segregated relationships, rejecting attitudes toward sexual relations are somewhat less frequent, and mildly positive feelings are more common (but this difference is not statistically significant) than is the case with whites. Apparently, lower class Negro women in segregated relationships are more interested in sexuality than their white counterparts. In both groups, however, the greatest difference between wives in intermediate and in highly segregated relationships is that the former show a strong interest in sexual relations almost five times more often than the latter. Such attitudes are slightly more common among that half of our lower class sample that enjoys intermediate conjugal relationships than among all middle class wives, although slightly negative attitudes are also somewhat more common. The mildly positive category of moderated enjoyment of sexuality, on the other hand, seems more common among middle class wives.

The differences, then, between lower class wives in intermediate relationships and their middle class counterparts are minor compared to the differences between both of these groups and the lower class wives in segregated relationships. In the first group, a majority take considerable pleasure in sexual relations and regard this as an important part of marriage; in the latter group, few wives have such attitudes and the majority have slightly to strongly negative attitudes toward sexual relations.

Among husbands, we find a similar pattern to that for wives though within a narrower range of responses. From Table 3–3 it is apparent that middle and upper-lower class husbands have stronger interests in and are more enthusiastic about sexual relations than are lower-lower class husbands. There is a consistent (but not statistically significant) difference between Negro and white at each lower class level: Negro husbands do not as often moderate their enthusiasm for sexual relations as white husbands, a response consistent with that of their wives. For each racial group, however, upper-lower class men are more likely to express strong interest than are men of the lower-lower class.

The difference between husbands in intermediate and in highly segregated conjugal relationships are in a similar direction (Table 3-4). Husbands in intermediate relationships are more likely to prove very interested in sex and to place a high value on the enjoyment they gain than are husbands in segregated relationships. (This difference is significant only for Negroes or for the two racial groups combined.) As with the wives, the lower class husbands in intermediate relationships seem to attach as much value to sexual relations as their middle class counterparts; while more men in the highly segregated group say of sexual relations, "It's O.K. when you

TABLE 3-3:
HUSBAND'S INTEREST IN SEXUAL RELATIONS

		Very Interested	More Mildly Interested
Middle Class	(56)	78%	22%
Negro Upper-Lower Class	(24)	87	13
White Upper-Lower Class	(32)	69	31
Negro Lower-Lower Class	(25)	56	44
White Lower-Lower Class	(34)	35	65

$X^2 = 20.25$ df = 4   T = .24   P < .0005

TABLE 3-4:
CONJUGAL ROLE ORGANIZATION AND HUSBAND'S INTEREST IN SEXUAL RELATIONS: THE LOWER CLASS

		White		Negro	
		Intermediate Segregation	Highly Segregated	Intermediate Segregation	Highly Segregated
Very interested		72%	55%	90%	56%
Mildly interested		28	45	10	44
	N =	(21)	(20)	(21)	(25)

Whites: not significant
Negroes: $X^2 = 5.38$ T = .34   P < .025

feel like it." Among lower-lower class whites, especially, this attitude is common; from their comments one gets the impression that the necessity to be close to their wives, even if only physically, takes most of the pleasure out of marital sexual relations.

Finally, a comparison of the level of sexual interest of husbands and wives specifies further the quality of their sexual relationship. Table 3–5 presents for each class a tabulation of the degree of consensus between husbands and wives on how much or how little they are interested in sexual relations. Among middle and upper-lower class couples, in about half of the cases husband and wife share the same general degree of sexual interest; usually both are either strongly or mildly positive toward sexual relations. In the lower-lower class, however, only about one quarter of the couples have the same level of interest. Only a few wives are more interested in sex than their husbands; and the pattern of greater enjoyment for the husband is increasingly common as one moves from middle to lower-lower class, increasing from one-third of the cases to two-thirds.

Within the lower class, the difference between couples in intermediate and highly segregated relationships is in a similar direction, and in this case there are no differences between Negroes and whites, since the greater frequency of mildly positive responses by Negro wives is compensated for by the greater frequency of strongly positive responses by their

TABLE 3–5:
COMPARATIVE ENJOYMENT OF SEX BY HUSBAND AND WIFE

		Husband Enjoys More	Equal Enjoyment*	Wife Enjoys More*
Middle Class	(51)	33%	59%	8%
Upper-Lower Class	(43)	47	51	2
Lower-Lower Class	(45)	67	26	7

*Combined for test.

$X^2 = 14.27$ df = 2   T = .27   P < .001

TABLE 3-6:
CONJUGAL ROLE-ORGANIZATION AND COMPARATIVE EN-
JOYMENT OF SEXUAL RELATIONS BY HUSBAND AND WIFE:
THE LOWER CLASS

		Husband Enjoys More	Equal Enjoyment or Wife Enjoys More
Whites			
Intermediate segregation	(21)	38%	62%
Highly segregated	(20)	80	20
Negroes			
Intermediate segregation	(21)	33%	67%
Highly segregated	(24)	75	25

Whites: $X^2 = 5.80$ $T = .38$ $P < .02$
Negroes: $X^2 = 6.20$ $T = .37$ $P < .02$
Combined: $X^2 = 11.40$ $T = .37$ $P < .001$

husbands (Table 3-6). The end result is that for about two-thirds of the Negro and white couples with intermediate relationships, the husband and wife have approximately equal interest in sexual relations, while among Negro and white couples with highly segregated relationships over three-fourths of the husbands indicate more enjoyment of sexual relations than do their wives.

As before, the results for lower class couples in intermediate relationships closely parallel those for intermediate middle class couples. However, because negative attitudes toward sexual relations are slightly more common among lower class wives with intermediate relationships, the *nature* of the divergence between husband and wife when it occurs is different in the two groups. Thus, for three-fourths of the middle class cases where the husband enjoys sexual relations more than the wife, the husband is strongly positive and the wife only mildly positive; for three-fourths of the lower class couples, the husband is positive toward sexual relations and the wife has negative feelings about them. Thus, although the amount of divergence is very similar, its quality is quite different, and reflects more conflict in the lower class group.

Taking all these data together, there is an apparent decline in interest in sexual relations as one goes down the social class scale; this decline is sharper for women than for men, and the largest difference is between lower-lower class men and women and those higher in status. These differences seem to a very large extent a function of the total conjugal relationship, since those lower class couples most similar to middle class couples in conjugal role-organization (that is, those with intermediate relationships) are only slightly different from their middle class counterparts. (As a corollary, it should be noted that the difference between joint and intermediate conjugal role-organization has no effect on the sexual relationship either in the middle class, where joint relationships are common, or in the lower class, where they are rare.) There is, in addition to these differences related to class and to conjugal role-organization as an intervening variable, a consistent tendency (not statistically significant in our sample) for lower class Negroes to be more positive in their attitudes toward sex in marriage than comparable whites. We have no immediate explanation for this difference, but examination of the qualitative data below may shed some light on it.

Table 3 – 7 presents a summary of husband-wife patterns of sexual enjoyment which compares middle class to lower class couples in each of the two conjugal role-organization types.

Since wives vary as much as they do in the stance they take toward sex in marriage, it is of interest to know how aware husbands are of their wives' attitudes, how accurately they assess the degree of enjoyment wives find in sexual relations. Table 3 – 8 presents these results for the couples in our sample in which the husband gave a clear statement of how he thought his wife felt. Among lower class couples in highly segregated role-relationships, we find husbands as likely to overestimate the amount of sexual gratification their wives have as to assess it correctly; the husbands either portray their wives as interested when in reality they have negative feelings about sex, or the husbands indicate strong interest on the wife's part when she herself indicates only

TABLE 3-7:
PATTERNS OF HUSBAND-WIFE SEXUAL ENJOYMENT

	Middle Class	Lower Class	
		Intermediate Conjugal Role-Relationship	Highly Segregated Conjugal Role-Relationship
	(51)	*(42)*	*(44)*
Both positive			
Both very positive	45%	57%	11%
Husband only very positive	25	7	20
Both mildly positive	12	2	7
Wife only very positive	8	5	2
Wife negative			
Husband positive	8	29	55
Husband negative	2	—	5

TABLE 3-8:
HUSBAND'S ASSESSMENT OF WIFE'S ENJOYMENT OF SEXUAL
RELATIONS

		Husband's Assessment Consistent With Wife's Statements	Husband Says Wife Enjoys Sex More Than Her Statements Indicate She Does
Middle Class			
Upper-middle	(23)	100%	—
Lower-middle*	(25)	84	16%
Lower Class			
Intermediate role-relationship*	(42)	79	21
Highly segregated role-relationship	(43)	49	51

*Combined for test.
$X^2 = 20.87$ df = 2   T = .33   P < .0005

moderate interest. Among lower class couples with intermediate role-relationships this kind of overestimation is much
less frequent. It is difficult to tell whether the lower class
husbands who make such errors are deceived (this seems
unlikely), are deceiving themselves (probably common), or
are trying to deceive the interviewer (also probably common).
In any case, these results suggest not only a lack of
communication and openness about sexual relations among
couples with segregated role-relationships, but also a tendency on the part of these husbands to conceal from themselves and others their awareness of the divergence between
their own and their wives enjoyment of sex. In this lower
(mainly lower-lower) class group, there is ample cultural
precedent for the husband to regard sex as mainly his pleasure, and the separateness of the roles of husband and wife
mitigates against embarrassing communication of conflicting
values attached to sex. But even here, husbands apparently
feel the need to present themselves as considerate of their
wives, as men who do not force their attentions on unwilling
mates, who do give pleasure as they take it. They do not want
to admit the extent to which their wives are grudging in their
participation in sexual relations.

Husbands in less segregated conjugal role-relations more
often know and are willing to say how interested their wives
are in sex; slightly over 85 per cent of these men are able to
portray their wives accurately. They know when sexual interest is more their own or is shared by the wife, and they
know when the wife would prefer not to engage in sexual
relations and is only seeking to please her husband. Since
they are willing to concede such unpleasant realities, these
husbands and wives are in a better position to come to some
compromise and to control more effectively the disruptive
force of lack of consensus about sexual relations. (We will see
below that only in segregated relationships do wives complain
that their husbands are inconsiderate concerning sexual relations.)

STRONG MUTUAL ENJOYMENT OF SEXUAL RELATIONS

A fuller understanding of what is involved when both partners indicate a strong positive interest in their sexual relationships can be gained from an examination of what these people actually say. Below, the comments of three couples with this pattern are quoted extensively. The first couple illustrates the typical middle class pattern; they are lower-middle class Catholics with a joint conjugal relationship. The husband is forty-three, the wife thirty-one; they have been married ten years, have four children and do not want more.

Husband:

I had been married before this time, and had had a few women friends between marriages, so I knew a lot from experience. It's been very satisfactory since we got married. We do it about four to six times a month. Of course, I travel so I have to be welcomed home a little more [smiles]. My wife and I both enjoy each other; we are compatible. The main satisfactions are physical, of course, and also emotional relaxation, and a sense of unity. That goes for both of us. She has an orgasm most of the time. Orgasm is the climax of emotion for a woman, but you can't always tell when a woman has one. Sex is very important; it is the way the family grows bigger and closer in feeling between husband and wife.

Wife:

I knew a girl was a girl and a boy was a boy. I knew about necking, and that there was such a thing as intercourse. I didn't learn much from my mother, mostly from reading and my high school hygiene course. I read a Church pamphlet and all they said was that you shouldn't pet. Two months before I got married a girl friend told me about her experience in detail. [How did you feel about this?] I was scared, nervous, scared that maybe he wouldn't be satisfied. It took a couple of months to get adjusted. I got pregnant immediately. My husband was very understanding. It was wonderful after the first couple of months and still is. It gets better and better. [Has there been any time in your marriage when things were not so good?] No, we always have a good time. We have intercourse once or twice a week because he travels. If he were at home more I would like it more. Of course, while he is away I could always put up a sign or something but I don't think I will. [How would you compare your feelings with your husband's?] We look at it similarly. Probably the majority of husbands and wives look at it differently; a few of the girls in my club give the impression that they have it only to please their husbands. They are always saying how they are so relieved when their husbands go away. I don't feel that way. I know that I am pleasing my husband, I can tell, and he makes me feel that I am the best thing in the world. I feel tired afterwards, but certainly not worn out. It makes him feel good, feel that he is a man and that he has made me feel good. I have an orgasm almost all the time. If I don't I feel sort of angry, frustrated, but it happens so seldom I really have to think to remember when I didn't have one. Sex relations are a very great percentage of our marriage. It ranks closest to being the most important. Because of it, everything else runs smoothly. You see how lucky I am, I have a wonderful man.

Both husband and wife are at pains to emphasize the "good time" they have in their sexual relations, and the importance of sex to them. As will be apparent in the next section, they are characteristic in their emphasis on both the physical and interpersonal gratifications which intercourse allows, and on the importance of both partners taking pleasure in the act. (Also characteristically, the husband is more restrained in his comments than his wife.) While the wife, unlike a good many lower class wives, does not feel she was totally ignorant about sex before her marriage, she feels herself to have been ill-prepared, and that the good relationship now enjoyed required effort on her part and understanding on the part of her husband, with the result that "it gets better and better." Not uncommonly, wives who are proud of their ability to find deep gratification in sexual relations speak disdainfully, as this woman does, of their peers who see sex as a duty rather than a pleasure; they feel a sense of superiority over women who have such "old-fashioned" feelings. It is clear from the ways these middle class women talk that they know a modern woman is supposed to enjoy sex; women who have not achieved a sense of self-confidence about their sexual role will indicate their frustration and sense of inferiority or failure when they admit that they do not achieve orgasm as often as they feel they "should."

One difference is qualitatively apparent between the lower-middle and upper-middle class groups. Few upper-middle class couples communicate the sense of joy about sex that this couple does. The higher group is more serious about it, as if they see the value placed on good sexual relations as an injunction which must be lived up to rather than taken for granted. In some ways, such upper-middle class couples seem less frank than lower-middle class couples. They try to be more "scientific" in discussing their sexual relations, with the result that what they say seems more impersonal. To what extent this is reflected also in their behavior is difficult to say.

Representative of the lower class couples in intermediate relationships, who also commonly have relationships of strong mutual enjoyment, is the following upper-lower class Protestant couple. The husband is twenty-six, the wife is twenty-five; they have been married for seven years, have three children and want no more.

The husband:
   I knew a little about sex from reading and talking with other boys. I guess I really never thought much about it. It made us closer together; sex is the basis for marriage. I'm still as active as I was when we first got married. We do it about twice a week, sometimes more, sometimes less. We get the same feelings and satisfaction when we do. It releases tensions, gives you a feeling of belonging. It's a good cure for insomnia, too. I'm aware when she has an orgasm, sometimes it's more than others, but I don't know exactly how often. Sex is very important to marriage. A man, if he's denied it regularly, it will cause trouble, disloyalty sometimes.

The wife:

I really didn't know much about sex. My mother told me just about all I knew. I knew what to expect, about the intercourse and how it was done. In school they taught us a lot, too. But I tell you I didn't know as much as I do now! I kind of looked forward to it as a new experience; I wasn't afraid. I think it's just bettered itself since then. It made me love him more. Of course when we first got married it was more frequent. I've refused Joe several times because I was afraid I'd get pregnant. If my period was late I would worry and know I wouldn't enjoy it and wouldn't let him do it. Since the last baby I haven't been half as bad because he doesn't want anymore kids either and he's been more understanding [i.e., used condoms regularly]. [How often do you have intercourse?] Maybe once or twice a week, sometimes more, sometimes less, and of course not at all when I have my period. He might like it more; I wouldn't care to have it more, or less, it's just right. We both enjoy it; sometimes he may enjoy it more but he's patient with me. He wants to make love to me because he loves me. I know he likes it because as far as I can tell he *never* went out on me. I have a climax most of the time. Not every time, but Joe must be a pretty smart old guy because he can usually tell even before we start whether I'm ready for it or not. He's real patient and gentle and he kind of builds me up. [How does it feel?] Well, it's hard to put in words. I just feel real full of pep, real good. Kind of like you was up on a star or something and everything beneath you — How did I get myself into this mess, I need a cigarette. Boy, what I'd do for humanity! — I kind of drift down, you know. Kind of like the rest of the world is blanked out, you know what I mean. It sorts of starts coming back into focus on the way down. [What about at the peak?] It's kind of like electrifying. It starts and then it goes from one point out all around; girl, I'm real busy about that time!

This woman manages to overcome her self-consciousness, though not without difficulty, to give a fairly vivid description of orgasm, which she says she has most of the time. Like the first couple above, this man and woman are proud of their sexual relationship, with the wife perhaps more proud because being sexually potent seems more of an accomplishment for a woman than for a man. Both of these people share the belief that if a man does not find sexual gratification at home he is likely to seek it elsewhere (less a preoccupation in the middle class), but the wife does not feel that she makes sacrifices in order to assure her husband's loyalty.

In both of these cases the emphasis on mutual enjoyment of sexual relations can be seen as an integral part of a conjugal role-relationship that is not highly segregated. The emphasis on sharing in such relationships extends to sex so that it becomes important that the wife also find enjoyment in sexuality, and that the husband not be "selfish" by taking pleasure only for himself. This imposes a responsibility on both partners. The husband must help his wife to achieve gratification, and the wife must achieve it to prove to herself that she is really participating as she should and to provide her husband with the fuller gratification that is believed to come when the wife achieves orgasm also. As has been suggested, upper-middle class couples seem to take all of this more seriously than other couples who indicate a similar level of enjoyment.

One final example illustrates that small proportion of lower class couples (11 per cent) in highly segregated relationships where both husband and wife maintain a strong interest in their sexual relations. In this lower-lower class Negro couple the husband is thirty-one, the wife is twenty-seven. They have been married twelve years and have seven children.

The husband:

Well, I knew a little about it, not too much. I learned some from experience and some I picked up from hearing older men. I don't think anything could beat it. It's always been good to me. There hasn't been much change since we got married; except that sometimes I don't go as long as I thought I could. [How often?] It varies, sometimes almost every night, then some nights we miss it. I'd say sometimes four or five times a week, sometimes less. We both enjoy it, it's something you just enjoy doing. I always come and I think she always do, too.

Sometimes it's not as long as other times. It changes but it's always good; sometimes I stay just a few minutes and then sometimes I go a long time without no letup. If two people like each other like that I think it's real important; you can tell how one feels about the other one.

The wife:
   All I knowed was just it was good feeling. No one told me anything about it. I felt shame at first. Mother had told me to keep my dress down. Then when I got pregnant I got married, like I already told you. I began to enjoy it better. My husband was a little big for me but after he broke me in it was much better. He got my cherry, you know. I guess that's why I love him. I still enjoy it; we're made for each other, right size and fit. I don't feel shame anymore; he's my husband now and I don't have to be 'shamed like I did when we courted. [How often?] Three times a week, sometimes more. When I'm pregnant I have my husband more, sometimes every night. I have it enough, he might like it more. When I'm pregnant I like it more. I don't have to worry about getting pregnant because I already am and it's better too. Used to be I would wear him out, I wanted it every night, but now only when I'm pregnant. He enjoys it more because he don't have to worry. We like to get our kicks, you know, go off together, but I worry about getting pregnant sometimes. I like to get my kicks, that's the main satisfaction. I don't like it when we don't get our kicks at the same time although I know that makes you pregnant. He enjoys it a lot but if he's kind of tired he don't last long and he don't like that. I always come. I really like for us to get our kicks at the same time but you really get caught when it is at the same time. The most important thing that it is, is sexual relations. That's why people marry, anyway. It holds a man and a woman together.

The sexual relationship provides this couple with one of the few mutual activities they enjoy. Although the husband is a steady worker and the family is not in daily financial danger, they are poor and their life is rather bleak. The wife indicates that she makes most of the decisions, that the husband simply brings home money and sometimes spends time with his sons. He spends a good deal of time away from home with friends, and the wife spends some time away, participating in church activities. Yet their relationship is stable and both seem satisfied with their own roles and with the performance of the other within the context of a highly segregated relationship. The autonomous interest that the wife takes in sexual relations (her desires are not at all dependent on his, she "would wear him out") is quite a typical for this croup, but it fits in with her independence in other areas of family life. She is used to having things her own way around the house, and apparently feels rather confident in this role. Her self-possession, combined with her husband's adequate support and his apparent lack of hostility allow a positive sexual relationship in a marital context which the experience of most other couples suggests is not really conducive to such a relationship. In this situation the wife's comment that sex "holds a man and a woman together" assumes more than casual significance. The sexual relationship is both an actual force for marital solidarity in a context where there are few other such forces, and a symbol that all is still well since, as the husband says, from how sex goes "you can tell how one feels about the other one."

MODERATE INTEREST IN SEXUAL RELATIONS

Not all husbands and wives who are positive about sexual relations are willing or able to find the enjoyment in intercourse characteristic of the couples discussed above; in about one-third of the couples in the total sample one or the other partner moderates his interest in sexuality, balances it off against other, more important, things, or in other ways indicates that sexual relations, while an accepted part of marriage, are not highly valued. These patterns, in which neither partner rejects sexual relations but one or the other moderates his interest, seem most characteristic of the middle class (45 per cent), quite characteristic of lower class couples (particularly Negroes) in highly segregated role-relationships (29 per cent), and are uncommon among lower class couples in intermediate role-relationships (14 per cent).

The following upper-middle class couple illustrates many of the themes that recur among middle class couples of this type. The husband is thirty-three, the wife thirty-two. They have been married eleven years and have three children. The wife works and is active in various clubs and associations.

The husband:

I knew a little about it but I was very shy; religion and companions had a lot to do with it. After we got married it was a problem learning about it but it's part of life and I had looked forward to it. We have a good relationship; it's gradually improved. Marriage took away all the mystery from sexual relations. I went from ignorance to understanding. It's about once a week now. It probably should be more frequent. I enjoy it so I'd like it more often. My wife feels the same but I think I place more importance on it than she does. We both feel that our feelings are mutually satisfying. It's emotionally satisfying, a completeness that is involved. It's the missing link in living. Cleanliness has a lot to do with it. You should both be very clean. If either party isn't clean it would be a difficulty — bathing before bedding. I think my wife is very satisfied. She feels she is doing something for me. She has an orgasm 99 times out of 100 I would say. It's similar for a woman as it is for a man; she doesn't ejaculate, it's a nervous reaction. It means as much to her as it does to me. [Your satisfaction always the same?] It changes from time to time. I don't know why; it's probably the mental approach. I think foreplay is important and it has an important effect later; if one doesn't function as he or she should it affects the culmination.

The wife:

I knew a little from my mother. Both Robert and I were anxious and wondering, neither of us had ever experienced sexual relations before our marriage. He is very understanding, not conceited or overly interested in sex. It is not a main factor in our marriage. [Have there been changes since marriage?]

We're more sure of ourself and have climaxes together. [How often?] Once a week. It should be more but we're, or I should say I'm, always too tired. I know I shouldn't be but when I've had a full day I'm just tired and Robert understands. We feel about the same except that he wants more than we have but he is very considerate and understanding. It gives pleasure, just pleasure, I guess. I usually have an orgasm except when I'm tired I don t. He seems to always react the same way; it doesn't vary for him. It definitely plays a part in marriage but it's more important to him, I guess he gets more satisfaction.

This couple have a relationship in which there is much emphasis on sharing activities and interests. Their values about sex clearly carry out this emphasis; both think it important that each partner have some satisfaction, that sexual relations occur when there is mutual willingness, that the husband be considerate and understanding, that he help the wife to achieve gratification. But unlike the couples discussed above, there seem here to be real interferences with sexual gratification—clearly for the wife and implicitly for the husband.

While most couples feel they were not well-prepared for the sexual aspects of marriage, this couple perhaps started off less well than most other middle class marriages. The husband notes that his religious background (Lutheran) made for some conflict, and his emphasis on cleanliness (unique among our interviews) suggests some continuing notion that sex is dirty. His effort to master these conflicting feelings by rationality and "understanding" is suggested by his rather anti-romantic statement that "marriage took away all the mystery from sexual relations." In general, his responses to the interviewer's questions present in exaggerated form the self-conscious, rational, mechanical approach which seems more characteristic of upper-middle class men and women; he goes "by the book." The wife, in her discussion, moves immediately to portray the relationship as equal—she takes pains to point out that her husband was as virginal as she, that he is not "conceited or overly interested in sex," and she places sex in its proper light as "not a main factor in our marriage." The husband is not willing to go this far in departing from how a man in our culture is supposed to feel but his remarks are quite consistent with the wife's view. The wife sees her other activities (work, outside interests, family responsibilities) as taking up most of her energy, leaving little for sexual relations. She makes it clear that she feels these other activities are more important, and recognizes that her husband does not completely share this view, though she expects him to be "considerate." Where other couples see in sexual relations a means of strengthening their marital relationship and of making it run more smoothly, this couple sees sex as something aside from the larger relationship—something, to be sure, that needs to be attended to, but not really an integral part of their life together.

The emphasis in the middle class on equality (sometimes carried to the extreme of equivalence) of the sexes would seem, then, to cut two ways. For some couples it means that the wife is freed from the traditional, Victorian view that sex is a duty for a woman, not a pleasure. For other couples, the wife's equality means that she is free to pursue her own interests, and less under an injunction to provide sexual services to her husband whether she wishes to or not. While few middle class women reject sexual relations completely, they do vary in the extent to which they take advantage of these two rather different ways of being their husbands' equals.

As noted above, among couples in segregated role-relationships, wives who have only moderate interest in sexual relations are more commonly Negro; white wives are slightly more likely to be at the very positive or the rejecting extremes. The 40 per cent of Negro wives in such role-relationships who indicate moderate interest and gratification in sexual relations communicate in their comments a sense of the acceptability of a woman's interest in sex that is different from the way white wives speak of their sexual roles. They communicate a sense of wanting to enjoy sexual relations, though they often find this difficult to achieve. Two examples will serve to indicate how Negro women in these groups speak, and the kinds of husbands' attitudes that provide the context in which they respond. In the first, an upper-lower class couple, the husband is thirty-one and the wife twenty-seven. They have been married nine years and have five children; they want no more but do not use contraception.

The husband:
   Well, when I got married I knew just about what I know now. I wouldn't say I knew what to do about getting in the mood. I didn't learn any place in particular, I just got it from older boys and used what they said for myself. My feelings haven't changed any except that I learned more about sex. Our feelings are pretty much the same about sex, you can't expect to be onesided and have a real good marriage. I like the thrills you get. If you finish before she does that's not good. Her satisfaction would be for her companion to provide satisfaction. First she has to be satisfied and second I do. Sex is the most important thing, say 95 per cent of marriage. Usually the man is not going to stay with his wife without that; he'd seek outside employment. The wife, if she's not satisfied, would do the same. So you see a lot depends on sex.

The wife:
   I didn't like to so well at first. I do better now than I did at first. I like it a little better at times. Then again, I don't know, I guess it's better. He likes it. Most of the time I feel more relaxed but it doesn't have to be so often. Sometimes I have a climax but not all the time. I'd say most of the time. He gets satisfied all the time. It's very important. He talks about it all the time.

This family is quite typical in the segregated role-relationship characterizing the activities of husband and wife. The husband works steadily and gives his wife money; she takes all the responsibility for what goes on at home and he helps very little. He plays pool or "just sleeps" in his spare time. For the husband, the sexual relationship apparently allows a kind of close mutual interest which little else in his married life provides. Sex, at least, is something which a man and his wife can (indeed, must) share. His wife does not completely agree with the picture he presents. She recognizes the potentialities for personal gratification in sex, but seems also to resent his sexual demands. Perhaps she resents the fact that this is the only area in which they do get together; she points out earlier in the interview that they have no common activities and that around the house "he don't help do nothing, just brings home the money." The wife, however, feels she can't complain; "nothing is really his bad points cause I don't have to work."

In our second, lower-lower class Negro couple, the husband is twenty-eight and the wife is twenty-four. They have been married seven years and have four children; they want no more children but do not use contraception.

The husband:
I felt good about it when I got married; I felt I had what I wanted and still feel that way about it. We have it twice a week. She want it just like we have it, she fuss when I say, when I ask her, she say she tired, just tired. I try to satisfy her, do like she wants to do. When we have sex I try to treat her nice, don't go the rough way with her. [Rough way?] Putting it in the buck. [Buck?] That's folding her legs up all the way over her shoulders. She feels she should get in bed and treat me like I treat her, nice, try to satisfy me. Ask me did I get satisfied! Sex gives a man's pleasure, makes him feel grand. She gets the same feeling. It's very important to me. One reason is I don't have to get up and go out in the street. And I don't have to be afraid to get anything cause I know there ain't nothing wrong with her.

The wife:
I didn't know anything until I got married. That was the part I dreaded, I guess I thought it was worse than it was. It was not as difficult as I thought it might be. I just had to get used to it. I guess I get satisfaction now, I'm used to being married. He just like to do that more than I do. Once a week would be enough for me but we do it two or three times a week. We both like to be petted; he never seems to be in a hurry and I

don't either. Sometimes I don't get any satisfaction cause I don't want to do it. I come but after a few seconds it's nothing. It makes you feel kind of strange and I know I have been satisfied. I guess it's very important. You get along better when you do that then if you don't. Look like it make everything go smoother. It's pretty important to me—all men say it's a part of love and all women want to be loved. It's real important to him; he act like he couldn't do without it if he had to so I guess it's real important.

This couple has a segregated relationship similar to the first couple, except that the husband does not start to work until 11:30 A.M. and therefore occasionally helps around the house. Mainly, however, "he don't do anything but lay down and sleep when he is at home." The wife says her husband does not want to go out with her, and that he is jealous and asks questions if she goes out by herself. He, on the other hand, complains that she does not want him to go out with her, or to go with him when he wants to go out. He feels she would be "gentler" with him if he earned more money (he earns $31.00 a week as a bus boy). This man seems more egocentric in his attitudes toward sex; he does not emphasize the importance of gratifying his wife, only that he should not be too rough with her. She, like the first wife, sees her husband as withdrawn from the family (he, too, "just sleeps" when home) and does not find it easy to shift from a compensatory indifference to him to interest in making love.

In both cases, the stability and security of the family and of the wife's role depend on coping with and compensating for the husband's apartness from the ongoing activities of family life. Having achieved some stability on this basis, both wives feel resentful and uncertain when their husbands wish to move closer to them—resentful because they suspect the husband is interested in his own pleasure, and because he pays little non-sexual attention to them; uncertain because their sexual role demands a receptivity and passivity they have foregone in other areas of relating to their husbands. (The lower-lower class Negro wife quoted above who shows strong interest in sexual relations does not seem to conceive of her sexual role as passive.) Nevertheless, these women, unlike over half of their sisters, do find some pleasure in sexual relations. They find this pleasure more despite than because of their husbands' attitudes (the Negro husbands' attitudes do not seem particularly different from those of white husbands).

When one compares the statements of women who have strong interest in sexual relations with those who have only moderate interest, one interesting facet of their attitudes toward their own physical gratification stands out. Most women in both groups say that they have orgasms "most of the time" or "almost all of the time," but their attitudes toward this fact differ considerably. The women in the moderate-interest category often seem to resent this vulnerability to sensuousness; they are made uneasy by their orgastic capacity and seek to moderate it. In the middle class, at least, they know they are supposed to experience orgasm but they are uncertain about it; often they talk as if they feel they should limit this pleasure, much as one might limit intake of candy for fear that too much is not good. Or, like the last woman quoted, they give the impression of psychic distance from the experience—"After a few seconds it's nothing. You feel kind of strange and I know I have been gratified." It is as if someone else had the orgasm. With respect to orgasm, then, the psychological difference between the strong and moderate-interest groups seems to be that the first group is better able to accept orgasm fully as ego-syntonic and is less anxious about the feelings and fantasies orgasm brings with it; for the moderate-interest group orgasm is a potent but potentially destructive force, an enemy within, that may be enjoyed only occasionally and must be kept well under control. Since, apart from individual psychological factors, a woman's ability to accept orgasm will depend on how secure she feels with her partner, it is understandable that women in less segregated conjugal role-relationships are more comfortable with this aspect of their femininity then are women in more segregated role-relationships, even if comparison is limited only to the women who have positive interest in sexual relations.

NEGATIVE AND REJECTING ATTITUDES
TOWARD SEXUAL RELATIONS

Less than 20 per cent of middle and lower class wives in joint or intermediate role-relationships have negative attitudes toward sexual relations, but 60 per cent of those in segregated relationships do. How do these women and their husbands talk about sex in their marriages? The examples which follow represent the range of attitudes encountered in this group.

We begin with an upper-lower class Catholic couple at the border between segregated and intermediate relationship (the husband has mixed feelings about how much he wants to "submerge" himself in his family; his wife wants to participate more actively in financial management and wants him to spend less time by himself). The husband is thirty and the wife twenty-seven. They have been married for four years and have one child although they have wished for more.

The husband:
I knew as much as I could learn before I was married and I think every young man should learn the way I did, going to a house of prostitution, but one that's run in a respectable way. I would take a son of mine to such a place to get the knowledge when he was old enough to want to have sex. I would tell him if he got a girl he was going around with in a family way he would have to marry her and support her and her baby and if he wanted this kind of thing to go where he could get it without taking any chances on spoiling his own life and a girl's life, too. Seems like it isn't the disgrace it used to be but I still think it's wrong for kids to start sex. I married a virgin and I knew that it was going to take me a little while maybe to teach her about sex, but she never did seem to take to the idea like I hoped she would.

It isn't that I don't satisfy her, I work on her until she gets the right response, she will tell you that, I'm gentle in working up to sex, she will tell you that, too, you ask her, but she got a notion as she grew up that it's a kind of an underhanded part of life, she won't see that it's necessary to a man to satisfy himself. It's always like she would let me go ahead when I want to but she isn't part of it, she is just letting me have my way. I think it's got to be a disappointment to a man to have his wife feel that way. It isn't because she doesn't want babies, she does.

[Have things changed since marriage?] They have never really improved. At first I kept on thinking once I had showed her how close it made a man and woman feel she would come to have the same urge I did, that's honestly what I thought, but I would have to say things have got worse instead of better. But a man has to have satisfaction once in a while if he can't get it at home. First I wanted her three or four times a week, then she began putting me off 'til it got to once a week, then all the time it was less and less. You might not believe it but sometimes it's a month between times; it's never more than once a week and a man's got a right to a better deal than that.

I think part of it is she wants to work until we get ahead and that way it might be that she's ready but still when she was using rhythm, when the priest said it was all right, she still was caring less and less for sex. She's sort of a cold woman, but she is crazy about our son. She just isn't ever really interested, never sort of coaxes me along and I wish she would.

Well, my feelings are those of any healthy man I would say —hell's bells it's one of the things you expect in your marriage and it's something a girl should expect, too. It might be hard for her just at first but she ought to grow more and more interested, not less and less. I don't think, even at the very start, she felt all sort of excited insides. A prostitute may not feel that way but she makes you think she does—it's part of her trade. [What are the main satisfactions?] Now you must'a been married a long time, you ought to know what the main satisfaction is to a man, I can't tell you any more than you know. You kind of work up to the climax, then it comes and you're tired but happy. You're not just tired, you're satisfied and kind of spent. There isn't anything that can make you feel as close to your wife as when you get her in your arms and love her up and then finish off with the sex act.

[How does she feel?] I guess she thinks, "There, I've done it again, and now he won't bother me anymore for a while," or maybe she just says to herself she's glad that's over. I hope when she thinks she really wants to be pregnant again she'll let herself go and it can be a mutual satisfaction. [Does she have orgasm?] I see to it she gets all the physical satisfaction there is, you ask her and she will tell you that same thing. I know I'm a big bruiser but I handle my wife carefully, she will say the same thing. I don't want to rape her, I want to have a sex life happy for both of us. I don't think she ever feels any different, any more interest or any more indifference, I never see any difference.

[What is the importance of sex?] Well, how are you married if you don't have sex? It's just getting a housekeeper and somebody to look after you and that's not for you if that's what you marry for. Sex was intended, it's the only way the animals produce isn't it.?

The wife:

I was the most naïve little lamb that ever said "I do." I knew of course there was a sex act connected with being married but that was the beginning and end of my information. It seems that now, if you believe what you hear, many girls have the sex experience before they marry, but I would have been so ashamed of a thing like that it would never have been possible. [How was it after marriage?] It was bad, I will tell you frankly. It was hard for Mike, I know, but it was terrible for me. There was this sort of deep down feeling that this was something we shouldn't do, it was physically very painful — I think you've talked with Mike and seen him and you will know what I mean, he is a big powerful man.

I knew it was part of my married life and I wanted to do all any wife should do but I just couldn't help dreading nights when he would want to make love. I will say for him Mike has been wonderful in building up to it and all but it doesn't give me the great physical satisfaction it gives him. I could live happily the rest of my life without any sex except that I want more children. Of course, it isn't painful any more but I am afraid it isn't pleasurable either.

I try to do my whole duty in the matter and I always expect to do that — I think that's only fair to your husband. [But you never, yourself, feel sex desire?] No, I don't, do you think most women do? [Yes, I do think that.] Maybe it's better that way, but how can you make your feelings change to that extent. [How often do you have relations?] I think maybe once a week, maybe a little less than that, three times a month maybe. I haven't kept any particular schedule about it. Unless there's some physical reason against it I try always to be willing. I think that's the way it is, probably, the husband is always in the mood, the wife isn't and I think it's just the way people are, men always eager, women not near as much so. Sometimes you just definitely don't want it, sometimes you don't mind that much. I suppose God made men that way. Mike really tries to give me a physical satisfaction; well he does, but it doesn't seem to do anything for me emotionally, or very little.

[What are the main satisfactions?] Just the feeling that I'm doing what is required of a wife, that this is my husband's privilege, that it was to him part of the meaning of being married and that I don't want to drive him away to some other woman. I have some friends — well, I just know this one girl, she feels that way about it, too, it's something you have to expect and accept. His satisfactions are those of any man, I guess, he gets wildly excited and then after the act, he feels relaxed and satisfied. He gets very eager, he has what he wants, he is contented. I hope in time I can understand just what this is, maybe after I quit working and want another baby, or maybe after I get pregnant again, whether I'm working or not, I'll have a greater desire toward him. I think there are times when it's difficult for me to have the [physical] response but usually I do get it, because Mike is willing to slow down and wait for me to get to that point.

[What is the importance of sex?] I think they are an important part — it's what makes marriage different from any other relation you can have. You can admire and love a man and all that but unless you're intimate you haven't gone all the way you're supposed to go for marriage.

The husband has proved a disappointment to his wife because of his irresponsibility in money matters; although he earns a good living she has had to work hard to keep him from deepening their indebtedness. Both would like to be mobile into the middle class (he works as a salesman) but his irresponsibility makes this difficult. The wife yearns for a stable, secure, family-centered, "Catholic" marriage. She is willing to do everything she feels is required of her to make a good marriage, but she clearly has strong moral resistance to sex that is exacerbated both by her husband's irresponsible behavior and by her inability to become pregant again.

The wife conceives of her sexual role as a sacrifice — "unless you're intimate you haven't gone all the way you're supposed to go in marriage." Although she indicates that she does have orgasm during intercourse, she does not like the idea at all and cannot begin to integrate sexuality into her sense of who and why she is; it is foreign, foisted upon her by nature and the demands of society. She observes her husband closely in this as in other areas of his behavior. She thinks she knows how he feels and does not consciously deny his right to be interested in sex. She feels that he is considerate and interested in helping her accept her sexual role, but she pulls back in confused regret. She is not able to see sex in marriage as really different from sex outside this sacrament, unlike the woman quoted on page 00 who says she felt ashamed of having intercourse before marriage but now doesn't have to be ashamed. Like other women who have these feelings, she tends to exaggerate the interest men have in sex ("The husband is always in the mood . . . men are always eager") and she seems to feel that sex carries with it the danger of being hurt (Mike is a "big and powerful man") unless she is on guard and he well-intentioned. His irresponsibility in other areas of life probably does not make it any easier for her to entrust herself to him sexually (not only has he made "bad investments" but she also believes he drinks and gambles too much).

It is interesting that the husband, too, touches on this theme of potential violence — he refers to himself as a "big bruiser," denies that he wants to "rape" her, and emphasizes that "I handle my wife carefully." Like his wife, the immorality of sexual relationships seems never far from his mind; he begins by referring to his early experiences with prostitutes, is concerned about kids who "start sex," comes back to the prostitute model in criticizing his wife for not even faking pleasure during intercourse, and hints at the temptation to engage in extramarital relations when he says, "but a man has to have satisfaction once in awhile if he can't get it at home." It is clear that he means more than the physical satisfaction of ejaculation; he wants to be accepted as a sexual being, admired for his prowess, and, hopefully, to feel "close."

In many ways, despite his seemingly constructive attitude toward marital sexuality, his attitudes mirror those of his wife. He wants to see marriage as converting the immorality of intercourse into a moral and legitimately gratifying expression for both man and woman. That his wife cannot accept this reinforces his more negative feelings about sex, and the division between "good" and "bad" women. Given his frankness with the interviewer (he seemed eager to talk to someone about his problem), it seems likely that many of these feelings and attitudes are also communicated to his wife, resonating with her own feeling that she must be "bad" to be a good wife, and that if she cannot do so, then she is a cold woman. This probably does not pain her as much as she suggests, since early in the interview she characterized herself in this way: "I like to keep house and get food for my men; I think I like to be a matron."

A somewhat different kind of rejection of sexual role is illustrated by the wife in the following lower-lower class couple. The husband is thirty-seven, the wife twenty-six. They have been married for nine years and have four children. The wife has just recently begun using a diaphragm regularly because they want no more children.

The husband:
I learned my knowledge in four years in the Army before I was married. If you don't have any relations there is no marriage; it's part of marriage. This is what brings you together originally. [How were relations in the beginning?] I couldn't disagree with any of them. Everything was fine; I was satisfied.

There was more satisfaction after marriage. [Since then?] I
don't think there's any change. No change in satisfaction. We do
it less often; two times a week. Running around taking care of
house and children and man's hard work—you just don't feel up
to it. If we're both not tired we both enjoy it. If one of us is
tired, we don't enjoy it. I feel that as long as the wife is in the
mood to have relations—we still feel the same about each other.
I get satisfaction. She always comes too. [How?] I couldn't put
it in words. I know when she is. It's different than for a man. I
think she experiences a greater thrill. It's different physically
and emotionally, especially emotionally. Once in a while there's
variation. It all depends on how you feel. Sometimes you feel
like talking and fooling around. I'd say half of marriage is sex. I
couldn't really answer for wife, but I think it's the same for her.

The wife:
[What did you know about sex before marriage?] Nothing,
not a single thing, not a single, solitary thing. I had a vague idea
of what it was from my stepfather, but he used words I didn't
understand. When I was 13, I took a sanitary napkin and waved
it in my hand all the way down Lincoln Avenue. I didn't know
what it was. I went home and my girl friend asked my mother to
explain to me what it was and when my mother got through
explaining, I asked my cousin and my girl friend how are you
supposed to fasten the Kotex across the breast—that's how well
my mother explained it to me. [And after marriage?] The first
time I was terrified because I had overheard girls in high school
talking and they said it hurt and I have always been terribly
afraid of any hurt. I guess after the second and third time [in-
tercourse] I began to enjoy it very much and I wondered if I had
heard the term overly-sexed.
He never satisfies me. I felt like I was left hanging all the
time. My husband told me to ask the doctor and I did. He
laughed and told me to douche with ice water after intercourse.
He said it would calm me down or suppress me. I did it for a
while—but then I learned to calm myself down. I put my mind
on something else—sometimes I got up and had a cigarette or
something. [Do you have a climax?] I had only one climax in
nine years—that's since I'm married. I still don't have a climax.
I used to always want it so bad—every night—and we did it

almost every night. Oh, he took all the time and patience and the knowledge that he had but it didn't help.

Now we do it about once a week. Now I could do without it. For the first three years I had that feeling of desire so intensely and with never being completely fulfilled, I felt like I'm waiting and waiting and it never comes and so I lost all my desire. Now, I feel I just tolerate it. I refuse him only during pregnancies. [How does he feel?] He couldn't believe it or understand it and things got to a point where I told him I did come to have a climax. He still thinks I have a climax, he always asks me and I tell him yes, he used to feel so bad when I told him "no." He's not too satisfied with once a week, sometimes it's more but he does it less often than at first. [Are there any satisfactions for you?] I think just from his caresses. Most of the time I condition myself and my mind to want it so that I enjoy it even though I don't come. He always has a climax.

[You said you had a climax once—what happened then?] It was a long time ago. I was on top of him and he had me turning across him and I turned all the way around until I was upside down with my head between his feet. I felt my pelvis bone rubbing him and then I had a climax. I asked him to let me do it that way, we were just experimenting. Since then he never let me do it again, he told me he never remembered such a thing happening and he believed it could not be done so I never mentioned it again. I felt wonderful—it was the first time I could completely relax afterwards.

Now, as a rule I don't think I'd ever miss it. Through my past experience, my marriage would be just as good without it. My husband couldn't live without it. For a long time, when my husband and I did start having arguments and disagreements and I'd get the feeling "boy, I could live without him"—up to four years ago I felt intercourse was the most important thing between us because we didn't agree on anything—that was the only thing we were close together in. You'll notice I probably contradicted myself, I've never been a very consistent person to do one thing, the same thing all the time. Now I'm extremely careful, I dream about being careful day and night. I use the diaphragm—ritually. That's all I know of that I can do. My husband never has the money to buy rubbers, he hasn't used one in six or seven years.

The wife here would like to find pleasure in sexual relations and apparently has made some efforts in that direction but to little avail. While she does derive some gratification from physical closeness and caresses, she also finds relations very frustrating, and apparently feels she would be just as well off without having to participate. The larger marital relationship is one in which there has been considerable conflict. The wife feels the husband buys things they can ill afford, resulting in their not being able to pay the rent. She also says he refuses to work sometimes when a job is available (he is a painter).

The husband is rather matter-of-fact in his attitudes toward sexual relations; he seems to regard sex as providing a routine kind of pleasure, and his comments about his wife's sexual interest suggest he is simply paying lip service to the value that sex should be gratifying to both. The wife, on the other hand, is obviously quite agitated in her feelings; she is both strongly attracted to sexual relations and strongly disturbed. Obviously she feels that her husband is as little understanding in this as in other areas of their life together. She hoped that sex could bring them closer together but then gave up and now says, "I lost all my desire. Now I feel I just tolerate it." She feels that sex makes no contribution to her marriage either by itself or in enriching the relationship generally — "Through my past experience, my marriage would be just as good without it." She apparently made one effort to find the kind of autonomous gratification in sex that the woman discussed on page 78 finds, but her husband would not tolerate this (to him, probably unnatural) way of making love. He wants his wife to keep her subordinate place in sexual relations; she apparently feels sufficiently subordinated in the larger relationship so that she rebels at this and increasingly rejects sex despite her obvious strong wish for gratification. To keep the peace she lies to him about having orgasms, but in herself she withdraws from the experience.

Obviously, to the extent that women wish for sexual gratification their ability to realize this is highly vulnerable to disturbances in their other relations with their husbands.

When they are unsure of their husbands' loyalties, when they feel the husband spends time away from home with his friends, drinking, gambling, or diverting money from the family, they tend to build up resentments which have repercussions in the sexual area. Since they start out in marriage with very mixed feelings about sex, they are likely to maintain acceptance and enjoyment of sex only in the context of good feelings about their husbands more generally.

As we saw in previous chapters, a majority of lower class couples in highly segregated role-relationships have serious, disruptive problems, centering mainly on the husband's tendency to divert his interest and resources outside the home. These themes are emphasized in the following lower-lower class couple, in which the husband is unemployed, the family on ADC, and the husband so frustrates the wife by drinking and running around that she has hauled him into court to seek to force him to support the family. He is thirty-six, the wife is thirty-three. They have been married for thirteen years and have eight children.

The husband:

I was well prepared for sex. When we first got married it was great. It was as important to her as to me. But since then she seems to have lost her desire quite a bit because of fear that she would have more kids. It seems every time she takes an interest in it we have another baby. I like to do it, but no more than any normal human being. She doesn't seem to get anything out of it. I guess she's had enough for her lifetime. She hardly ever has a climax. It plays an important part in anybody's marriage. Everybody wants to have their bodies close together, but there's times when they're wore out and they don't want it.

The wife:

I didn't know nothing about it. I had intercourse with my husband before I married him. I didn't think it was right but I was wantin' him so bad I didn't want to go against anything he wanted to do. I don't get satisfactions. I used to but not now. I just don't want my husband because of the things he does. If it was up to me I would never do it. Since that time we separated [a year ago] I don't have the desire any more. It's been two or three months since I've felt anything at all. It hurts me too much.

The husband gives the impression in his interview that he increasingly spends his time away from home. He doesn't know what has gone wrong but he feels somehow that his wife does not like or respect him any more. As a result, his comments suggest that his sexual interest has waned, and he finds pleasure more in the company of his male friends than in bed. The wife now feels that he has no interest in her:

> The way I look at it he just married me to get kids and take care of the house; I don't get nothin' else. . . . Ever since I've been married I've had it this way. I kept waiting for him to change. I've seen men go along for a few years and then change, which my daddy was one, but my husband didn't. I made up my mind I won't have any more kids because he treats me so bad when I'm pregnant. He slaps me and hits me when I'm pregnant. He doesn't want me to tell him about things that need to be done. He doesn't work and when he works he doesn't take care of the family right.

Yet these people have been married for thirteen years. Though the wife is very dissatisfied, she is reluctant to separate from the husband permanently and he does not want any change in status at all. The marriage can be maintained on a highly segregated basis, but the wife can find little to recommend in sexual relations, given both her fear of pregnancy and her dissatisfaction with her husband.

Not all women, of course, start marriage with a wish to find sex pleasurable and then find experience moving them in a more negative direction. The following lower-lower class couple illustrates the situation in which sex has from the beginning been of interest only to the husband. This couple has been married for fifteen years and have four children. The husband is thirty-five and the wife thirty-two. Theirs is a stable relationship, and aside from her "coldness" neither complains a great deal about the other, although she does feel that he gambles (in card playing) more than he should.

The husband:
Before I was married, I knew what sexual relations were. I knew how it felt and what was done, but that's about all. I guess I thought it was done just for fun. All I ever knew I learned from other boys, just hearing them talk about different things they had done, and that I should try it too, that it was a lot of fun, but that maybe I would have to get married first. I guess we're like everyone else. We have relations, I guess, two or three times a week. [How does your wife feel?] She doesn't have any desires to be aware of that I have ever known. She just doesn't ever want any part of that if she can help it. She always knows when I am thinking about it she says. Things haven't changed that way at all since we were married, she has always been like that. I don't know why it is. Well, I don't know just how important they[sexual relations] are, but it's something I feel is important, and that is why you get married. To me it is just as important as any other part of marriage. I can't say what they do for me other than just to satisfy my desires, I guess, the same as they do for any man. I would prefer them more often, I think, if my wife didn't fuss about it so much. They could be much better for me, I think, if my wife got any pleasure from them at all. They are not at all important to her, in fact, she says if she never did it at all it would suit her fine, then she wouldn't have anything to worry about. I don't know why she feels that way, I wish I did know; she has always been like that. [What are the differences between you?] The differences are that I do it because I enjoy it, she does it because she feels it's her duty, I guess. Certainly not because she enjoys it.

The wife:
I didn't know anything about sex at all, I had heard older kids talk but I never knew what they were talking about, except that it was something you weren't suppose to talk about, that only married people did, but I didn't know what it was. I never was very curious about it like a lot of the kids were. I guess I really didn't even think about that at the time I was married. One thing

I do remember is that the first time, I bled so much I thought he had killed me, that he had done something to me and I was going to bleed to death. Maybe that's when I began to feel the way I do now about sex. I have always had a dreading of having to do that. I guess it is something that is done because my husband wants to. He acts like it is something he could not live without but I sure could. I'm aware of his desires all right, he sees to that, but as far as I am concerned I don't have any, other than to be left alone, where that is concerned. I can't say that things have changed any in that way since we've been married. I know when he wants to, and I usually say well go ahead and get it over with. They aren't the least bit important to me but it does cause me a lot of worry. That's the one thing I wish I never had to do. It's just plain disgusting to me. If I had my way I would prefer never to do it. I don't think there is any way it could be any better for me, the only way would be if I didn't have to do it at all, I would like that better. To him, they are very important, he says, but I can't see why. I wouldn't know what they do for him, he acts like its something he can't live without. I sure don't know why he feels that way, I've wondered that for years. [Who is it important to?] My husband, there is no doubt of that. It is for sure not important to me. I could go from now on without any of that. He acts like his life depends on sex life or relations, and it is of no interest or pleasure at all to me. It's a worry for me all the time, as to whether I am going to get pregnant or not.

This wife's rejection of sex is based less on disappointment with her husband than on her conception of herself as a hard-working woman who tolerates no nonsense. She finds little pleasure in life and seeks little. She is not morally embattled like the first woman discussed in this section; rather, she simply sees her life as that of a mother and homemaker and thinks of sex as something unfathomable which interests only men. Her sense of separateness and autonomy is very strong; she comments about marrying in the first place:

I don't think I ever loved him, or at least I never had the feelings people say you're supposed to have when you're in love and, for that matter, I've never had them since. I think the main rea-

son I married him was because of his sisters. He had been going
with some other girl that his sisters wanted him to marry because
her family had more money.

Marriage came more from competition with sisters than from
interest in the potential mate. In short, she makes her life in
terms of a female role that is sexless, that relates to mothering ("it's more important for the children to have a mother
than anything else I can think of") and to being a housekeeper for the man who brings in the money that supports the
household and allows the children to be reared. This sense of
who she is, of what she will and won't do, seems to have
arisen early in her life, since her memory (and his) of their
"courtship" period portrays it as unromantic as the present.

Frequency of intercourse

Given these various levels of enjoyment of sexual relations, we turn to the effect of interest in sex on frequency of
intercourse. Table 3 – 9 presents the relevant data.

Given some of the other differences in sexual attitudes
among social class groups and between those in intermediate
and segregated role-relationships, it is of interest that frequency of intercourse does not vary sufficiently among these
categories to approach statistical significance. Instead, the
frequencies mentioned are approximately the same in all
groups. There is little difference in the overall distribution of
frequencies given by men and by women. Half of both groups
indicate a frequency of once or twice a week and the balance
split more or less evenly between greater and lesser frequencies. Among the couples in our sample there is agreement
between husband and wife about frequency in 70 per cent of
the cases, and in only 5 per cent of the cases does one partner
indicate a frequency of less than once a week and the other
partner more than twice a week.

Most people indicate that there is considerable variation

TABLE 3-9:
FREQUENCY OF INTERCOURSE

		Less than once a week	Once or twice a week	Three or more times a week
Total sample:				
All men	(148)	22%	54%	24%
All women	(174)	19	52	29
By level of sexual enjoyment				
*Men**				
Very positive	(101)	11%	56%	33%
Not very positive	(47)	45	49	6
Women†				
Very positive	(68)	6%	50%	44%
Mildly positive	(47)‡	23	54	23
Negative	(59)‡	30	56	14

*$X^2 = 23.52$ df $= 2$ T $= .34$ P $< .005$
†$X^2 = 18.48$ df $= 2$ T $= .27$ P $< .005$
‡Combined for test.

in how often they have intercourse, and often resist answering by saying, "We don't have a schedule, we just do it when we feel like it." Most men, and a good many women, say they would like to have intercourse more often but do not do so because of the press of responsibilities, tiredness, or other distractions. Members of the middle class sometimes feel that manual workers have intercourse more often because "brainwork is so tiring." The latter, however, often feel that white-collar workers probably have intercourse more often because "their work doesn't tire them out" since they do not use up their physical strength on the job. Like active sports, sex may relax and refresh, but most people seem to feel that to gain these gratifications you have to have enough energy to start with. There is widespread awareness that frequency of intercourse declines with age and length of marriage, but there is considerable variation in this. The respondents are inclined to console themselves on this score by saying that "now it's quality instead of quantity."

As might be expected, frequency of intercourse is related to the level of interest each partner has in sexual relations. Only 11 per cent of the men who have strong interest in sexual relations have intercourse less than once a week, compared to 45 per cent of those who are not so strongly interested. Among women, 44 per cent of those with strong interest in sex have intercourse more than twice a week, compared to fewer than 20 per cent of those who are less interested. Overall, the association between frequency and interest is slightly stronger for men than for women, as would be expected given the fact that men more often take the initiative. (That the association is not even stronger for men indicates the extent to which women can moderate frequency when they wish.) The somewhat greater influence of husbands is apparent when one compares the cases in which the husband is more interested in sexual relations than the wife with the few cases in which the wife is more interested. Where the husband is more interested, only 26 per cent of the couples have sexual relations less often than once a week and 21 per cent have intercourse more often than twice a week, whereas when the wife is more interested 57 per cent have intercourse less often than once a week, and none have a frequency of more than twice a week. When both are strongly interested, only 9 per cent have a frequency lower than once a week, and 54 per cent have intercourse more often than twice a week.

On the other hand, the wife's rejecting attitude *per se* seems to have little effect on frequency. Where the wife's attitudes are negative but the husband is strongly interested, 39 per cent of the couples have intercourse more often than twice a week and only 11 per cent have a frequency lower than once a week. Where the husband's attitude is not strongly positive, only 10 per cent have intercourse more often than twice a week, and 45 per cent have a frequency lower than once a week. The wife's attitudes do have an indirect effect, however, in that with time her negative feelings tend to lower her husband's interest and he then becomes less demanding. Finally, as might be expected, where the husband's interest is strong and the wife's only moderately so, the average frequency predominates; 58 per cent of this group have intercourse once or twice a week. In general, then, frequency of intercourse can be viewed as the resultant of both partner's attitudes, with the husband's predispositions having the stronger influence, most dramatically so when the wife's attitudes are negative.

The husband's role as initiator

For almost all couples, sex is an activity in which the husband's interest and initiative is regarded as appropriately central, though the wife may share this interest, fully or only moderately. Much of the discussion in the interviews therefore revolves around what the husband does or does not do to make intercourse more pleasant or acceptable to his wife. Several of the views that husbands and wives express on this score have become apparent in the extensive interview excerpts given in the previous sections. In this section we will discuss some of the issues that are central to this problem.

Some men reflect in their comments a belief that it is important that sexual relations be mutually gratifying to both husband and wife. Others talk in ways that suggest, either explicitly or by implication, that they are not concerned with whether or not their wives find gratification in sexual relations; their comments are oriented only to their own personal gratification. Still others, while not specifically mentioning the wife's gratification as important, do reflect a concern about the wife that is not inconsistent with a desire that she be gratified.

Tables 3 – 10 and 3 – 11 present distributions of these categories of response, first for three class and religion groupings and then for the two conjugal role-relationship types in the lower class. In our discussion of levels of sexual interest and frequency of intercourse no mention has been made of reli-

TABLE 3–10:
HUSBAND'S CONCERN THAT SEXUAL RELATIONS BE MUTU-
ALLY GRATIFYING

	Specific mention of mutual gratification	Not specifically mentioned, but response not inconsistent with mutual gratification	Specific suggestion of disinterest in wife's gratification
Middle and upper-lower class Protestants (59)	85%	12%	3%
Middle and upper-lower class Catholics (35)	46	43	11
Lower-lower class* (46)	37	24	39

*Includes Negroes
$X^2 = 34.71$ df = 4 T = .35 P < .005

gion because no differences were apparent in the data between Catholics and non-Catholics at each class level. However, as shown in Table 3–10, religion does seem to make a
difference in the extent of concern with mutual gratification
above the lower-lower class level. Among Protestants, 85 per
cent of the husbands specifically comment on the desirability
that sexual relations be gratifying to the wife. They often
mention mutual orgasm and more often still say that they
think it important that their wives find sexual relations generally satisfying. While the number of Catholics and Protestants
that talk in ways that suggest a real indifference to this question is about the same, only 46 per cent of Catholics in our
sample specifically comment on mutual gratification as a
desideratum of sexual relations. They apparently think of sex
somewhat more egocentrically than do Protestant men, although we will see below that middle class Catholic men
consider sex less as a purely physical gratification than do
middle class Protestant men. At this point, we can suggest

TABLE 3–11:
CONJUGAL ROLE-ORGANIZATION AND HUSBAND'S CONCERN THAT SEXUAL RELATIONS BE MUTUALLY GRATIFYING: THE LOWER CLASS

		Specific mention of mutual gratification	Not specifically mentioned, but response not inconsistent with mutual gratification	Specific suggestion of disinterest in wife's gratification
Intermediate organization	(43)	74%	14%	12%
Highly segregated	(46)	35	22	43

$X^2 = 13.07$ df $= 2$ T $= .32$ P $< .005$

that these Catholic men tend to think of sex more exclusively in terms of a movement toward the wife, and are less concerned than Protestants about her movement toward them and finding pleasure in the closeness that results.

Illustrative of the way men talk who are specifically concerned with mutual gratification are these comments:

I guess learning to climax together is one of people's greatest desires, learning to control together has been the main change since we got married.

If she gets enjoyment I know I will get a lot more. I manage to stay until she has an orgasm, too.

We get a lot of satisfaction from being together, it's a mutual thing, a deeper feeling of belonging together.

At the other extreme are the lower-lower class husbands, 39 per cent of whom talk in ways that suggest that they do not give much thought to the question of whether sex should be gratifying to the wife as well as themselves. When we look at the breakdown by type of conjugal role-relationship for the lower class (Table 3 – 11), we see that 43 per cent of those in highly segregated relationships reflect such attitudes compared to only 12 per cent of those in intermediate relationships; 74 per cent of the latter specifically mention the desirability of mutual gratification compared to only 35 per cent of the former. Illustrative of these two tendencies are the following comments:

Husbands in intermediate relationships:
We both enjoy it a lot. She always has a climax. If mommy don't enjoy it, I don't either!

It was good when we got married. Like when you're first married you try to wear it out but you don't. It was new to my wife and I had to teach her, help her to enjoy it. As time goes on you try to get better satisfactions, new ways. What you do is look for different ways to arouse feelings, different positions and like that. We're pretty well matched. She erupts in a way so it's the same as for a man. I usually try to make it so it happens before I do, sometimes you have to wait for her. She usually comes before or during when I come.

Husbands in highly segregated relationships:
I think with a woman it's mostly just to satisfy her husband and then she's happy. I think if she feels he is satisfied she is satisfied. She has an orgasm about half the time, I guess. [What does sex mean to her?] I really don't know. I don't think it makes her no difference other than to satisfy me.

I think that we are satisfied with one another as much as anyone else. She comes sometimes, sometimes she don't. Actually, a woman is not as much interested as a man in sex.

I enjoy myself; I can't say for her but I think she enjoy herself. I think she come, too, but I can't be sure.

Often men in segregated relations talk as if the wife's enjoyment is her own problem—let each partner take care of himself. They are not necessarily hostile to the idea that their wives find pleasure in sex and often say that their wives do find it pleasureable (although we have seen that half the husbands in segregated relations overestimate the pleasure their wives find in intercourse); but they do not accept the idea that they should be concerned or make efforts to insure that their wives find sexual relations gratifying.

A more specific test of the importance of mutual gratification involves the question of whether the husband makes conscious efforts through foreplay or "waiting" to ensure that his wife is gratified when they have intercourse. Some men speak about such techniques and other do not; wives, too, sometimes comment that their husbands make specific efforts to help them achieve orgasm. Table 3 – 12 presents these results for social class groups (role-relationship types within the lower class are not different here). It is not surprising that fewer than 20 per cent of lower class husbands or wives mention this kind of specific help by the husband, since not many of these husbands seem concerned about mutual gratification in sex. The fact that half the lower-middle class husbands or wives mention husbandly techniques compared to very few of the upper-middle class spouses is not so readily understood. Upper-middle class husbands seem equally interested in the wife finding gratification, yet apparently they are not expected to be as concerned about their

TABLE 3 – 12:
SPONTANEOUS MENTION THAT HUSBAND ENDEAVORS TO ENSURE HIS WIFE'S GRATIFICATION

	Husband		Wife	
Upper-middle class	(25)	12%	(29)	7%
Lower-middle class	(26)	42	(29)	48
Upper-lower class	(43)	23	(63)	19*
Lower-lower class	(46)	6	(70)	14*

*Combined for test.
  Men: $X^2 = 12.14$ df = 3   T = .22   P < .001
  Women: $X^2 = 15.89$ df = 2   T = .24   P < .005

role in insuring gratification as are lower-middle husbands, whose wives talk in this way:

> Some nights when I wouldn't particularly have any desire about it if he starts love making pretty soon I find my pulse accelerating and my own desire rising.

> I have an orgasm about three-fourths of the time. It's what goes before that brings it on, the love play, he rubs the clitoris and there's the kissing of the breasts.

> He sees to it that I do (have orgasm). It took us a couple of weeks to hit it off right but now we do. The penis is hard and you wouldn't want him to quit until you've reached it. You just kind of explode. Things have to be just right for me to enjoy it. If one of the children was sick I could never make love.

These women suggest, in mentioning foreplay, control, and the like, that the husband actively assists the wife to achieve gratification. It may be that upper-middle class women are expected to require less specific attention from the husband to achieve gratification. Like lower class women, they are autonomous with respect to orgasm, but unlike lower class women, they are expected to achieve it without special effort on the husband's part. Technique may loom larger for lower-middle class couples because of their belief that the wife is less freely sexual, more dependent on her husband for stimulation and consideration. The individualistic emphasis of upper-middle class conceptions of husband and wife may mean that each is expected to bring a more ready sexuality to the relationship; the wife is expected to learn this during the early years of marriage and then to require less careful attention from her husband.

Some wives complain that their husbands are not considerate in their sexual behavior. The wife who indicates this may say that her husband does not help her achieve gratification, or that he demands intercourse too often or when she does not feel like it, or that he rides roughshod over her negative feelings about sex and does not try to reach some mutually acceptable compromise. Table 3 – 13 presents the proportion of women in the middle class and in each role-relationship type in the lower class who voice these complaints. Apparently only lower class women in highly segregated role-relationships have these feelings. We have seen in earlier chapters some of the ways in which wives in such relationships view their husbands in other areas; here we see an extension of such views into an area about which these wives have many other negative feelings.

It is not surprising that these women are the only ones very likely spontaneously to say that they engage in sexual relations with their husbands only because it is their duty, a duty about which they either feel resentful or which they fulfill in order to show their love but without finding any pleasure for themselves (Table 3 – 14). Given these attitudes, it is understandable that these women feel they have a special right to demand considerateness from their husbands since they are making "sacrifices" for the husband by permitting themselves to be available for intercourse.

TABLE 3 – 13:
WIFE'S FEELING THAT HUSBAND IS INCONSIDERATE OF HER WISHES IN CONNECTION WITH SEX

Middle class	(58)	— *
Intermediate organization	(44)	7%*
Segregated organization	(48)	40%

*Combined for test.
$X^2 = 32.37$ $T = .46$ $P < .0005$

TABLE 3 – 14:
SEX AS WOMAN'S DUTY, NOT FOR PLEASURE

Middle Class	(55)	13%*
Lower Class		
Intermediate organization	(42)	14*
Segregated organization	(45)	38

*Combined for test.
$X^2 = 9.57$ $T = .26$ $P < .005$

Functions of sexual relations

Men and women recognize that sexual relations "do" something for people, that they satisfy particular needs, although the degree of clarity people have about the functions of sex varies considerably. In the interview excerpts quoted earlier in this chapter, the husbands and wives indicated something of why they feel sex is of value. In this section we will examine more systematically a few of the functions which appear most often in people's spontaneous comments. (We emphasize spontaneity, because these specific ideas were not sought in the interviews but arose in response to questions about the satisfactions each partner finds in sex and the importance attached to sex in their marriage.)

Two common themes stand out. One is that sex provides what we will call "psychophysiological" relief—it gets rid of tension, relaxes, gives physical release ("it's like the back pressure on a car that you have to get rid of") and provides positive pleasure in the form of orgasm, etc. The other theme emphasizes, instead, the social-emotional gratifications that come from closeness with the partner, a growth of love, a sense of oneness, of sharing, of giving and receiving. Almost all of the respondents (over 95 per cent) who speak of the functions of sex in these terms noted that it provides psychophysiological relief, but many mentioned this only and did not talk about the gratification of social-emotional closeness. Table 3 – 15 presents a tabulation of type of gratification for middle class Protestants and Catholics and for the two conjugal role-relationship types in the lower class (no religious differences were apparent at either lower class level). Middle class Catholic men and all middle class women emphasize social-emotional as well as psychophysiological gratification. The quality of their conceptions is illustrated by the following comments:

> I feel that it is an immense emotional experience, an act of unity, to me it has a deep and holy significance.

We're both receiving and giving; it gives you a feeling of being wanted.

There's the feeling of closeness and the expression of love for each other.

It's a complete union, you both get physical and emotional satisfaction.

It's a mutual feeling of love between you and your wife, a matter of conveying love.

We noted earlier that fewer Catholic men mentioned mutual gratification in their discussion of sexual relations,

TABLE 3–15:
PSYCHOPHYSIOLOGICAL AND SOCIAL-EMOTIONAL FUNC-
TIONS OF SEXUAL RELATIONS

| | Middle Class | | Lower Class | |
| | | | Intermediate Organization | Highly Segregated Organization |
	Catholic	Protestant		
Husbands				
Sexual relations provide social-emotional closeness and exchange	95%	63%*	52%*	16%
Sexual relations only provide psychophysiological relief and pleasure	5	37	48	84
Wives				
Sexual relations provide social-emotional closeness and exchange	89%†	89%†	73%	32%
Sexual relations only provide psychophysiological relief and pleasure	11	11	27	68
*Combined for test (N =)	(21)	(35)	(40)	(31)
†Combined for test (N =)	(27)	(19)	(33)	(22)

*Combined for test (N =) (21) (35) (40) (31)
$X^2 = 29.42$ df = 2   T = .40   P < .0005
†Combined for test (N =) (27) (19) (33) (22)
$X^2 = 21.22$ df = 2   T = .39   P < .0005

yet we find here that almost all of them, and significantly more of them than middle class Protestants, mention social-emotional gratifications in addition to these purely psycho-physiological. In contrast, 85 per cent of Protestant middle class men mention mutual gratification, but fewer mention social-emotional functions. Putting these two sets of findings together, we suggest that middle class Catholic men seek complex psychic gratifications from sexual relations with their wives, and that these gratifications involve the wife as a person as well as a body. These men, in short, reflect in their specific attitudes toward sex the religious conception of the conjugal act as sacred, and they seek a sense of sacredness in sex that is not so prevalent among middle class Protestants.

At the same time, they show less concern with reciprocal gratification on the wife's part, perhaps because the shift of emphasis from physical orgasm to social-emotional closeness and unity seems to make it not particularly relevant. The middle class Protestant men, on the other hand, do not so unanimously emphasize interpersonal as well as internal gratifications. This subgroup stands out in its emphasis on purely psychophysiological gratification, which in most cases they specifically say should be mutual. Sex for them thus partakes less of the sacred and is more of a straightforward sensual pleasure like other pleasures. It is interesting that for wives there is no difference between religions; wives in both groups place importance on non-physical gains, and in their extended remarks it is clear that for many, perhaps most, of them the physical pleasures of sex are possible only because of the feelings of love and closeness which sexual relations express.

In the lower class, couples in intermediate role-relationships approach the middle class Catholics (and Protestant women) in their emphasis on the interpersonal functions of sex, but for those in segregated relationships the gains are heavily physical and internal (somewhat less so for women). This is, of course, consistent with separateness in the marital relationship generally; if a low value is placed on co-operation and sharing in the relationship generally, it is not likely that such values will be manifested in the sexual area in particular. Concentration on physical aspects is apparent both in the comments of couples in which the wife enjoys sexual relations and in which she does not, as the following excerpts illustrate:

> I get kind of worked up when he begins on me and pretty soon I'm all for it. I give and he takes, but I take, too. It gives you something you can't get any other way. That's when it's the right man and the right night and all that—maybe some men aren't very good at it; you look at some of these little shrimps sometimes and think maybe they wouldn't give you the kind of satisfaction but Joe is good. Without sex any marriage would break up or else he would be out cheating on her. When they take their time and you put your mind on what you're doing it makes you feel good when you're finished, it just makes you feel real good.

> It makes me feel good. When a guy gets heated up and after he has it he feels good. It takes the crabbiness out of you, you don't yell. Sometimes she can't sleep but after she gets it she sleeps better. When a woman comes it makes her feel better.

> He thinks sex is very important. It gives him some kind of pleasure; it makes him happy. He couldn't live without it, I guess. It's just getting the sexual urge out of him. He wets from it, you know, it comes out. Me, I could do without it; our feelings are completely opposite.

In this kind of situation, the wife's interest in sexual relations will depend much more than in the other groups on her ability to find personal gratification of a more physical kind, since neither she nor her husband think of sex as providing other kinds of gratification. Since, as we have seen, few husbands in this group evince interest in helping their wives to achieve gratification, the wife's isolated position in intercourse requires her to bring strong interest to the situation if she is to find it gratifying.

Some couples say that frequent sexual relations make married life go more smoothly, make the partners less tense and "crabby." If we had probed specifically for this concept, probably a good many more men and women would have mentioned it than did so spontaneously. Nevertheless the results are interesting. Among men, 28 per cent of those in the lower-middle class mentioned this as one of the functions of sex, one of the gains from it, compared to only 8 per cent of all other men. This greater interest among lower-middle class men in the friction-reducing function of sex is consistent with their strong familial emphasis; for them any activity which preserves the even tenor of married life is valued. However, lower-middle class women do not similarly emphasize this function. Instead, among women, such gains from sex are most frequently mentioned among the lower class (21 per cent compared to 9 per cent of the middle class). The quality of comments in the two cases is different, however. The lower class women are often specifically concerned to keep their husbands from complaining and "making a fuss" about being kept on short rations; the lower-middle class men emphasize instead the positive gains that come from mutual participation in sexual relations.

One final function of sexual relations we should consider has to do with preserving the marital relationship itself. Both husbands and wives sometimes comment that sex is important in marriage because if there were not a satisfactory sex life the couple would either separate or one or both partners would engage in extra-marital affairs. One woman offered this view from direct experience:

> Sex is pretty important in a marriage. I know he was running around with other girls. I didn't care much for sex and that's what started him running around. He said, "If you don't want me around the house. . . ." But if you discuss it you can get together. I like it much better now — he stays home now.

Others made similar remarks without such threatening experiences in the background:

> Sex is 80 per cent of a happy marriage. The average man likes sex and the woman must satisfy him to be a good companion. That's the main cause of divorce today; he finally gets satisfaction outside the home.

> I feel sex is the most important thing, say 95 per cent of marriage. Usually he is not going to stay with his wife without intercourse; he'd seek outside employment. The wife, if she's not satisfied would do the same. So you can see a lot depends on the sex relations.

Such views are more common among the lower-lower class (Table 3–16), and probably reflect something of the all-or-none attitude about marriage that seems more prevalent at that class level. The sense of disruptive force in marriage is stronger there and the danger of dissatisfaction (mostly on the part of the husband) is apparent. When husbands say that sex is important in this way, they usually indicate that they feel husbands have a right to expect satisfaction or to leave if they do not receive it. When wives note the same possibility, they reflect the feeling that this is merely another danger from unpredictable husbands that has to be coped with. While middle class people also recognize the disruptive potential of poor sexual relations, they tend to think of marriage as held together by many forces and of difficulty in any one area as

TABLE 3–16:
SEX KEEPS A HUSBAND OR WIFE FROM STRAYING

		Men	*Women*
Middle class	(58 and 55)	12%*	7%
Upper-lower class	(53 and 62)	17*	24*
Lower-lower class	(51 and 69)	33	31*

*Combined for analysis
Men: $X^2 = 6.55$ T = .20 P < .025
Women: $X^2 = 8.17$ T = .21 P < .005

TABLE 3-17:
EFFECT OF SEX ON MARRIAGE PARTNERS (MEN AND WOMEN COMBINED)

		Holds Husband Only	Also Holds Wife
Middle Class	(11)	22%	78%
Lower Class Negroes	(26)	54	46
Lower Class Whites	(36)	83	17

$X^2 = 13.64$ df $= 2$ T $= .36$ P $< .005$

subject to compensation from others; the relationship is thought to have a resiliency that makes it less vulnerable to any one disruption, however basic.

As the interview excerpts suggest, some of those who think of sex as important because of its potential threat to the stability of the marriage think of the threat as coming only from the possibility that the husband might "step out" or leave permanently, while others think this is a possibility for either husband or wife if one of them is dissatisfied (only 1 per cent mention it as a possibility only for the wife). There seems to be a systematic variation in whether the person thought likely to take leave is only the husband or both partners (see Table 3-17, which, because of the small numbers involved, combines men and women). The few middle class people who mention sex as a holding force in marriage refer to it as holding both partners. This is in keeping with their emphasis on equality, and their belief (and the reality) that women are often as interested in sexual relations as their husbands. In the lower class, Negroes are more likely than lower class whites to think the wife, too, would seek sexual gratification elsewhere if relations did not go well. The fact that almost half the Negroes who bring up this issue mention the wife's potentiality for straying, is consonant with the greater acceptance of wifely sexual interest that seems to characterize the group, as noted earlier in this chapter. This idea seems, on the other hand, to occur to few lower class whites; 83 per cent of them mention only the husband's potentiality for straying. That he might do so would be in line with his general tendency (at least among those in segregated role-relationships) to spend time away from the family in pursuit of his own interests and pleasures.

4
Family size preferences

RESEARCH IN many different societies suggests that in most of them men and women have fairly clear ideas about the number of children that would be most gratifying and suitable for them. Despite mixed feelings (particularly those occasioned by the belief that one really cannot affect how many children Fate decrees), people in most societies develop ideas about how many children are too many, how many are too few, how many are just right.

An understanding of the distribution of preferences for particular numbers of children is one important element in predicting or understanding population trends in a given society. In the United States, Freedman, Whelpton, and Campbell (1959) have shown how such preferences can be taken into account to predict population trends without having to use arbitrary estimates of future fertility (the full range of factors necessary to an "analytic framework" for the analysis of fertility has been described by Davis and Blake, 1956). One can, then, inquire of the members of a population in the child-bearing ages their desires and expectations concerning the number of children they will have. In a society like the United States, where a very high proportion of the population uses contraception, answers to such questions will provide a fairly reliable indication of the trend of population

118

growth. Where few couples have available to them effective means for limiting their families, the answers to such questions serve more as an index of the extent to which family size goals are frustrated. In either case, an understanding of fertility must start with an examination of the wishes of families about family size, and the factors that condition those wishes. In this chapter, therefore, we will examine how American couples of different social groups feel about different family sizes, and the social context in which individual preferences are held.

Ideal and personally preferred family sizes

The United States stands rather high in the family size ideals of its citizens, compared to other countries for which data are available. Table 4–1 summarizes data from several studies in Europe, the Caribbean, and Asia. The United States outranks all industrially developed countries in the average size of its ideal family, and also outranks several less developed countries – Puerto Rico, Jamaica, and certain urban centers in India. While women in America do not have as many children as women in Chile, Lebanon, India, Jamaica, or Puerto Rico, they average larger family ideals than in any of the European countries. In the less developed countries many women end up with more children than they think ideal; in the United States a good many of them, for physical or other reasons (Freedman, Whelpton, and Campbell, 1959) have fewer children than they want. The spread in actual fertility, therefore, is wider than in ideal fertility.

In this country, conceptions of ideal family size seem to have varied considerably over the past twenty years. Thus, a 1941 Gallup Poll found that 27 per cent of women thought that four or more children were ideal for the average family; by 1955 Freedman, Whelpton, and Campbell found the proportion had risen to 49 per cent. Similarly, in 1941 fully

TABLE 4-1:
IDEAL FAMILY SIZE IN FIFTEEN COUNTRIES

	Average no. of children considered ideal	Proportion of families with ideal of 4 or more children
Canada[a]	4.2	70%
Chile (Santiago)[b]	4.0	58
Lebanon[c]	—	50+
India[d]		
City	2.6 – 3.7	—
Non-City	4.0 – 4.7	—
United States[2]	3.4	49
Netherlands[a]	3.3	39
Jamaica[f]	—	30
Norway[a]	3.1	25
Great Britain[a]	2.8	23
Switzerland[a]	2.9	22
Italy[a]	3.1	18
Puerto Rico[g]	3.0	18
France[a]	2.8	17
Germany[h]	2.6	12
Austria[a]	2.0	4

Sources: [a]Various Gallup Polls reported by Glass (1962:244)
[b]Tabah and Samuel (1962:389)
[c]Yaukey (1961:74)
[d]Bogue (1962:504)
[e]Freedman, Whelpton, and Campbell (1959:223)
[f]Blake (1961:184)
[g]Hill, Stycos, and Back (1959:72)
[h]Freedman, Baumert, and Bolte (1959:141)

40 per cent of women thought a one- or two-child family ideal, compared to only 19 per cent in 1955 (results of both surveys given in Freedman, Whelpton, and Campbell, 1959: 233). Three children is apparently always a popular size; the variations occur in the proportions wanting a larger or smaller family.

Thus in the United States at present many couples think a four-child family is ideal for the average American family, many see three children as ideal, and a rather small proportion think of two children as ideal. The data from this study's

TABLE 4-2:
IDEAL NUMBER OF CHILDREN FOR THE AVERAGE AMERICAN
FAMILY

| | MC | | LC | | UL | LL |
	Prot.	Cath.	Prot.	Cath.	Negro	Negro
Women						
N	31	20	30	29	24	28
1-2 children	7%	5%	23%	7%	25%	14%
3 children	74	40	10	28	12	18
4 children	19	25	44	41	63	39
5+ children	—	30	23	24	—	29
Total	100%	100%	100%	100%	100%	100%
Men						
N	30	23	38	34	22	25
1-2 children	17%	9%	21%	18%	36%	8%
3 children	67	39	32	26	23	20
4 children	13	30	37	38	27	52
5+ children	3	22	10	18	14	20
Total	100%	100%	100%	100%	100%	100%

sample, however, suggest a wide variation among couples in terms of their class and religious membership (Table 4-2). Within the middle class, the differences between the upper-middle and lower-middle sub-classes are small, but the differences between Catholics and Protestants are large. Over 80 per cent of middle class Protestant men and women have an ideal of no more than three children, while a little over half the middle class Catholics offer an ideal of more than three children. The differences between the two religious groups are trivial in the lower class whites.*

These ideals do not necessarily correspond with the desires men and women have for their own family size in their

*These differences cannot be accounted for as rationalizations of existing conditions, that is of one group already having more children than another since only 8 percentage points separate Protestants and Catholics of the middle class in terms of already having four or more children, but over 35 points separate them in ideals. A rationalization factor may operate, however, in the case of the high proportion of large family ideals for lower-lower class Negroes, since 59 per cent of them already have four or more children.

own present circumstances. Table 4–3 presents data for the actual number of children desired by the couples in our sample. It is necessary to report these results in detail since the differences among class and religious groups are marked. At all levels but the lower-lower class, Catholics indicate a larger desired number of children than Protestants (this difference is statistically significant at the lower-middle class level for men and women, at the upper-lower class level for men only). There seem to be only slight differences in desired family sizes among white Protestants at the top three class levels, but lower-lower Protestant men desire larger families more often by a rather large margin, and women of this group by a somewhat smaller margin, than Protestants at the higher levels. For Catholics the differences among classes are quite small.

In summary, neither religion nor race seem to make much difference in desired family size at the lower-lower class level. At higher status levels, Protestants want fewer children than Catholics, and within religious groups there are only minor differences among social classes. This contrasts with our results concerning ideal family size: middle class Protestants do not

TABLE 4–3:
NUMBER OF CHILDREN DESIRED AT PRESENT

		Men				Women		
	N	0–2	3	4+	N	0–2	3	4+
Whites								
UM Protestants	20%	30%	50%	20%	18	33%	39%	28%
UM Catholics	9	33	22	45	11	27	9	64
LM Protestants	15	27	46	27	16	31	38	31
LM Catholics	17	–	24	76	15	–	27	74
UL Protestants	18	44	33	23	20	40	20	40
UL Catholics	20	15	25	60	22	9	32	59
LL Protestants	27	30	11	59	31	23	16	61
LL Catholics	20	20	20	60	18	22	11	67
Negro								
UL	23	22	26	52	25	20	28	52
LL	23	13	9	78	28	18	14	68

see four or more children as ideal as often as lower class Protestants.

To what extent are ideal and personally desired family size identical for individual couples? What changes take place in family size preferences as a couple progresses through marriage and family building? Table 4–4 summarizes data on these points. It is apparent that a majority of couples hold desired family sizes consistent with the ideal American family they imagine, but the variations among social classes are notable: lower-lower class men and women have a lower level of consistency than upper-middle class men and women and the other classes fall in-between. Similarly, a much lower proportion of lower-lower than upper-middle class men (and to a lesser extent, women) say that early in marriage they had an idea about how many children they would like. For those who did have an early preference, the variations from higher to lower status are not so systematic. Lower-middle class men and women are less consistent than either the class above or below them; lower-lower class women are low in consistency also, as are upper-lower Negro men and women and lower-lower class Negro women.

TABLE 4–4:
CONSISTENCY OF DESIRED FAMILY SIZE WITH IDEAL FAMILY SIZE AND SIZE PREFERRED EARLY IN MARRIAGE

| | Desired size consistent with ideal | | Proportion expressing early preference | | Of those expressing an early preference, proportion consistent with present desires | |
	Men	Women	Men	Women	Men	Women
White						
UM	87%	80%	73%	81%	90%	83%
LM	72	61	71	68	63	52
UL	79	64	64	77	83	70
LL	58	42	42	62	76	52
Negro						
UL	61	52	50	54	62	60
LL	64	48	32	61	80	48

TABLE 4–5:
DIRECTION OF INCONSISTENCY BETWEEN DESIRED FAMILY
SIZE AND IDEAL FAMILY SIZE

| | | Men | | | Women | |
	N	Ideal Larger	Ideal Smaller	N	Ideal Larger	Ideal Smaller
White						
Protestant	21	52%	48%*	25	52%	48%†
Catholics	14	14	86	21	19	81
Negroes	17	18	82	26	42	58

*P < .05 exact test (whites only)
†X = 3.95   T = .23   P < .05 (whites only)
White men and women combined X^2 = 9.11   T = .33   P < .005

More interesting, however, in the direction of the inconsistencies when they occur. Table 4–5 indicates the direction of deviation of presently desired family size from ideal size. Because neither Protestants nor Catholics differ from one class to another, the analysis is made by comparing the two religious groups. Catholic men and women are more likely to offer a smaller ideal size for the average American family than they want for themselves than are white Protestant men and women — over 80 per cent of the Catholics who offer an ideal different from their own desired size offer a smaller number, while among white Protestants only 48 per cent offer a smaller ideal. These Catholics, in other words, are saying that the average American family does not have to live up to their own religiously-informed desires. Negro men, but not Negro women, present a similar pattern, indicating that they want more children than they consider the ideal size to be.

The differences in direction of change from earlier desired sizes occur in connection with social class rather than religion. Table 4–6 compares the direction of change for the middle class with the direction for the combined white and Negro lower class (differences within these groups are negligible). These results suggest that when middle class men and women shift their family size preferences as time goes on they do so in

TABLE 4–6:
DIRECTION OF INCONSISTENCY BETWEEN DESIRED FAMILY
SIZE AND SIZE PREFERRED EARLY IN MARRIAGE

		Men			*Women*	
	N	*Earlier Size Larger*	*Earlier Size Smaller*	*N*	*Earlier Size Larger*	*Earlier Size Smaller*
White Middle Class	13	77%	23%*	19	69%	31%†
White and Negro Lower Class	21	19	81	38	28	72

$*X^2 = 9.03$ T = .52   P < .01
$†X^2 = 6.82$ T = .35   P < .01

the direction of a smaller size; when lower class people shift it is in the direction of a larger size. The middle class shifts represent a scaling down of earlier desires in line with an appreciation of some of the realities of child rearing, as these quotes from interviews suggest:

Upper-middle class Protestant woman:
When I was first married I liked the idea of a big family; I wanted six children. Now I've decided to take it more as we go. First I cut it down to four and now to three. I didn't think enough of the future in terms of education and things like that, and managing the work load.

Lower-middle class Catholic man:
At first I wanted ten children. However, my friends have children and I found that too many children got on my nerves. I wondered how I could take so many children emotionally. I want disciplined children; my relatives' and friends' children were unruly and upset me. Since then I've scaled down the number I want.

Lower-middle class Protestant woman:
I always thought I'd have four. I really think that would make a happy family. I think with four you don't have as much compe-

tition among the children; I think with just two they get too demanding. Now that I have three I guess that's all we'll have. I'm just real happy with them. I don't see how we could support a fourth one after seeing the expense of this last one, and we're getting older, too.

Lower-middle class Protestant man and woman:
[*Man*] We thought the more the merrier, six or more. Now I can see how foolish we were. We didn't consider the work or the finances involved. Also, if you had that many it might lead to less care and less time for each one. [*His wife:*] We thought at the time six was a good number. We thought we'd have a ball with that many. We came down to earth and decided on three because we're practical now. With large families they don't even get to know each other.

Upper-lower class Protestant woman:
I thought maybe I'd like five because that's what Moms had and I thought that was a good number. After that first one I thought one was the best I could have! Now the three I've got is enough. I didn't consider everything when I wanted five. It really isn't because there's always conflict — the middle child, you know. It's just that we can't afford another one and I just don't believe I could go through having him — him!

Most of the couples who have scaled down their ideas of how many children to have started off with rather high expectations; a few have come down from three to two, more from four to three, most from over four to three or four. This latter category includes about equal numbers of Catholics who started off with wishes for really big families of seven to ten children and quickly recognized the unreality of these enthusiasms, and Protestants who started off with wishes for four to six child families and found such numbers beyond their financial and psychic means. Apparently this sort of thing occurs most often in the lower-middle class; about a third of the lower-middle class men and women in our sample have scaled down the family size they envisioned early in marriage.*

On the surface, the most compelling reason for reducing initial aspirations is financial — some couples find the medical expenses of having children hard to bear, others are worried by gradually mounting costs as each additional child requires clothes, food, recreation, and education.

But behind these easy justifications for reducing initial aspirations is a factor that often pinches even more. The respondents quoted above mention "managing the work load," "too many children get on my nerves," "we're getting older," "the conflict (between children)." In other words, these people come to believe that having as many children as they initially wanted would be a psychological burden of demands, emotional control, attention, and giving which they would find difficult to manage. They would, in short, be spreading their energies, both physical and emotional, too thin. The quick or tangential way in which these concerns are expressed suggests that the respondents are somewhat loath to admit the emotional force behind them (as will be discussed more fully in the next two chapters).

The couples (predominantly lower class) who have shifted their family size preferences upward in the course of married life tell a different story:

Lower-lower class Negro woman:
I thought I might have four, two boys and two girls, but I got to outdo the thing! My mother had four so I said I'd have four or

---

*Our impression is that most of the changes dealt with in this analysis take place from the early marriage period to after the first or second birth. That is, the experience of having one or two children suffices to moderate earlier enthusiasms. It should be remembered that these estimates come from recollections about early desires. Very likely this underestimates the extent to which couples changed their views in the early period of marriage. Only a longitudinal study such as the one in progress by Westoff and his colleagues can accurately estimate the amount of change that takes place, or its direction (see Westoff, *et al.,*1961, pp. 339 ff.).

five. I always wanted an even number. Now I've got seven. Talking and having is different. Now I want eight, though, four boys and four girls. That's a plenty. The doctor said I was good for ten, but I don't want no more than one more to even the number. I have had my share.

Upper-lower class Negro woman

We only wanted two. I'm an only child; I was stupid enough to think if you came from an only child family you could only have one. My husband is an only child, too. I wanted a boy first and I got a girl. I always used to say only two children. Now I have three but I don't think three is a good number. If I only had one more it would be right.

Lower-lower class Catholic woman:

I wanted three. I thought that with three you can dress them better. My husband always wanted a lot of them. He only had a sister. He plays with all the children in the neighborhood. Now I have four and after the youngest is about five and he's in school I'd like to have more, about six children. I think it's nice to have that many. They grow up and they're a lot of help around the house.

Upper-lower class Protestant woman:

I always wanted about two, a boy and a girl. I wanted twins. Now I've had a boy and then I'd like a little girl. If my husband gets a better paying job and I can stay home and take care of them I'd like three.

Lower-lower class Protestant man and woman:

[*Man*] I wanted four, we ended up with nine but two died. That's all right with me because God gave them to me. Naturally you love the children; there is no money or anything that can replace them. When God gives you a child it's a blessing. [*His wife:*] I wanted a boy and a girl. So the first three were girls and I still wanted a boy so I just kept having girls and then I finally had a boy. Now I have seven and that's enough.

Lower-lower class Protestant woman:

I wanted two actually. I always wanted a boy and a girl. But I love children and they just kept coming. As my husband said, "The more they come the sweeter they are." I think we have enough now with five. You should have your children while you're young.

Lower-lower class Negro woman:

I always said I wanted two boys and two girls. For a while I didn't think I would have any but after a while they started coming so fast. We soon passed the four mark, but it's God's will I suppose. They came so fast. I'd like to quit now with these eight because I don't feel so good with this baby. We really can't afford any more, we have enough.

Two main themes are represented above. First, some men and women start marriage with fairly modest expectations about the number of children they will have and as they experience having and rearing children find that they would like more than they originally thought. These lower class men and women are often rather worried when they marry about their ability to care for and support children, they are somewhat intimidated by the responsibilities of a parental role. If things go well for the husband in his work and the wife finds more gratification than worry in rearing their children, they become more confident and want more children.

Such cases of relatively planful choice represent a minority in this group, however. More representative of what is involved in the shift toward a larger family are the first and last two quotes. In the majority of cases, passive acceptance of a string of children is more apparent than active choice or wish. Sometimes the children are accepted with pleasure, at other times only with resignation. One has the impression that after each pregnancy the wife (and, to a lesser extent, the husband) says to herself, "This is enough, no more," but that when she becomes pregnant again she reacts with pleasure ("The more they come the sweeter they are") or resignation ("It's God's will, I guess"). The extreme of this passivity, of course, is reflected by those who did not early in marriage even think about the number of children they would like to have.

Combining those who had no early preferences with those who have had to revise them upward, we find that slightly over two-thirds of Negro and white lower-lower class and Negro upper-lower class men and women fall into this passive category, but slightly less than 40 per cent of white upper-lower class men and women. In sharp contrast to the lower-middle class in which as many as one-third of the respondents revised their initial expectations *downward,* and the upper-middle class, in which few men and women changed their initial expectations at all, about one-third of the lower-lower class women had shifted in the direction of larger families. For both of these groups, the ease with which children are conceived comes as an unpleasant shock, a shock which some can then cope with by regarding their almost yearly conceptions as "God's will." Rather than face the frustration of confronting their desires for a smaller family with the reality of continuing pregnancy (and risk the hostility toward the children that might follow), these couples seek gains and gratification in the larger family and tell themselves that "Naturally you love the children; there is no money or anything that can replace them."

Several of the respondents quoted above mentioned a desire for a particular number of boys or girls in connection with their earlier or present family size desires; how often does concern about the sex of children enter into attitudes toward number of children? Table 4 – 7 shows the distribution of references to the sex of children in connection with the respondents' discussion of family size. (Since these are spontaneous references, the findings must be accepted tentatively and as an index of the degree of concern about sex, rather than as true measures of frequency.) Concern about the sex of children seems to be at its low point in the upper-middle class and at a high point (mainly through the contribution of husbands) in the white upper-lower class. Overall, and out-

TABLE 4-7:
REFERENCES TO THE SEX OF CHILDREN IN CONNECTION
WITH DESIRED FAMILY SIZE

	Husband is Concerned		Wife is Concerned		Husband or Wife Concerned (couples only)	
	N	%	N	%	N	%
White						
UM	28	7	28	11	26	18
LM	31	26	30	14	28	37
UL	38	39	45	24	22	64
LL	48	19	48	15	24	33
Negro						
UL	22	27	23	35	22	41
LL	28	29	29	24	28	47

side of the highest status group, at least a third of the couples express some concern on this score, with a very slight tendency for men more often to be concerned than their wives. That the desire for children of both sexes has a slight influence on whether couples want another child has been shown by several previous studies, most recently by Deborah S. Freedman and others (1960:141-46).

Awareness of the trend toward larger families

To what extent are men and women aware that there has been a change toward a larger family ideal over the past two decades? It is possible for such a change to take place without penetrating the public's awareness; what is the case here? The men and women interviewed were asked: "Do you think people want larger or smaller families than twenty-five years ago, and why do you suppose that is?" Table 4-8 presents the results. The higher the class status, the greater is the tendency to see people as now preferring larger families. There is also a tendency, most apparent in the lower-middle and upper-lower classes, for women more frequently than men to

TABLE 4–8:
DO PEOPLE WANT LARGER OR SMALLER FAMILIES THAN
25 YEARS AGO?

		Men			Women	
	N	Larger	Smaller	N	Larger	Smaller
White						
UM	23	78%	22%	24	83%	17%
LM	27	44	56	27	67	33
UL	21	19	81	19	47	53
LL	16	25	75	13	23	77
Negro						
UL	23	13	87	22	27	73
LL	23	4	96	25	20	80

see a trend among couples generally toward larger families. (Within classes there are no differences between Catholics and Protestants.) Middle class women strongly perceive a trend in the direction of larger families, a view shared by the upper-middle but not the lower-middle class men. Lower class men, equally strongly perceive a trend in the direction of smaller families now, a view shared by all groups of lower class women except those in the upper-lower class. These perceptions seem generally in line with the realities of shifting preferences in family size: middle class people have moved toward a larger family ideal while lower class people are, if changing at all, striving to get away from early patterns of very large families. Where the middle class sees a shift from a two- to a four-child ideal as a shift in the direction of larger families, the lower class sees a shift from a six- or seven-child reality to a four-child ideal as a shift toward a smaller family. An examination of the reasons people give for their opinions allows a fuller understanding of what is involved.

When people express their opinions about whether couples want more or fewer children they inevitably also express some of their feelings about the ease of living in urban America today. In the lower-lower class there is a strong tendency to feel that times are very hard now and that therefore couples do not have as many children as formerly:

> Smaller families now 'cause times are getting so bad. The older people has bigger families and they tell the young ones not to and they put them wise how not to.

> They want less kids. It costs more to live, even though we're making more money. They don't want their kids to go through the hardships they are going through. It's harder to live now.

> Well, women didn't seem to mind larger families then, but they do now. The cause is because of the men, because some men leave them. Some women like to go too much and don't want many children to keep them at home. Some men don't like the responsibility so most women are scared to have too many for fear the man will run off. You can't hardly get them to pay child support so they want small families.

> I think they want smaller families. They can get a better place to live if renting, cost of living is high and jobs are getting harder to find.

> I think they want smaller ones. When I was growing up I never heard nobody complaining about babies. Now, nobody wants a lot of babies. It seems like times are too hard.

> They're having smaller families. There are a lot of working mothers now. If they work they don't have large families. Things cost more these days.

These people are saying that life is tough, and if you have many children it's even tougher. They postulate a heavily negative motivation for having smaller families; their emphasis is on the problems thus avoided rather than on the values thus achieved.

Another theme, less common perhaps in the lower-lower group than in the upper-lower and lower-middle classes, is that people have smaller families in order to be able to enjoy some of the fruits of a higher standard of living. That is, they do not see the problem so much as avoiding basic deprivations as gaining material or leisure-time benefits:

> I think the change has been from larger to fewer because of people's attitudes, people's pleasures. With fewer children they have a chance to do more. They think that larger families get in the way. It would be easier to find a sitter for one or two than for five or six.

> They had larger families then. According to when I was a little girl, most of my playmates had five or six brothers and sisters. Now they are more modern. They are fussier as far as dentists, eye exams. In my husband's family they didn't have no doctor, people just lived.

> Families are definitely getting smaller. People can't afford large families and provide for them like society expects them to.

> Smaller families and a greater desire for offering the kids more materialwise. You get less for the dollar and it costs more to live and therefore you can't offer your children as much. I think children were happier then 'cause now the first thing a child asks if you go somewhere is "what did you bring me?"

Here the emphasis is on affording better medical care, better education, more time for the parents to spend by themselves, etc. There is often a critical note in the characterization of this trend, as the last quote by a lower-middle class woman indicates. Those who see a tend toward smaller families not infrequently indicate ambivalence—they say times are bad, or that you need fewer children to take advantage of what prosperity has to offer *but* parents and children are thereby more self-centered, selfish, or unloving.

Regardless of underlying negative feelings about the trend to smaller families, most lower class respondents see the trend as a response to the economically more demanding life of the city today. For the lower-lower class there is the pressing problem of job instability and low earnings, for the upper-lower class there is the felt pressure to educate ones' children and try to live up to the new standards of an official prosperity — a better home, better clothes, relatively new automobiles, and the like. It is interesting to note that about half of lower-middle class men share these views; their particular version of the rationale for smaller families these days is aptly summarized by the man quoted above: "People can't afford large families these days and provide for them *like society expects them to.*" Apparently both lower-middle and upper-lower class men more often than their wives feel burdened by the problems of providing for a family at the standard of living they accept as fitting. (We have seen above that there is a tendency for men of these two classes to offer an ideal family size smaller than their wives do.) In contrast, the wives seem more often to feel that it is possible to indulge oneself as the mother of a larger brood than the parental generation's.

What, then, are the views of those who believe families are larger these days?

> It looks like everybody wants a big family now. I think as life gets easier for people and as they get better educations they realize what it can mean to the future to have a great many children to carry on the faith.

> I think there are larger families today, even if there's talk and articles about overpopulation. I think it's a myth. I think it's a feeling people have; people are concerned less with material things. I think it has a lot to do with Christian values, turning more toward Christian ideals. Twenty-five years ago people were concerned with other things. I think people worked more then, had to work harder. They were scared more than now even if we are scared about the atomic bomb.

> It seems to me the trend is very definitely toward larger families, especially among the well-educated group, and I think it indicates

that people have an increasing sense of responsibility and that they regard children as blessings. Of course, in times of depression there is undoubtedly a tendency on the part of the people who are hard hit to think it's a misfortune to have the expense of having a baby. But, in my adult life we've had prosperous times for the most part.

My Lord, my impression is that bigger families are more fashionable now. Almost as fashionable as 50–60 years ago. In the 1930's it was indecent to have a lot of children, now it's fashionable.

I would say people are having slightly larger families. Maybe our economic standards are rising all the time and people can afford larger families now. I've heard my mother and daddy talk about the depression and how terrible it was.

I think larger families. People are optimistic about the future. This generation hasn't known want unless they are from an extremely poor family. They haven't been through the depression. I think optimism might be the answer.

Although disapproval of the trend toward larger families is sometimes expressed ("They get married so young and expect their mothers and daddies to help them raise their kids"), the usual tone is one of approval. People can have larger families because life is easier and more secure. And the proposition can be reversed: having larger families is a sign that times are good, that things are going well for us—people "were scared more (then) than now, even if we are scared of the atomic bomb." Whether this change is viewed (as by some Catholics) as a return to Christian values, or simply as an indication of well-being and good feelings, the emphasis on optimism, security, absence of materialistic striving and anxiousness is apparent.

Implicit in most views—regardless of whether the trend perceived is toward larger or smaller families—is the belief that when people are well-off and secure they will have more children than when they are not. That is, most of these people express in their responses to this question an underlying belief that people really want large families if they can afford them. This is a theme to which we return in the next chapter when discussing contemporary norms about family size.

It would be interesting, given the above information concerning beliefs about trends in family size, to know the relationship between the size of husbands' and wives' families of orientation and their preferences for their own families. We have these data for men and women in our sample who spontaneously compared the size of the family in which they grew up with the family they want for themselves. The numbers are small, since only a few respondents (about 20 per cent of the sample) mentioned the size of their families of orientation. However, these are presumably the individuals to whom size of the parent's family is most salient. Table 4–9 presents these data. Clearly those middle class people who orient themselves to their parents' families when thinking about their own want either to have their families as large as the parents' or larger. A considerable minority of lower class men and women, on the other hand, are concerned with having a family not as large as their parents'. For this group of people, at least, the awareness of broad trends in the society is reinforced by personal evaluation of their own parents' experiences.

In summary, then, most men and women are able to perceive trends in family size. Understandably, such concerns are not only the professional concerns of the demographer but also of interest to men and women in all social classes.

TABLE 4–9:
OWN FAMILY SIZE & PARENTAL FAMILY SIZE

		Want family smaller than parent's family	Want own family as large as parent's or larger
Middle class whites	(25)	8%	92%
Lower class whites and Negroes	(39)	39	61

$X^2 = 5.66$ $T = .30$ $P < .025$

The perception of these trends, however, varies strikingly from one social class to another. Middle class women and upper-middle class men overwhelmingly believe that people want larger families now than before World War II, and most of them believe people want larger families because they can afford to enjoy whatever pleasures a large family affords. In contrast, lower class men and women (except for upper-lower women) overwhelmingly believe that people want smaller families now either because of financial risks or because with a large family the family cannot enjoy some of the luxuries-become-necessities that American life offers the postwar generation of parents. With this latter perception not infrequently goes some concern over being selfish and ungiving.

5
Rationales for family size

WHAT ARE the common understandings in American culture about why individuals want large or small families? These imputed motives or rationales say something about the social meaning attached to being a parent of a large or a small family, about the kind of person one signifies oneself to be through procreation and child-tending. From these imputations it is possible to deduce something of the norms which govern family size preference — vague, imprecise, and conflicting though these norms be.

Rationales for large and small families

In our interviews, a series of questions probed what men and women thought were the reasons for varying desires for large or small families.* The responses to all questions bear-

*In addition to inquiries about ideal family size, family size preferred now, and whether families are smaller or larger than 25 years ago, these questions were: (1) Why do you suppose that families with the same income may still have different ideas about the desirable number of children? (2) What do you think are the main reasons a person would want more than one or two children, the main satisfactions he would get from a large family? (3) What are the main things about your children in the way you feel about them, and how would this be different if you ended up with two more children than you want, with fewer children than you want? (4) With whom have you discussed the question of the number of children a couple has, what sorts of ideas do these others have and why do you suppose they feel that way?

139

ing on how many children people want to have were coded as one unit, summarizing the reasons offered by each individual. It is important to keep in mind that most respondents offered reasons why couples would want both a large and a small family; that is, most were able to impute motives for both goals, not necessarily the motives they consciously felt they themselves had.*

The most general level of evaluation of those who prefer large or small families is nicely illustrated by a technique used in our exploratory study of attitudes of lower class whites. In an early interview guide, four sentence completion items were included which asked respondents to characterize a woman who wants respectively no children, one child, three, and seven children. There was universal rejection of the woman who wants no children as either totally self-involved, childish, neurotic or in poor health. The woman who wants three children was generally regarded as an average, good, and loving person. It is the contrast between the characterization of the one-child and seven-children woman (both extremes in terms of the women interviewed) that highlights the general evaluation of large and small families. Of the fifteen respondents who completed these sentence completions, 80 per cent made a positive characterization of the woman who wanted seven children (although one-fourth of these also included some negative comment), but 80 per cent had only negative comments about the woman who wanted only one

*In general, only positive characterizations were coded. For example, if a respondent said that people who want small families "don't like children," this was coded as a large family motivation, "likes children." Similarly, if a respondent said that people who want large families "don't understand how much it costs to educate children," this was coded a small family motive, "better able to educate children." In this way the characterization of rationales for the two family types was considerably simplified without doing violence to the underlying ideas involved. The one area in which this was not done involved the simple assertion that those wanting a small family are "selfish," since this negative characterization carries the underlying assumption that such people want small families because they can have more goods or time for themselves.

child, and over half the women said specifically that she was "selfish." The characterizations run along the following lines:

Woman who wants one child . . .	*Woman who wants seven children . . .*
doesn't want to be tied down	could only have great love for children and nerves of steel
it is self-centered, she wants no responsibility	a good woman, a good housekeeper, a good manager and a lot of patience
very selfish, or very sick	kind hearted, very sweet person, other people would like her very much, must be wealthy
a deep thinking person, determined, self-reliant, I wouldn't care for her, she would be kind of cold	happy-go-lucky, not a perfectionist, loves her husband very much, liked by other people

To what extent do these simple and relatively straightforward images of the woman with a very small or a very large family hold up when men and women speak of more ordinary sizes that can be called small or large? Here the picture is more complex, although this basic theme of selfishness versus loving does not disappear.

First, for whose benefit do couples want a small family? Table 5–1 presents a tabulation for those men and women in the sample who gave at least one rationale for a small family that could be characterized as mainly for the benefit of the parent or for the benefit of the child. Cases in which more reasons were given for parental benefit than for child benefit are called "parent dominant" and the reverse situation is called "child dominant;" some respondents gave an equal number of reasons suggesting both.

Among men, dominance or equality of child benefits is most apparent for the upper-lower class whites and, to a

TABLE 5-1:
DOMINANCE OF PARENT- OR CHILD-ORIENTED RESPONSES
IN RATIONALES FOR A SMALL FAMILY

		Men				Women		
	N	Parent-Dominant	Equal	Child-Dominant	N	Parent-Dominant	Equal	Child-Dominant
White								
UM	(17)	65%	—	35%	(19)	26%	26%	48%
LM	(20)	60	15%	25	(23)	65	9	26
UL	(13)	8	23	69	(18)	56	17	28
LL	(14)	50	—	50	(13)	69	—	31
Negro								
UL	(15)	33	7	60	(18)	11	—	89
LL	(16)	56	—	44	(14)	71	—	39

lesser extent, upper-lower class Negroes. These two groups are least likely to see preference for a small family as mainly motivated by what parents gain for themselves; they are more impressed by the gains of the child in education and goods. Men of other classes are more likely to think in terms of the parents' gains in goods, time to themselves, and less responsibility.

For women, the picture is rather different. Among whites, it is the upper-middle class women who are most likely to see children as primary or equal in benefiting from small families, and least likely to see parental benefits as dominant in the thinking of those who want small families. Upper-lower class Negro women show this tendency even more extremely; they are significantly different both from whites of the same class and from Negroes of the lower-lower class.

What are the particular rationales that are offered for small families? Tables 5-2 and 5-3 present a more detailed tabulation of reasons why couples are thought to prefer a small family. It is apparent that financial reasons loom very large; over three-quarters of the sample give at least one economic reason. Middle class men are less likely to give financial reasons than are lower class men: of the total number of codable reasons given, 51 per cent of those given by middle class men were financial compared to 77 per cent of those given by white and Negro lower class men. It is noteworthy that generalized statements about times being "bad", the cost of living too high, are given by 37 per cent to 50 per cent of lower class men but by only 10 per cent of those in the middle class.

White upper-lower class men seem particularly preoccupied with the gain of children in small families in having more goods; for them the most compelling reason for having a small family is that one is then better able to feed, clothe, and otherwise care for the children. We saw earlier that these men

TABLE 5–2:
REASONS COUPLES HAVE SMALL FAMILIES ACCORDING TO MEN

	White				Negro	
	UM (19)	LM (22)	UL (16)	LL (18)	UL (21)	LL (19)
Parent gains						
More goods for adults	16%	27%	–	17%	–	16%
More time, less responsibility	32	50	25%	11	19%	37
Generally more selfish	27	41	6	17	5	5
Man can accomplish more easily	5	–	6	–	5	–
Better for woman's health	5	–	6	–	10	–
One or more parent gain	*63*	*73*	*44*	*39*	*33*	*53*
Child gains						
More goods for children	10	18	63	39	43	37
Better education for children	37	27	25	17	33	26
Better care for children	–	–	6	–	–	–
More love and appreciation for children	10	–	–	–	–	–
One or more child gains	*42*	*41*	*69*	*44*	*48*	*42*
General economic reasons						
Times are bad now, cost of living too high, etc.	10	9	50	39	37	37
Avoids housing problems	21	5	13	11	14	10
One or more economic reasons (child, parent, or general)	*74*	*77*	*94*	*94*	*76*	*74*

TABLE 5-3:
REASONS COUPLES HAVE SMALL FAMILIES ACCORDING TO
WOMEN

	White				Negro	
	UM (17)	LM (23)	UL (18)	LL (14)	UL (20)	LL (21)
Parent gains						
More goods for adults	12%	22%	33%	29%	—	5%
More time, less responsibility	47	31	39	21	—	38
Generally more selfish	12	35	22	36	5%	24
Man can accomplish more easily	—	—	—	—	5	—
Better for woman's health	—	—	6	—	—	—
One or more parent gain	*65*	*70*	*67*	*64*	*10*	*48*
Child gains						
More goods for children	41	26	29	29	70	19
Better education for children	59	26	6	36	25	5
Better care for children	6	13	6	7	5	—
More love and appreciation for children	—	9	6	—	—	—
One or more child gain	*76*	*57*	*38*	*57*	*80*	*24*
General economic reasons						
Times are bad now, cost of living too high, etc.	—	26	17	21	30	38
Avoids housing problems	—	9	—	14	15	10
One or more economic reasons (child, parent, or general)	*88*	*74*	*78*	*86*	*95*	*67*

were most preoccupied with the gains of children in a small family; we now see that these gains are mainly in terms of goods. For the middle class, the preoccupation is more in the direction of future educational demands, especially in the upper-middle class. It is interesting to note that very few men in the sample suggest non-financial child gains from a small family (and indeed, only a few women do so).

In general, middle class men suggest more parental gains with fewer children than do lower class men. They show little concern with more goods, somewhat greater concern with educational gains, and speak much more frequently of parents' desires for more time and less responsibility, or of "selfishness" (note that 50 per cent of the lower-middle class men give this reason). Simply stated, middle class men seem to say that people have small families because they prefer the advantages they gain from this; lower class men seem to say that people have small families because they cannot afford to give more than a few children the things the children need. There is a significant minority of lower-lower class Negro men who hold to the theory of parental avoidance of responsibility; these are mainly men with quite large families.

Among women, the upper-lower class Negroes stand out as seeing the small family almost exclusively in terms of the gains for the children, primarily in terms of more goods. Only 10 per cent of these women offer any motivation for parental gain in explaining why couples have small families. Upper-middle class women are most impressed by the problem of educating children and secondly of providing them with the goods they need, but unlike the Negro upper-lower class women, they also see that the parents gain in having more time and less demanding responsibilities. They are less likely to characterize the parents' gains as selfish than are other whites.

Interestingly, whereas the white upper-lower class men are most likely to give child-oriented reasons for small families, among white women the upper-lower class is least likely to do so. This suggests that in some of these families, husbands and wives have conflicting concerns, the husbands preoccupied with providing for children and the wives not particularly concerned about this problem.

Overall, it seems that the selfishness concept of motivation for a small family (in the sense of all parental gains, economic and psychological) is held most often by middle class men, by a smaller but significant group of lower-lower class men, by a considerable number of white lower-middle and lower class women, and by a somewhat smaller number of Negro lower-lower class women. Upper-lower class men, upper-middle class and Negro upper-lower class women seem most strongly to reject this conception and to say instead that the children's needs dominate in a desire to have a small family.

What of the rationales for large families? Table 5–4 presents a tabulation of responses that can be categorized in terms of whether the parent or the child benefits from a large family. Among men, the upper-middles, the Negro upper-lower, and white and Negro lower-lower classes share a similar pattern. Over three-fourths see a desire for a large family as motivated solely by the parents' desires for some reward for themselves. Whites of the lower-middle and upper-lower class are more likely to see gains also for the children in terms of companionship, and of being less spoiled, more co-operative, and more responsible. Among women, only the Negro upper-lower class women stand out as different from other groups. They see little gain for the children in having large families, a response congruent with their strong concern with the gains for children belonging to small families. Negro lower-lower class women more often mention children's gains from large families, but not so often as do middle class women. The upper-middle class women, particularly, see gains for the children— 61 per cent of those who have a child- or

TABLE 5–4:
PARENT- OR CHILD-ORIENTED RESPONSES IN RATIONALES FOR A LARGE FAMILY

		Men				Women		
	N	Parent only	Both	Child only	N	Parent only	Both	Child only
Whites								
UM	20	80%	15%	5%	18	39%	44%	17%
LM	21	29	62	9	23	48	48	4
UL	14	43	36	21	20	55	25	20
LL	14	72	21	7	16	56	31	13
Negro								
UL	18	78	11	11	19	90	—	10
LL	22	86	14	—	19	69	21	10

parent-oriented reason mention that children benefit from large families.

What, specifically are the parent and child gains people mention as motivating a large family preference? Tables 5–5 and 5–6 detail these rationales. Middle class men (and, to a lesser extent, women) are somewhat more likely to mention reasons that bear on neither parent nor child gains but on

TABLE 5–5:
REASONS COUPLES HAVE LARGE FAMILIES ACCORDING TO MEN

	White				Negro	
	UM (25)	LM (25)	UL (19)	LL (14)	UL (19)	LL (23)
Extrinsic pressures						
Carry on religious tradition	40%	40%	21%	7%	5%	13%
Carry on family tradition	8	8	5	21	5	4
Fashionable now	12	4	–	–	–	–
One or more extrinsic pressures	*52*	*48*	*21*	*28*	*10*	*17*
Feel comfortable about standard of living	12	20	5	–	16	–
Parent gains						
Like, love children	64	54	52	79	52	78
Accomplishment, sense of fulfillment	16	36	5	14	26	9
Have children around longer, make old age nicer	8	20	20	14	5	26
Family name survives	24	20	–	21	5	13
Children help around the house	–	8	10	7	5	17
*One or more parent gain**	*72*	*68*	*53*	*86*	*69*	*78*
Parent-child gain						
Happier or closer atmosphere in home	36	32	10	21	32	13
Child gains						
Children more responsible, cooperative, less spoiled	8	36	31	21	16	13
Children have companionship, more fun	12	28	21	14	5	4
One or more child gain	*16*	*60*	*42*	*29*	*21*	*13*

*First two items only

TABLE 5–6:
REASONS COUPLES HAVE LARGE FAMILIES ACCORDING TO
WOMEN

	White				Negro	
	UM (25)	LM (27)	UL (21)	LL (20)	UL (23)	LL (24)
Extrinsic pressures						
Carry on religious tradition	36%	26%	14%	10%	–	8%
Carry on family tradition	4	–	10	10	–	–
Fashionable now	12	4	5	–	–	–
One or more extrinsic pressures	48	30	24	20	–	8
Feel comfortable about standard of living	8	30	10	5	30%	25
Parent gains						
Like love children	24	70	62	55	71	62
Accomplishment, sense of fulfillment	36	33	19	15	8	–
Have children around longer, make old age nicer	8	26	5	20	8	8
Family name survives	4	4	–	20	9	4
Children help around the house	8	7	5	10	9	21
*One or more parent gain**	48	77	72	60	61	63
Parent-child gain						
Happier or closer atmosphere in home	32	26	24	15	35	21
Child gains						
Children more responsible, cooperative, less spoiled	28	37	29	35	4	21
Children have companionship, more fun	20	22	24	15	9	8
One or more child gain	44	45	43	35	9	25

more "unreasoning" and extrinsic factors; they are likely to mention religious tradition (usually saying that Catholics have more children because of their religion) or that it is fashionable now to have many children. Often when middle class people give these reasons they are saying simply that some people have large families not so much because they really want them as because they feel social pressure to do so. It is interesting that as many upper-middle class women give this type of reason as mention either a parent or child gain, in sharp contrast to all of the other groups of women. This suggests that more upper-middle class women feel alienated from the idea of large families, or at least that they do not believe that most of the people who have such families do so for individualistically relevant reasons. This seems also to be the case for many of the middle class men. However, very few of the respondents give only this kind of reason, so it appears that most men and women believe that there are also more personally grounded reasons for wanting large families.

As noted above, among men, lower-middle and upper-lower class whites emphasize more the effect on the child of having a number of siblings; they say that children are less spoiled, more co-operative, more responsible, enjoy the companionship and have more fun than do children with only one or two siblings. Apparently the men in other groups do not see these advantages as especially compelling. The variation among groups in terms of parental gain is not great, but upper-lower whites do not so often suggest such gains as rationales for large families, perhaps because they tend wholly to reject the idea of a large family as reasonable.

Among women, those in the Negro upper-lower class stand out in that they cannot offer much of a rationale for larger families beside the vague notion that people who want many children must like them, and perhaps it makes for a happier home. Their reasons for small families seem so pressing that they do not have a strong sense of reality about motives for large ones.

Upper-middle class women avoid the simple idea that couples have large families because they "like" or "love" children. Perhaps they feel such a statement is redundant, perhaps they are reluctant to make the ready assumption that a woman who has four children is more loving than a woman who has two. Rationales dealing with the gains of the children, with a generally happier and closer atmosphere in the home, and with the parent's sense of accomplishment and fulfillment, loom larger for this group than for others. Just as these wives are more impressed by the material gains for children in a small family than are their husbands, they are more likely than their husbands to see advantages for children in a large family.

Looking at the total pattern of rationales for large and small families, we can abstract one central norm: one shouldn't have more children than one can support, *but one should have as many children as one can afford.* To have fewer is regarded as an expression of selfishness, ill health, or neurotic weakness; to have more is an expression of poor judgment or lack of discipline. Implicit in the comments of the great majority of respondents is the idea that when people are financially able to have a large family, they want a large family. The "good" person does this; the person with moral failings stops short of the number he could afford in order to have something extra for himself or for his children. These extras tend to connote selfishness in the parent and cause it in the child. The latter gains from being a member of a large family in being less spoiled and selfish, more co-operative and giving, and he has more fun because of this. The parent gains from a greater chance to love and be loved, and he lives in a happier milieu because of this. The "stingy" parent lives, instead, with his small family according to a life plan that emphasizes goods for himself and his children, time and freedom for outside interests, and education for the children. In living by this he deprives himself and his children of other moral, social, and personal advantages.

From their comments, it seems that most men and women regard a two-child family as too small to offer the desired advantages; a three-child family offers these advantages to a considerable degree, and a four-child family represents the maximum gain. On the other side, a four-child family makes very heavy demands on financial resources, three children represent a bearable or almost bearable burden, and two children can be managed by almost anyone. Thus, three children represents a popular compromise. At the level of ideals, then, few couples want fewer than three children; in our sample, only in the two hardest pressed groups — the

lower class white Protestants and the upper-lower class Negroes—do even as many as 20 per cent of their members
suggest an ideal smaller than three children (see Table 4–1).
However, larger proportions of most of the groups say that
their own personal preferences—as against ideals—are for
two children. These men and women feel they have jus-
tification for less than ideal aspirations because of a special
pinch in income; often they hope that if things really improve
for them they can afford a third child. For middle and upper-lower class Protestants particularly, the third child brings
the advantages of a large family in sufficient measure; for
Catholics it is only a starter—almost 60 per cent of the middle class Catholics say they want five children or more, a
sentiment in which their lower class co-religionists, most of
whom would stop at four, do not join them (only 20 per cent
want as many as five.)

The pro-natalist sentiments of men and women of all
classes are apparent in the rationales they offer for large and
small families. The good person in a good world has a large
family. In the next chapter we will examine some of the motives behind this view. At this point it is worth noting that this
sentiment gives every evidence of stemming from deeply held
beliefs and values, that it does not reflect simply a passive
response to the "widespread, vocal and highly influential
'fertility cult' which tries to stimulate the continuation of high
birth rates for its own self interest" (Population Reference
Bureau, October, 1960: 136). Similarly, while a thoughtful
observer looking on from the outside may assert that "The
(socio-psychological) advantages of belonging to a large
family are no longer as apparent as they once were, and the
disadvantages are certainly greater than they have been"
(Susannah Coolidge, 1960:149), men and women in our sample seem to feel that the advantages are exactly the same as
before but that now more people have a chance to enjoy them
and to provide their children with them. So long as parents
see such clear moral and social gains from a large family, and
so few other than "selfish" gains from a small one, it seems

likely that family size preferences will fluctuate simply as a function of prosperity, of the availability of necessities and "necessary" luxuries. Only if the smaller family comes to have meaningful value apart from its relation to economic scarcity would the situation change.

Discussion of family size with persons other than spouse

The ideals, personal preferences, and norms of family size discussed so far presumably are not results simply of each couple coming to their own conclusions. Rather, like most other aspects of life these views are the grist for conversation and sanctions within the intimate circles in which these couples participate socially. Respondents in our sample were asked to indicate who beside their spouses would care about how many children they had, and how these persons would feel if the couple had more or fewer children than they themselves want. They were also asked to indicate with what persons other than those cited above they have discussed the question of having children.

These questions were designed to probe first the area of sanctions, in the sense of views of others expressed with some vigor and personal interest, and second, the less intense area of exchange of views on family size. (Of course, in the sociological sense, sanctions are expressed in these latter discussions as well but we questioned at both levels in order to avoid the common reaction that "How many children we have is no one's business but our own.")

In only a very small number of cases was anyone but a relative named in answer to the question about who "is interested enough and close enough to you to be concerned about how many children you have."Thus, most people believe that a relative may properly express interest and concern about this question, but friends and neighbors are confined to disinterested conversation regarding their feelings about

TABLE 5–7:
EXTENT OF SANCTIONS BY RELATIVES CONCERNING FAMILY
SIZE

	White				Negro	
	UM (24)	LM (27)	UL (21)	LL (21)	UL (24)	LL (28)
One or more relatives expresses views about family size	71%	78%	81%	95%	75%	57%
No relative expresses views	29	22	19	5	25	43

family size. Table 5–7 indicates that about three-quarters of the couples named at least one relative as having expressed a view about family size. An examination of the nature of their concern indicates that 76 per cent of these relatives were quoted as saying, in essence, "don't have too many children." A comparison of the results by social class (there were no religious differences) indicates that lower-lower class Negroes are least likely to report sanctions by relatives, and lower-lower class whites are most likely to do so. The former group is perhaps more mobile and therefore more likely to have moved away from the influence of family. Overall, however, it is clear that at all social class levels relatives are likely to put a word in about family size in such a way that the couple knows what their families' preferences are.

Who are the relatives who express their views? Table 5–8 indicates the major categories mentioned, first in terms of whether they come from the husband's or the wife's side of the family and then in terms of the specific relative mentioned. In the middle class (and among upper-lower class Negroes) there is equal mention of both sides of the family. Among couples in the white lower and Negro lower-lower class there is more mention of relatives from the wife's side than the husband's. Apparently in the lower class family, size concerns are organized more around the wife and her line than around the husband's. This emphasis on women, of

TABLE 5-8:
TYPES OF RELATIVES EXPRESSING VIEWS ABOUT FAMILY
SIZE

	White				Negro	
	UM (17)	LM (21)	UL (17)	LL (20)	UL (18)	LL (16)
Relative from						
Wife's family only	23%	24%	35%	45%	28%	38%
Wife's family mainly	–	–	12	10	5	6
Both families equally	54	52	53	20	39	44
Husband's family mainly	–	10	–		–	–
Husband's family only	23	14	–	25	28	12
Specific Relatives						
Mothers:	94%	100%	100%	75%	78%	81%
Wife's mother	65	85	95	65	50	56
Husband's mother	76	72	53	40	39	50
Fathers:	65	43	47	35	28	25
Wife's father	53	33	42	25	22	18
Husband's father	41	39	36	20	28	6
Any Siblings	–	10	18	45	11	37

course, carries over to the sex of the relative, and mothers
are mentioned more often than fathers. The husband's mother
is more likely to express her views in the middle than in the
lower class; lower-middle and white upper-lower class wives'
mothers are most likely to express theirs. In the white lower
class this gives the preponderance of weight to the wife's
mother compared to more equal voicing of views by middle
class mothers. Negroes of both classes and lower-lower class
whites are less likely to mention a father of either side than
are upper-middle class whites. Siblings (mostly sisters and
mostly on the wife's side) are most often mentioned by the
white and Negro lower-lower class. They compensate for the
relatively lower proportion of couples in these groups who
mention mothers of either side. Overall, then, couples in all
social classes find their relatives often expressing sanctions
about how many children they should have—usually enjoin-
ing them not to have too many. In the lower class, relative to
the middle class, these injunctions come more predominantly
from the wife's side of the family and more heavily from

females than from males. This in in keeping with the greater separation between the man's and the woman's world characteristic of the lower class (see chapter 2).

As noted, most of the sanctions expressed by relatives are in the direction of limiting family size. There are some differences in the types of relatives who express limiting versus expansive values. Relatives from the wife's more often than from the husband's side say that the couple should be careful not to have too many children. Among the few couples where a relative is mentioned as encouraging the couple to have more children the converse is true—the husband's side is more often mentioned.

Thus, it is the wife's relatives who bring to bear most forcefully whatever influence they have in an injunction to be reasonable; the difference is most dramatically apparent for the lower-lower class. Usually this means that the wife's mother counsels limitation while the husband's mother is silent or concerned that she have enough grandchildren.

How about discussion outside the extended family? Table 5 – 9 shows the distribution of husbands and wives in terms of general discussion of family size. Men vary more than women by social class. Upper-middle class men are least likely to have discussed family size only with relatives, and most likely to have had discussions with non-relatives. Overall, the higher the status the more likely it is that there has been discussion with non-relatives. In the lower class, discussion with relatives is significantly more frequent than discussion with non-relatives; in the middle class both are of about equal frequency. Discussion with no outsider is most common among lower-lower Negro men, least frequent in the lower-middle class.

At each class level, fewer women than men have had no discussions. Higher status women are more likely to have had discussions with non-relatives than are lower status women, but within classes the differences between those discussing with relatives and those discussing with non-relatives is significant only for lower-lower whites.

TABLE 5-9:
HUSBANDS' AND WIVES' DISCUSSION OF FAMILY SIZE

	White				Negro	
	UM (24)	LM (27)	UL (21)	LL (21)	UL (24)	LL (28)
Husband discusses with	*100%*	*100%*	*100%*	*100%*	*100%*	*100%*
No outsider	29	11	19	24	29	43
Non-relatives only	17	18	5	14	8	7
Relatives only	–	30	33	48	38	32
Both	54	41	43	14	25	18
Total relatives	54	71	76	62	63	50
Total non-relatives	71	59	48	28	33	25
Wife discusses with	100%	100%	100%	100%	100%	100%
No outsider	12	7	5	15	25	21
Non-relatives only	21	15	14	–	4	18
Relatives only	4	15	29	35	21	29
Both	63	63	52	50	50	32
Total relatives	67	78	81	85	71	61
Total non-relatives	84	78	67	50	54	50

All of the above results suggest, in somewhat simplified form, the following pattern: at the lowest status levels the wife's mother, and sometimes other females in her family, form the core of those concerned with how many children the couple has, and relatively few others are involved. At successively higher status levels members of the husband's family become more involved, and also friends outside the family are more often included in these discussions. Thus considerations of family size are interpersonally more complexly conditioned at higher than at lower status levels.

Whether one discusses family size only within the confines of the extended family or also outside it should have an effect on awareness of shifts in family size norms and preferences in the larger society. If one talks about these things only with one's parents, then presumably one will be less aware of generational shifts in preferences than if one also discusses family size with friends, neighbors, and work colleagues.

Table 5-10 presents a tabulation of proportions of husbands and wives in the sample believing that people want larger or smaller families than twenty-five years ago according to the kinds of people with whom the individual has discussed family size. The three top classes in the white group, all of whom should be exposed to the general shift in preference toward larger families, show a significant association between discussion with non-relatives and belief that people now want larger families. (And this association is present for each of the sex groups at each of the three social class levels.) Overall, 65 per cent of the husbands and wives who have discussed family size with non-relatives think people want larger fami-

TABLE 5-10:
RELATION OF DISCUSSION OF FAMILY SIZE PREFER-ENCES WITH NON-RELATIVES TO BELIEF THAT PEOPLE WANT LARGER FAMILIES

		People want larger families than 25 years ago	*People want smaller families than 25 years ago*
*Three classes averaging 56 per cent saying people want larger families (UM, LM, white UL)**			
Have discussed with non-relatives	(94)	65%	35%
Have discussed only with relatives	(26)	31	69
Have discussed with no one	(19)	53	47
Three classes averaging 17 per cent saying people want larger families (white LL, Negro UL and LL)			
Have discussed with non-relatives	(48)	12%	88%
Have discussed only with relatives	(36)	17	83
Have discussed with neither	(37)	24	76

*$X^2 = 8.36$, df = 2. T = .21 P < .025

lies, compared to 31 per cent of those who have discussed with relatives only. Among the other three class groups in which only 17 per cent believe people want larger families, there is no relationship with discussions of family size, as would be expected since peers will only mirror parental admonitions to keep family size down.

6

Motivations for large and small families

IN PREVIOUS CHAPTERS we examined the "numbers game" of family size—"How many do you want?" and "How many should Americans have?"—and then discussed the rationales for the numbers people choose. In this chapter we want to look in detail at the meanings and functions of particular family sizes for particular couples—at what motivates couples to decide that two, or three, or five children is a good number *for them*. For the time being we will hold in abeyance the question of how well couples are able to realize their goals, how effective they are in limiting the family to a size on which they can agree. Because middle and upper-lower class couples are more successful at keeping goal consistent with reality, our analysis of motivations will concentrate on them.

Husband-wife agreement about family size

First, however, it is necessary to see to what extent husband and wife agree about family size since an examination of motivations assumes an understanding of *what* each partner wants as the basis for examining *why* he wants that. Table 6–1 presents various categories of husband-wife agreement and disagreement for two stages in the growth of the family:

TABLE 6-1:
HUSBAND-WIFE AGREEMENT CONCERNING PRESENT FAMILY SIZE

		Family Below Desired Size for Both Spouses		
		Both Want Same Number	*Husband Wants More*	*Wife Wants More*
Middle Class	(28)	64%	11%	25%
White lower class	(16)	63	12	25
Negro Lower class	(10)	30	40	30

		At Least One Spouse Has Enough Children					
		Both Have Number Wanted	*Husband Wants More*	*Wife Wants More*	*Both Have Too Many*	*Wife Has Too Many*	*Husband Has Too Many*
Middle class	(19)	58%	11%	21%	—	5%	5%
Combined upper-lower class	(23)	48	13	17	13	—	9
Negro lower-lower class	(23)	13	17	9	31	17	13
White lower-lower class	(19)	26	21	5	26	16	5

first, before the family has reached a size desired by either and, second, the stage at which at least one partner wants no more children.

Among those couples in which both partners want more children, about two-thirds of the whites agree on the number of children required to complete their preferred family size. Where there is disagreement, it is the wife who tends to want more children (although the subsamples are quite small, the data suggest that it is mainly in the lower-middle class that this is true). Among the Negroes, there is much less agreement between spouses (again, the samples are small but the data suggest that it is upper-lower Negroes who disagree — only one of seven respondents agree on their preferred family size.

Among those couples where at least one partner wants no more children, the greatest divergence among classes, as would be expected, is in terms of whether the number of children at present is just enough or too many. Middle and upper-lower class respondents are least likely to indicate an excess of children for either partner; in contrast, 47 per cent of the white lower-lower and 61 per cent of the Negro lower-lower couples have at least one partner who feels that there are too many children. In the white lower-lower class the push toward larger families seems disproportionately the province of the husband — 37 per cent want more children than their wives, and the converse is true in only 10 per cent of the cases. There is a difference in the same direction for Negro lower-lowers but of smaller magnitude.

Overall, then, the degree of agreement between partners should not be exaggerated. Once the family has reached a size desired by one of the partners, agreement occurs more often than before this stage, yet still only slightly more than half of the couples agree, and there are no significant differences among classes in this respect. Apparently, however, in the middle class, the partner who wants the smaller family more often retains a veto if he cannot persuade his spouse to change her mind, perhaps mainly because his desires are allowed to have an effect on the consistency of contraceptive practice in the middle but not in the lower-lower class.

Family size motivations in complex perspective

Within the small range (two to five children) which includes the family size preferences of almost all the couples in the sample, there are strong feelings about which particular number is most satisfactory from the husband's or wife's point of view. It will be convenient to discuss motivations in terms of small, medium, or large families. For Protestants, a small family is defined as one with two children, a medium sized family has three children and four or more make up a large family. Among Catholics, both two and three children make a small family, four make a medium size family, and five or more make up a large family. The middle class Protestants in our sample are rather evenly divided among these alternatives, about 30 per cent want a small family, slightly over 40 per cent a medium sized family, and less than 30 per cent want the four children that for them represent a large family. Among Catholics, about one-third want a two or three child, "small" family. Among the women, most of the remainder, 61 per cent of the total, want five or more children, but the men split evenly between the medium and large sizes, approximately one-third of the Catholic men prefer each size. Freedman, Whelpton, and Campbell (1955: 288 ff.) found that young, better educated Catholic wives want larger families than their less educated co-religionists, but that these desires are very likely to be moderated as time goes on. Apparently their husbands have more modest expectations from the beginning.

Because the matter is complex and subtle, a full look at the ways couples talk about their family size preferences will be useful. There follow complete excerpts of answers to the questions about family size from interviews with three couples of rather similar status who want different family sizes. The first couple, an upper-middle class officer of a small firm and his wife, have decided they want only two children. Like the two couples to follow, these people live in a substantial house in a good suburban neighborhood. The husband is forty-two and the wife thirty-two. Like the other couples, both attended college, belong to country clubs or other kinds of social and civic organizations.

Husband:
Three's ideal. I was raised in a family of three. [Why is three your ideal?] Oh, [chuckle] back to the theory of the growth of the country. If families don't raise an average of three we will start back down population-wise. [Would you prefer two or four children?] I guess two because you can give two more than four. You can send them to college. The average family could not

give four very much. Saying two is probably selfish on my part; for the good of the country probably an average of four would be better. Two is all we can support adequately. My wife wants just two, too. Occasionally we see a little baby and she wants to have another one. The other night we went over to some friends and she picked up their baby, a real cute little red-headed baby, and was playing with it when I came in the room. She said, "You'd better get me out of here!" I feel the same way sometimes when I see a cute baby on TV or in a magazine. I guess if our second child had been a girl we would have felt different. Our youngest boy is very wild. He almost killed himself on several occasions, like falling off the air-conditioner with screwdrivers in both hands and wild things like that. I don't know if we would want another one like him or not. Oh, I love him just as much as the older boy but I guess he has just been more difficult to raise.

Wife:

I think three's ideal; I don't know. I guess it's because that is the number that was in my family. I have two brothers and it seemed our family at home was ideal. Would you prefer two or four children?] Two, but if I had loads of money I would want loads of kids. I wanted three when we first got married because I came from that kind of family; three makes a nice little crowd. If I had lots of money, enough for full-time help, and plenty of room I would like half-a-dozen or more. If by any wild accident I did become pregnant it would be fine but it is two now and will probably stay that way. [How does your husband feel?] Every once in a while when we see a particularly cute little girl in a TV commercial we will mention how nice it would be to have one but one or the other of us usually manages to talk us out of the idea. The other day I was holding a baby my mother-in-law was keeping and my husband told me to get that gleam out of my eyes and I said, "You had better get me out of here then." [This interview was conducted simultaneously with the husband and wife in different rooms.]

Husband:

[Why do some couples want small families, and others want large families?] Because of the way they were raised. I don't know if you are a Catholic or not but all Catholics believe in large families. People from large families want large families and only children want only one child; if they have more it's a slip, somebody goofed. It also depends on their ideas about children. Some people don't want to have large families because to have more would deprive them of the luxuries of life. [How do you feel about your children?] I couldn't begin to name all of the pleasures. This little one here is always getting into trouble. But, just one little thing at night, just one little word, and everything he has done during the day is forgotten. It's very hard to get the little one to mind; he is extremely opinionated for the age of five. He has been spanked four times as much at five as the older boy has at eight. I have very little discipline problem with the older boy; the little one challenges or tests my authority all the time. I keep a ruler on the icebox and I use it as a reminder to him. [How would you feel if you had more?] Well, it's really a matter of conjecture. I suppose there would be less discipline problems with three or four children; they would work out their problems on their own. I know I let my boys fight it out now and then if one of them doesn't have a hammer in their hand. My wife just walks away but she doesn't say anything. I think three or four would be much easier to raise unless they were all like our little one. If they were all like the older boy it would be OK. [How would you feel if you had fewer?] It would be much easier to raise one, but an only child has a tendency to be mothered. The mother has a more protective instinct than the father; she still wants to help it make decisions even after he gets married. I have a friend who is an only child and he was 44 years old before he got married; when that girl married him she married his mother, too. [Why do some people want more than two?] The main reason would be the pleasure derived. If I got two times the pleasure I get from these two I would be slap-happy with ecstasy. It takes a very patient man to have several children. He must be an optimist; if he is pessimistic about a child dying or losing his job then he couldn't have a large family and enjoy it. [Do people want smaller or larger families now?] Oh, I think larger families; I've heard different opinions expressed and they all say that families are getting larger. [Why?] Well, the Catholics are on the rise; that might be one reason. I have a Catholic friend in Dallas, a lawyer, who has five. People

are optimistic about the future. Your generation hasn't known
want unless they were from an extremely poor family. I think
optimism might be the answer.

Wife:
[Why do some couples want small families, others large?] Not
counting income it would depend on what kind of people they
are. Some are just crazier about kids than others are. Also,
there are men that are very demanding; I have a Catholic friend
and I don't think it's just their religious convictions either because he impresses me as just being a beast and would have all
those children regardless of his religion. And, of course, there
are people who are just plain careless or so oversexed they
don't think of the consequences. [How do you feel about your
children?] I had my last child naturally. I read Dr. Reid's book
and was determined to go through my delivery fully conscious
so I would know all about it. My doctor tried to talk me out of it
but I stuck to my decision and I'm glad I did; it was wonderful
and after nine months of being nauseated it was nothing. I think
my children are amazing; they are so different. I thought I had it
all figured out that I could mold them but now I know that
children are born individuals. My oldest son is thoughtful and
studious; the young one is a natural-born mechanic. I think that
is what is interesting about a family; it's the variety you get in
personalities and dispositions. [How would you feel if you had
more?] It would be rather upsetting, I'm sure. My husband has
everything planned and arranged for our two sons' college. Now
I'm able to be free to be active in things. I just can't imagine
how it would be to have four but I can conceive of three. I was
glad to get to the point of getting out of the house and I don't
think at this point I would be too thrilled to go back to diapers
and formulas, etc. [Why do some people want more than two?]
I remember visiting friends recently and the youngest is about
three. The husband said it would be nice to keep it going so they
could always have one at this age. Some women are just natural-
born mothers. With me it had to grow on me; I remember after
my first child and they brought him to me I kept waiting for
this wonderful mother-love to start flowing over me but it didn't.
I kept thinking, "What am I ever going to do with this little
red wiggly baby?" [Do people want smaller or larger families

now?] I think we are in a cycle of larger families now. I think preferences change from one generation to another. [Why large now?] Oh, I don't know, sometimes I think it is a matter of keeping up with the Joneses in the number of children as well as the old-fashioned things. I hate to say it but I think that's some women's idea of the best way to hold their husbands.

Husband:

[Who cares about how many children you have?] Nobody. [Who have you discussed the question with?] No one; that's where we draw the line.

Wife:

[Who cares?] I'm sure both families are interested, especially my mother-in-law; she had four [sic?] and always said that was too many. I know she would be vitally concerned if I had even one more than I now have. I don't think my mother would mind, but she's not here. [Have you discussed this with others?] Of course with friends it has come up in numerous conversations. There seems to be a wide variety of opinions on the subject. One of my best friends had five and wants another but her home is in wild disorder and this would drive me crazy.

This couple's youngest boy is five years old but it is clear that neither the husband and wife are thinking seriously about having more children. They invest a good deal of emotional energy in their two children, both positively and negatively. That is, they seek enjoyment in relating to each child, but they also worry about them a good deal. The husband is specific in talking about each boy, each one stands out for him as a very different individual with different needs and offering different rewards to him as parent. The wife is not so concerned with the children individually and is more impressed by the general problem of emotional demands which additional children would represent. In other parts of the interview, both husband and wife indicate that they have quite active outside interests, devote considerable time to these, and hope to devote even more time. In this household, the husband has the dominant voice according to both principals;

he is the main decision-maker and authority, and his wife consciously caters to him in a way that is not typical of other women in her class. As the husband is aware, he is rather conservative and pessimistic about life; although they live well he worries about the future, is unwilling to take prosperity and good health for granted. Apparently he communicates these feelings forcefully to his wife since she is aware of, although she does not seem to fully share, his sense of need for caution and prudence in handling the family's affairs.

One result of all of this is that neither husband nor wife feel up to having more children. In this it would seem that the husband is the more adamant, he feels more children would represent an intolerable emotional pressure and an unwelcome financial burden. In the former case, at least, given his complex and intense concern with the upbringing of his two sons, he is probably right. The wife, were she married to a different husband, or allowed her own way, would be tempted to have one more child in spite of the gains she feels she has from no longer being mother to a toddler. In her, the balance is close between the attractions of mothering a very young child and the restrictions and nervousness that come from having several children. She does not find it easy or "natural" to be a mother; she could be tempted to have more children to "prove" that she is a normal woman and mother were it not for her husband's insistence that they cannot afford more children.

The second couple have three children, one boy and two girls; the youngest is two years old. The husband is a thirty-seven-year-old small business man, the wife is thirty-four years old. Both have been socially mobile from their parents' upper-lower class position. They live in a comfortable eight room house in an upper-middle class suburban neighborhood.

Husband:
I think two is ideal for the average American family based on an average income of $5000.00. I don't see how they could properly provide for more children. Personally I'd take a dozen

if I could afford them. I wanted four when we got married, or as many as the family income could support. We talked about how many we would have but not a definite goal, that's relative to how the family progresses. We have what we want as a family now; the children are what we can take care of now. [Would you want fewer?] Not on your life, love 'em all! We've talked about it and my wife is in complete agreement with my views, I think. [Aren't you sure?] Oh yes, she is not the kind of person to hide what she thinks.

Wife:
I think four is ideal, I was an only child; that's not right. With four there is more of a family feeling, two is still not enough. I spent some rather lonely hours. [How many did you want early in marriage?] I liked the idea of a big family, six. Later I decided to take it as we went. My husband wanted children but not that many. We didn't talk about it much then. I cut down to four, and then to three. I didn't think of the future in terms of education and all that, and managing the work load. We talk about it occasionally. He is satisfied with the way it is now.

Husband:
[Why do some couples want small families, others large?] Some people don't plan for the future, they have children as they come. Those with one or two have that number primarily for economic reasons, age limitations or some physical reason. Housing has a lot to do with it. [How do you feel about your children?] Respect for other people is an important value. I want them to be informed, have a good family environment. We have no difficulties except our share of childhood sicknesses. [What pleasures do you have from them?] Have you got a week! We've had all pleasure. It gives you a complete family life and happiness to see them grow and accomplish and basically to feel their love. [How would you feel if you had more?] It would be about the same. [If you had fewer?] Naturally we wouldn't have the same financial responsibilities now and in their future education. [Why do people want more than two?] Well, I like children, they are a blessing, not a burden. I think that I wanted

more than a couple for that reason. A man naturally likes to see his family live and grow and prosper. [How has this changed in 25 years?] Not much. The conditions of each family make the difference. I know that a large number of children can make housing a problem and there are also wives that work; they can't work and stay home to have and raise children, too.

Wife:
[Why do some couples want small families, others large?] Partly attitude; each day will take care of itself and don't worry about ten or fiteen years from now. They have no worries about putting the children through college. Different religions, too. We're all used to living different ways; the ways we live, the ways in which we bring our children up, are determined by the way in which we were brought up. [How do you feel about your children?] The pleasures are their love, appreciation of what you do, fun in seeing them grow up. The difficulties are getting the little one trained right. With the boy it's trying to get him to be more of a boy; he's easily pushed around, too whiney, get him to stand on his own feet. He's leery of new situations, going to school, new Sunday School, ill-at-ease meeting new people. [How would you feel if you had more?] The difficulties over time increase; there is less time for each one—there is a great demand that way already with three. But you can't call all the shots. The little one would enjoy a brother. The good points increase, too, as the disadvantages increase. [If you had fewer?] That would be like saying I had just the two older ones. There would be a lot of bickering. The pleasures wouldn't be as great. The kids love the new baby; there's less bickering now. They spend more time with her than I thought they would. [Why do people want more than two?] I suppose it's the same reasons I have—the differences in the children, different ideas, say different things, the fun of raising them, seeing them develop. [People want smaller or larger families now?] I wonder if it has changed very much. Farm families had a lot of children; fewer farm families now. Probably hasn't changed much. Today there are fewer couples with one or two, more with three or four. [Why?] I don't have any idea but being raised an only child it's fun to have a brother and sister.

Husband:

[Who's concerned about number of children you have?] No one. [Who have you discussed it with?] Family study groups, church discussion, informal presentation of ideas. They all just talk generally, say about four children is ideal. Everybody talks to someone about family problems from time to time. It's hard to pinpoint anything. Most of the people I know have about the same views that I do.

Wife:

[Who's concerned?] Both our mothers are. They think we have enough with three. But I don't think they would speak out too strongly if there is another one. [Have you discussed this?] It's come up in conversation but not discussed seriously. Some of them are flabbergasted about people having seven or nine children. If they have one child they want more. Usually they want two or three; this is what they can manage, taking care of the children and the work load. I've never really discussed it with anyone in detail.

Both husband and wife are attracted to the idea of a full family. The husband is proud that his accomplishments allow him to have more than the two children he feels is reasonable for the average man, and both would like to have another child if they felt they could provide for four children adequately. The husband is most impressed by the financial problems that would be involved; he shows little of the concern over emotional demands that the first man experiences in dealing with his two children. The wife is concerned both about the financial and the responsibility aspects of having more children. She clearly expresses the idea that three children represent the best combination of the advantages of large and small families. She can give individual attention to each child, as she fears she could not with four; but the three children do not bicker and are not as selfish as they would be if there were only the older boy and girl. She values her three children because each has his own individuality and each provides his parents with a different experience, and she is concerned that she could not enjoy them as individuals if she had more children. The wife sees all of this as making up for the companionship and family-feeling she feels she was deprived of in her own childhood; she wants a family in which neither she nor her children are lonely as she was as a child. In short, she feels more alive because of the variegated emotional exchange, both giving and getting, which her five-person household allows her. She still is attracted to the idea of adding another to this group, but feels that this would not be a reasonable thing to do.

The husband apparently does not feel as deeply this attraction to a large family. Like most other husbands, he treats the family more as a group—he speaks of a "complete family life" and uses "they" without the concern with individuality that his wife shows. Both because it is his responsibility to provide and because he is less complexly involved with the children, it is easier for him to conform to the dictates of reason that he perceives in their situation.

The third family has five children, apparently a cause for some conflict between husband and wife. The youngest child is one year old. The husband is forty-five, and she is thirty-five years old. Both are Catholics; he is active in church organizations, she in non-sectarian groups. They live in one of the best suburban areas in an eight room house which the interviewer described as "very lovely."

Husband:
I think five children is ideal. I was raised in a family of five. Even though we were pretty broken up [his mother died when he was quite young] five was a nice secure number. When we were all together it was very pleasant. It's a real nice family size, a nice challenge. There are differences in children and you watch the children develop and help them; you recognize the children as individuals. I've always thought about five, even before I was married. I don't think my wife would have gone along with this when we were married; she would have been shocked out of her shoes because she comes from a family of two. Many of my wife's relatives had large families and she felt

that they had many problems, and that she could never cope with that many. But, she was wrong, she could cope with all those problems. I still think that five is best. [How does your wife feel?] She is perfectly satisfied with five now. When I first mentioned it to her it was a shock, but I don't think it was much of a problem after we had three.

Wife:

I think three is ideal because I feel this is all most people are equipped to raise, to give a good education and send them through college. [Suppose you had to choose between two and four children?] I'd choose four. We talked about how many children to have when we were married but we never came to any agreement. He always wanted four or five and I thought that two or three would be plenty. We discussed it occasionally but that's the extent of it. We said we would just wait and see. Now I've got five and that's enough. I'm getting too old to have another baby. I just don't have time to help them grow up. With just the little day-to-day things I can't be in five places at the same time. Without my mother (who recently moved to a distant city) I feel the younger ones are going to suffer because she gave the older ones a lot of love and attention. [How does your husband feel now?] He would like more but I feel they become part of a group rather than individuals. Everything here is a real production.

Husband:

[Why do some people want small and some want large families though they have the same income?] They have different feelings; I think it's more fear than anything else. I don't think they feel the ability of handling so many children. It's like Roosevelt's idea of the fear of fear. It may be an unwillingness to accept the responsibility of raising, training, and educating children. [What are your feelings about your children?] It's mostly pleasurable; the hardships are minimal. I don't think there are any hardships that can't be surmounted by parents. [Hardships?] Primarily it's social, for some it may be financial. I think there's an unwillingness to cope with problems that children have as growing humans — adjustments to school, community, playmates. The real purpose of marriage is to have children; it's a God-given right and responsibility. With fewer you're really not extending yourself. It's an easy way out; I think you have a tendency to become self-satisfied and complacent. (Suppose you had more?) Well, I don't have any major objection to more. Considering our children's ages, as soon as our 4th and 5th are in school, I don't think there would be any great hardships with having more. [Do people want larger or smaller families now than 25 years ago?] Fewer children were desired then because of the economy. That was 1936; we were just coming through the depression and heading for a recession. This was followed by war babies. There were quick marriages and the war itself. Postwar-wise there is an improved economy, more homes, more jobs, more mobility—these all gave rise to larger families.

Wife:

[Why do people have large or small families on same income?] People feel different about what they should spend money on. Some feel they should do what they can for their children. [How do you feel about your children?] They are different personalities. The baby's needs are straightforward—just love, food, and clothing. The older ones have different interests. The second one was born jealous. The older one is much more responsible; she is much more mature because she had to accept responsibility. I don't know if this is good for her or not; I'm concerned about how she will feel about a large family. [How would it be different if you had more?] I would just put more responsibility on the older ones and I doubt whether this would be good or not. With five children they have quite enough now. [How would it be different if you had fewer?] I might have been able to give them more material things but I really don't know; a large family makes for a lot of togetherness which is good. [Why do some people want more than two children?] Many people enjoy watching a baby grow up. I think larger families find more enjoyment within the family and enjoy doing things together. [Do people want smaller or larger families than 25 years ago?] Larger families from what I have heard. The depression years made people want fewer children because money problems were so great.

Husband:

[Who else is concerned about number of children you have?]
My wife's parents. They are wonderful and gracious—they
never interfere and they are helpful. Knowing her family, they
would have been concerned if it were a question of my wife's
health and welfare. It wouldn't make any difference to them
if we had fewer children. I've discussed this with neighbors,
friends and business associates. [What are their ideas?] Well,
a couple I know had two children but their contribution to
the world was just a reproduction of themselves; they had a boy
and a girl and that was enough for them. I can think of another
couple, friends, that have one child. Since the husband is an
only child one was enough for him. He grew up alone and this
guided his decision on the number of offspring.

Wife:

[Who else is concerned about the number of children you
have?] My father and mother; they are very concerned about
the welfare of the children and my physical welfare and about
the money aspects of it. If we had another they would love the
child, but not the idea. I've talked about this very generally with
friends and very seriously with my husband but I've never
really gone into it with others.

In this family the husband argues for a large family and
the wife for moderation. Much of what each says in the interview seems to be a replaying of justifications each has used
in arguing his views with the other—the husband has undoubtedly told his wife that she is afraid of responsibility and
the wife has told him that it's not fair to her or the children to
have so many. It comes as no surprise, then, to learn that the
fifth child was an unwelcome "accident" from her point of
view. The husband takes religion more seriously than his
wife; he more often speaks of it in connection with issues that
come up in the interview, and the wife tells us that they have
argued about his wish that the daughters go to a Catholic
school. The husband does not approve of their using mechanical contraceptives (condoms earlier and the diaphragm more
recently); the wife has no qualms on this score. The husband

has come around to the point that he is willing to accept contraception as a way of spacing children, but he still feels that they should have another child when the youngest is in school.

For the husband, several streams of experience come together to influence him to prefer a large family. He values his religion and takes seriously the injunction to be fruitful. He grew up in a large family and found it a source of security in the difficult situation of being motherless. He sees in a large family a source of security and stability now, and a proof both that he is a competent, confident, and prosperous man and that he is meeting the challenges of life without selfishness, complacency, or laziness. He has been mobile from a lower class background; having a large family may give him some sense of continuity with his past and a feeling that he has not moved into an effete world of selfindulgent rich. (He probably feels that this is his wife's difficulty; she attended an Eastern finishing school and comes from an upper-middle class family.) In his conversation about his children, one gets the impression that he is more interested in his large family as a symbol of something than he is in relating to them individually. In describing himself and the way he functions in the family he notes that he does not have much time to spend with the children because of pressing career and community responsibilites. In the excerpts quoted above he spends relatively little time talking about his children and considerable time speaking more abstractly of the rights, duties, privileges, and values involved in having a large or small family. Neither he nor his wife mention any duties he has in connection with the children other than that he is "very strict about morals and ethics" and that "the children are only allowed to associate with children whose families he knows and approves of." In the couple discussed previously, the husband says that one of his main responsibilities is to "love my family" and the wife mentions that he spends much time with the children.

The wife, although clearly not wanting as many children as she now has, has mixed feelings about the desirability of a small family or one with four children. In terms of her own personal needs and interests she apparently feels attracted to a small family of two or three children, but she also feels that a family of four offers much to the children *if* there are enough adults around to pay attention to them. Because she is very active in community and social affairs, she finds her family burdensome, and she notes that the daughter whom she characterizes as "born jealous" is "always telling me I don't have any time for her." She finds it difficult to reconcile her conception of herself as a modern woman—socially active, well-educated, sophisticated—with the necessity to supervise a household with seven persons in it. But she insists on pursuing her interests; apparently these are so meaningful to her that she seeks the necessary give in her familial role rather than her community roles. She notes that if she had more children she "would just have to put more responsibility on the older ones." She says that she is concerned over the effect such responsibility and the lack of Mother's time will have on her older daughters, but she regards these hardships as necessary because she is not able to give up her high level of activity outside the home. (Her comment that she is concerned about the effect of these experiences on her daughter's feelings about a large family can be interpreted as meaning that she is teaching her daughters not to have as many children as she has had, is giving them an object lesson.)

Much of what she says is reminiscent of the way the first woman quoted talks about her interests in home and community. Were her husband like the first woman's husband it is quite possible that she would have had a small (for a Catholic) family of three children. In any case, her resentment (in which she is probably supported by her parents) at the effect of her husband's desires is clear. Such a pattern is unique among the middle class cases (Protestant and Catholic) in our sample. The reverse situation, in which the husband is talked into having more children than he wants, is perhaps more common, but also less likely to make for resentment since the husband is not confined in the same way by having more children than he wants. Thus, in one Protestant couple the husband, who would have preferred two children instead of the four (or five) his wife has insisted on, regards children as a "nuisance and an expense" but he says that he is rather selfish in his views and that if his wife feels she can manage four or five children he is willing to go along. He tries to see to it that the children do not restrict his "freedom to come and go" any more than is absolutely necessary, or his desire to have time at home to pursue his intellectual interests. His wife, a very energetic woman, manages to enjoy her family and work part-time at a job which she enjoys, but she does not have active social interests otherwise and looks to her children for companionship, stimulation, and a sense of being absorbed in something worthwhile and distinctively her own.

Specific motives for small and large families

The six men and women who have been quoted above, cover in their comments most of the things which middle (and lower) class people have to say about their preference for a small, medium, or large family. The combinations in which the various views are put differ greatly from couple to couple, but these six reflect the dominant attitudes. In chapter 5 we examined the rationales offered by men and women for why different people might prefer families of different sizes. Do the rationales that are offered vary depending on how many children the respondent wants? The tables below indicate that for men there is considerable variation; for women the variation is much less because women seem better able to put themselves in the shoes of those who want different numbers of children. That is, women who want large families are better able than men with similar preferences to understand what motivates the person who wants a small family and vice versa.

TABLE 6-2:
REASONS PEOPLE WANT SMALL FAMILIES ACCORDING TO
MIDDLE CLASS MEN

	Respondent's wants		
	Small Family* (19)	Medium Family* (20)	Large Family (14)
Parental convenience or selfishness only*	27%	25%	57%
Best for children	37	45	(—
Both*	5	15	14
Parents are "selfish"	16	15	57
No response	31	15	29

*Combined for text X^2 (without NR) = 6.81   T = .41   P < .01

From Table 6-2 it is apparent that men who want large families see those who want small families most often as simply catering to their own convenience and as selfishly concerned to have more goods and time, less responsibility, as parents. Over half of the men who want large families specifically characterize those who want small families as "selfish." Presumably part of their desire for large families stems from a wish to avoid such an identity and to be regarded (by themselves and others) as men who are willing to give of themselves and able to give because they are achieving. On the other hand, a majority of those who offer rationales for a smaller family and themselves want a small or medium-sized family place the emphasis instead on how the children benefit, primarily in terms of goods, secondarily in terms of future education (college). They emphasize thereby that they are persons of good judgment who know enough not to indulge themselves to the detriment of their children's needs for goods and costly education.

Interestingly enough, women are not influenced by their own preferences in the rationales they offer for a small family; many women who want large families understand that others who want smaller ones are concerned about providing for their children, and are less likely than men who want large families to see only selfishness on the part of such parents. Wives who want small families feel more justified than their husbands in emphasizing the fact that a small family cuts down on the pressure of household and mothering duties, perhaps because a large family does mean a greater increase in work and demands for them than it does for their husbands. On the other hand, the division of labor in the family means that the husband is more likely to be concerned about the financial burden involved. Kiser (1962:150–51), summarizing the results of the Indianapolis Fertility Study, notes a finding that bears on this point:

> Among couples. . . . who had no pregnancies except those that were deliberately planned. . . . there was a direct (instead of inverse) relation of fertility to socio-economic status. . . . Fertility rates were directly related to feelings of economic security and of personal adequacy. The relationship to economic security persisted in rather strong form after socio-economic status was controlled.

In other words, at any given status level those who felt more secure economically had more children, conforming to the norm that "you should have as many children as you can afford."

If the central meaning of selfishness for the small-family parent has important social reality we would expect that those who nevertheless with to have only two children will be quite sensitive and protective of their own attitudes. They will emphasize the objective necessity for so limiting the family. Given the larger social meanings that attach to having a small family—selfishness or poverty—one might expect that those who want only two children would be less likely to discuss their preferences with family and friends than those who want more children, and that they would also be more likely to "misread" the family size trend in the middle class and to believe that people want smaller rather than larger families than formerly. Tables 6–3 and 6–4 present the data bearing on these hypotheses. From the first table it is ap-

TABLE 6-3:
PREFERRED FAMILY SIZE AND DISCUSSIONS WITH OTHERS:
THE MIDDLE CLASS

	Respondent wants	
	Small Family (26)	Medium or Large Family (76)
Respondent has discussed family size with		
No one*	23%	11%
Relatives only*	19	13
Friends only*	27	17
Both relatives and friends	31	59

*Combined for test X^2 = 5.18   T = .23   P < .02

TABLE 6-4:
TREND TOWARD SMALLER OR LARGER FAMILIES AND DE-
SIRED FAMILY SIZE AS PERCEIVED BY THE MIDDLE CLASS

	Respondent's wants		
	Small Family (35)	Medium Family* (33)	Large Family* (33)
Compared to 25 years ago, people want			
Smaller families	52%	18%	21%
Larger families	48	82	79

*Combined for test X^2 = 9.50   T = .31   P < .005

parent that husbands and wives who want two-child families
are much less likely to discuss family size extensively with
relatives and friends than are others. Apparently people who
want small families keep their own counsel, thus avoiding
experiences likely to communicate to them the low esteem in
which most of their peers hold couples who thus limit their
families (avoiding, that is, implicit accusations of selfishness
or denigration as not prosperous enough to afford a family of
fitting size). Table 6-4 shows that people who want small
families are much more likely to believe that couples prefer
smaller families than 25 years ago, while those who want

medium or large families overwhelmingly believe that the trend is toward larger families. (The relationship is significant for men and women separately as well as together.) We can only hypothesize that in this way, too, people who want small families protect themselves from a feeling of being out of step with others in their generation.

We saw above that men, but not women, perceive the rationales for large or small families differently depending on their own desired family size. What about the rationales for large families? Tables 6–5 and 6–6 present data for men and

TABLE 6–5:
REASONS PEOPLE WANT LARGE FAMILIES ACCORDING TO MIDDLE CLASS MEN

	Respondent's Wants		
	Small Family (19)	*Medium Family (20)*	*Large Family (14)*
Specific immediate parental or child gain	37%	65%	86%
Parent Gain	(21)	(55)	(66)
Child Gain	(26)	(35)	(57)
Parents just like or love children	58	25	7
Neither	5	10	57

X^2 (Without NR) = 7.64, df = 2 T = .33 P < .025

TABLE 6–6:
REASONS PEOPLE WANT LARGE FAMILIES ACCORDING TO MIDDLE CLASS WOMEN

	Respondent's Wants		
	Small Family* (17)	*Medium Family* (15)*	*Large Family (21)*
Specific immediate parental or child gain	53%	60%	86%
Parent Gain	(29)	(53)	(62)
Child Gain	(41)	(33)	(52)
No specific gain	47	40	14

*Combined for test. Exact test: P < .05

women on this point. Both men and women who want large families are much more likely to mention specific immediate parental or child gains from having a large family than are men and women who want smaller families. The specific parental gains are a sense of accomplishment, the pleasure of watching children grow and develop, and the generally happier atmosphere and companionship that children provide their parents. Only about one-fourth of the men and women who want small families see this as a reason for having many children compared to over 60 per cent of those who want large families. Those who want a large family are saying, in short, that they enjoy having more than two or three children around; it provides them with a sense of human involvement. Often when they speak of what they get from their children it is as if a large family is more fun and more entertaining than television—they will say that "something new is always happening" or "there's never a dull moment around here."

Among men there is also a clear difference between groups in the perception of benefits to children from a large family. The large-family fathers more often say that children gain from the companionship and training in sharing, cooperation, and responsibility that the large family provides. That is, children profit both by having available to them the same kind of pleasures that the parents value, and they also have experiences which develop character and make for a more moral person. Few small-family fathers perceive these advantages, but the small-family mothers often do. These mothers feel that their two (or for Catholics, three) children would profit from having companionship and from the necessity to share and work out one's own difficulties with one's siblings, but they feel that other needs, their own or their children's, overshadow these gains.

The small-family fathers more often offer as the reason why some people want larger families simply the notion that they "like" or "love" children more, or that they "like having children around" and offer no more specific content for these assertions. That is, unlike the large-family parents, they are unable to imagine specifically what parental or child advantages the large family offers its fanciers. Small-family mothers more often offer instead a variety of other reasons less specifically tied to parental or child gains—they mention religion, or that having a large family makes the man feel more of a man, the woman more of a woman, or that the family name is surer to survive. In general, they offer motives that are less praiseworthy than the specific parental gain suggested by the large-family mothers.

Table 6–7 presents data on reasons for preferring a large family in which Protestant and Catholic middle class men respond differently. Among Protestants, men who want small families are more likely to offer one of three extrinsic (to them) pressures for having a large family—that the parents are Catholic, that they have a family tradition to maintain, or that large families are fashionable now. Protestant men who want medium or large families do not offer such rationales.

TABLE 6–7:
REASONS FOR WANTING LARGE FAMILIES

	Middle Class Protestant Men	
	Wants Small Family (11)	*Wants Medium or Large Family* (18)
Offers extrinsic pressure (religion, fashion, etc.)	55%	17%
Does not offer such pressure	45	83

	Middle Class Catholic Men		
	Wants Small Family (8)	*Wants Medium Size Family* (6)	*Wants Large Family* (10)
Offers religious tradition	50%	17%	90%
Does not offer such reasons	50	83	10

(Protestant women do not differ according to preferred family size; overall, about 40 per cent offer extrinsic rationales.) Among Catholics, few women (21 per cent) offer religious tradition as a reason why some people might want a large family. Catholic men, however, vary according to the size of family they want. Nine out of ten men who want a large family include religion as one of the reasons, suggesting that this is an important part of their motivation. Only one of the six men who want four children (a medium-size family by our definition) offers religion as a reason. At the other extreme, half of the men who want a small family offer religion, but here they are expressing this as a reason external to their own motives; they are saying that they will not be guided by religion, and also that those who do want a large family are more often guided by religion, and/or a vague liking for children, than by specific gratifications they seek for themselves or their children.

Personal and role factors in the desire for small and large families

These specific, relatively conscious motivations for wanting a large or small family must be understood in terms of their functional relations to other characteristics of the husband and wife as individuals, and of their marital functioning. The history of reasearch into the social psychological bases for American couples having small or large families has not been particularly encouraging and the yield of findings has been small (Kiser, 1962: 149–66). Fertility is so complexly determined by biological, psychological, intimate interactional and broader cultural forces that this is not surprising. A recent paper by Lois Hoffman and Frederick Wyatt (1960: 235–44) sketches a set of theoretical propositions about social changes over the past thirty years which they believe have the effect of encouraging couples to have larger families. Further, since the changes and attributes posited in the theory are not uniformly distributed among couples, these propositions also provide a starting point for examining variations in desired family size among couples. The authors offer three areas in which they believe there have been social changes affecting family size preferences: areas of change (1) in the woman's role (and, by implication, the man's role, since roles have meaning only in relation to other roles), (2) in the parent role, and (3) in increasing loneliness and alienation in American society. Although this research was designed before the writer became acquainted with the Hoffman–Wyatt paper, much of the data collected bear on their hypotheses. Therefore we will summarize these propositions, elaborate them at some points to increase their generality, and then examine findings from this study which bear on these hypotheses.

First, Hoffman and Wyatt discuss the changes in the woman's role brought about by technological advances. They note that housework has become less time-consuming, duller, and less creative through the availability of labor-saving devices and products (such as packaged mixes) which require less labor on the housewife's part to produce what the family consumes. Concurrent with these changes, more married women have entered the labor market and in most cases "it is more economical for the woman to work for wages and buy commercial products than to spend her time making the products at home for her own family." At the same time women have come to feel that they have a right to personal happiness and self-fulfillment based on their own choices and preferences; they feel they are not required simply to fulfill homemaking roles decreed by society. Further, in our society neither women nor men are allowed to be simply idle, one must justify oneself in terms of some productive or creative activity. Thus, the woman with a small family confronts the fact that when her children enter school she will not have a full-time job at home. If she does not find the idea of going to work attractive, she must face the possibility of not having enough socially-approved responsibilities to be regarded by herself, her husband, and her peers as a constructive person. One way out of this conflict, say Hoffman and Wyatt, is to have more children since mothering is clearly an acceptable, creative, and demanding activity. Having three or four children postpones for a long time the point at which the wife cannot feel fully occupied with her functioning at home.

The direct opposition between mothering and employment which dominates these authors' argument perhaps states the situation more simply than is realistic. Let us summarize the hypothesis, and at the same time fill it out with other possibilities open to the woman: (1) Because non-maternal homemaking functions take less time and energy than formerly, women do not derive the same sense of worth and prestige simply from keeping a household running; neither housekeeping nor cooking are now as demanding or offer as many opportunities for self-expression and self-validation. (2) Women, therefore, can have more children than formerly without overburdening themselves as housekeepers. In doing so they may make up, by being more fully mothers, some of what they have lost by the loss of skill in their homemaking role. (3) If the woman does not occupy herself with having children or does not substitute some other absorbing and socially valid activity for large-family motherhood, she runs the risk of seeming lazy, parasitical, and socially unworthy. (4) Equally important, she may simply be bored, with all the psychodynamic implications this carries for not being engaged in activities which provide constructive and anxiety-free impulse expression. Her increased leisure thus seems doubly threatening to her—others will think poorly of her and she will be threatened internally by impulses which an occupying routine does not channel.

What choices does she have if she does not have more than one or two children? First, she can try to devote herself to homemaking and rise above the deskilling pressures society brings to bear. That is, she can devote great energy to decorating the home, or to becoming a gourmet cook, or to gardening. These activities, however, are likely to be rewarded only at upper-middle class levels; at lower status levels the emphasis is on an adequate home, not a fancy one. Even at the upper-middle class level, the woman probably runs some risk of being regarded as self-centered if she devotes herself so single-mindedly to house and garden rather than to people.

Second, she can devote herself to her husband, catering to his interests and spending her time doing things that will please or be helpful to him. She can become his full-time social secretary, for example, devoting herself to entertaining his business associates and others who are important to him. Again, this is a functional alternative only at higher status levels, and even here it is doubtful that there is really enough work to keep the wife busy after her children are in school. The couple that devotes itself single-mindedly to such pursuits and interests also runs the risk of appearing selfish to others.

Finally, the wife can turn her interests to the world outside the home; she can take a job or in some other way become active away from home. The comment by Hoffman and Wyatt that by taking a job the wife puts herself in a position of potential competition with her husband and thus runs the risk of threatening at the same time "the woman's femininity, the man's masculinity, and the integrity of the marriage", applies almost as well to non-occupational alternatives for outside activity. Whether the wife goes to work or becomes active in clubs or service organizations, she develops interests and relationships which compete with those her husband wishes her to have. She develops a competence and accomplishments that may conflict with her husband's and are very likely to make demands on her time and emotions which conflict with the desires of her husband and children.

Purely from the wife's personal point of view, functioning in the outside world may involve other threats — she must deal with strangers, she must compete with other women as well as men (for example, she must dress better than she would have to do as simply a homemaker), she must make a kind of narcissistic investment in herself which she may find both burdensome and anxiety-producing ("I am somebody important because I work at an important job" and "I am somebody important because I am Chairman of our League of Woman Voters"). This narcissistic investment is threatened by society's implicit refusal to take women very seriously in the non-home world — women workers are too emotional, women leaders of voluntary organizations are well suited for cartoon subjects, etc. Functioning in the outside world, particularly on the job but also in certain kinds of voluntary association activity, may expose the woman to sexual liaisons (either flirtatious or more serious) which make her anxious and threaten her relation to her husband. Finally, for middle class women, particularly those of higher status, their own jobs often carry status implications inferior to the ones they have by virtue of being their husbands' wives. Wives of middle class men seldom match their husband's job status when they work, and this can be a source of irritation and frustration as they must accept interactions in which their more basic social status is denigrated. As middle class women marry younger and less frequently begin serious careers before they start raising their families, it is less and less easy for them to achieve an above average white-collar job level when they go back to work. The refusal to take women very seriously in civic activities may have the same effect — the corporation president's wife may have difficulty getting the mayor to take her as seriously as head of the local hospital welfare league as he would in her role of the wife of an important man.

All in all, though our society no longer officially maintains that a woman's place is only in the home, many of the forces which operate in the day-to-day interactions of the wife who goes out of the home serve to tell her that home and husband's-side are probably the safest places for her. Hoffman and Wyatt hypothesize that having several children cements the wife's status as dependent on the husband and thus both gratifies her and reassures him. At the same time, having children may be the most legitimate way for the wife to establish herself as independent of her husband and his demands—that is, she must worry about the children, attend to them, invest in them, and therefore is able legitimately to fend off desires on his part to have her at his beck and call. This is simply to say that having a large family can be multifunctional for the wife, and for the husband (if she is caught up in dealing with the children she may make fewer emotional demands on him).

We have outlined above several alternatives for wives to having a large family as a way of absorbing energies and giving lives meaning. We have pointed out for each of the alternatives some of the factors which can mitigate against its effectiveness for the wife. This is not meant, however, to obscure the fact that many wives may put together a combination of these alternatives (for example, devoting themselves both to helping the husband in his career and to outside social activities) that functions well for them, or at least seems superior to having larger family.

The second and closely related set of propositions that Hoffman and Wyatt offer to account for the growing popularity of larger families has to do with changes in the parent role:

> In the past decade the United States has become increasingly a child-centered culture, and a closely related development is the popularization of psychology. . . . The stress on child rearing and the widespread conviction that a child is what his parents have made him have had two important effects on the parental role. First, they have added challenge and importance to the child-rearing function, making it a creative and ego-involving area, for mothers at least. . . . At the same time, and largely because the skills for being a good mother are not being communicated at the same rate as is the emphasis on being a good mother, the child-rearing function is fraught with anxiety.

The interviews quoted in this and the previous two chapters certainly underline the value which men and women place on their parental roles as creative and ego-involving, although this is less true of men as one moves from middle to upper-lower to lower-lower class. The parental role, then, is increasing in attractiveness at the same time that the housewife role becomes more taken-for-granted and, very likely, as the husband's bread-winner role becomes more secure and thus less anxiously preoccupying.

Hoffman and Wyatt argue that anxiety about child-rearing, about doing a good job as mother (the logic applies equally well to father), "may operate as a motivation for reproduction, particularly later pregnancies." The parent seeks either to do a better job with succeeding children or at least to become absorbed in the activity which many children require, and thus fend off awareness of guilt, anxiety, and disappointment about discrepancies between how her children actually behave and the ideal, well-reared and well-adjusted child. They note that performance of parental functions probably does improve with practice; thus this solution is reinforced by reality. Further, we have noted previously the fairly common belief, particularly held by those who want larger families, that each additional child contributes to the socialization of the others by helping to create an atmosphere that at once builds character and makes for fewer demands on the parents since the children can make demands on each other. In other words, in large families, the children themselves do part of the parents' job.

The way people who want large families talk about the effect of the larger number of children on the family atmosphere suggests that they value both the increased individuality each child shows in contrast to all the others and the lesser emotional involvement they have in each individual child. At a deep level, one of the functions of having many children may be to moderate reciprocal Oedipal attachments; from the parent's point of view, several children lessen the intensity of incestuous involvements and diffuse them in ways that result in less anxiety. Not uncommonly, parents mention as advantages of the large family that one is protected against loss should one of the children die, and that one has children around longer in the life cycle. This suggests a greater continuity of Oedipal gratifications on the parents' part at the same time that these gratifications are made safer by diffusion. They are not only safer for the parents (in the sense of producing less guilt and anxiety) but also for the children, since the large family, many people believe, prevents pathological attachments to and dependence on the parents. This, too, assuages parents' guilt, since they can feel that they have created a situation in which their incentuous desires are not damaging to their children.

To what extent do our data support the Hoffman-Wyatt model outlined and elaborated above? We have already noted some of the themes of conscious rationale that seem in line with this model. We can deduce some further consequences for which our data provide a test. At the simplest level, it should be true that women who see themselves as oriented either to their husbands or to outside interests should not want as large families as women who think of themselves mainly in terms of interest in children and homemaking for them. From the tabulation of traits women ascribed to themselves when asked to tell what kind of persons they are, we can see to what extent this hypothesis holds. Table 6–8 presents these data. There is a strong association between family size desires and how exclusively the wife sees herself

TABLE 6–8:
MIDDLE CLASS WIVES' SELF-DESCRIPTIONS IN RELATION TO THEIR DESIRED FAMILY SIZE

Self-description		*Small Family*	*Medium Family*	*Large Family*
Solely oriented to outside interest or husband as companion	(19)	63%	16%	21%
Equally oriented	(20)	20	45	35
Solely oriented to children and home	(14)	7	21	72

$X^2 = 13.81$, df = 4 T = .34 P < .01

as oriented to husband and outside interests as opposed to children. This cannot be due solely to her current maternal functioning since about two-thirds of these women have not yet had more than a small family. Even so, almost three-quarters of the women who mention only their mothering functions want a large family, while almost two-thirds of those who mention only outside activities want a small family. Those who mention both kinds of characteristics want either medium or large families. Looked at another way, we see that 90 per cent of those who want a small family mention outside or husband orientations, compared to three-quarters of the medium-family mothers and only 45 per cent of the large-family mothers. In contrast, over 80 per cent of both medium and large-family mothers mention orientation to children compared to only 30 per cent of small-family mothers. It seems, then, that in the middle class, women who want small families do manage to find gratifying outside activities to keep them from feeling lazy, that those who want large families instead keep their interests focused on home. Those who want medium-size families appear to combine both orientations—their medium-size family preference represents a compromise that allows both ways of validating themselves as worthwhile women.

Another relationship that can be hypothesized has to do with desired family size and conjugal role organization. If the model outlined above is valid then the wife should be more likely to want a large family in a medium-segregated than in a jointly-organized conjugal relationship, since in the former she and her husband would live more separate lives and she would be less likely to find relating to him and sharing activites with him a source of validation as a woman, and more likely to seek this in mothering. Women in joint relationships, on the other hand, are more involved with their husbands in common interests and activities, and more identified with the husband and his accomplishments. Table 6–9 presents the data bearing on this point. In this table the couples with a joint relationship are subdivided into two groups. In one, the

TABLE 6-9:
MIDDLE CLASS CONJUGAL ROLE-ORGANIZATION IN RELA-
TION TO WIVES' DESIRED FAMILY SIZE

Joint Organization		*Small Family*	*Medium Family*	*Large Family*
Husband's concerns dominant	(9)	78%	22%	–
Husband's concerns not dominant	(26)	27	38	35
Medium Segregation	(19)	16	16	68

$X^2 = 13.14$,   df $= 4$ T $= .35$ P $< .02$

"husband's concerns dominant" group, are a small number of
couples who were isolated in this fashion because the husband seemed to be much more the focus of both family
goal-orientation and authority than was true of the other
couples. Whatever the wife's activities might be, they were
more subordinate to the husband's interests and concerns
than was the case with the other couples in jointly-organized
relationships. It is apparent that there is a strong relationship
between the three categories of role-organization and the
three family sizes. Almost all of the small group of husband-
dominant wives want a small family; two-thirds of the wives
in medium-segregated relationships want large families.
Looked at the other way, over 80 per cent of those who want
small or medium-size families have jointly-organized conjugal
relationships, while about 60 per cent of those who want
large families have more segregated conjugal relationships.
We can say then that the more interwoven are the interests
and concerns of the husband and wife the more likely the wife
is to want a small or medium-size family; the more separate
are their interests and concerns, the less they see their marital
roles as interpenetrating, the more likely the wife is to want a
large family. In our data the relationship is in the same direction for Catholics and Protestants and for upper-middle and
lower-middle class couples, though the sample is not large
enough for these subgroups to show a significant relationship
between the variables in each group. Further, the relation-

ship, unlike the others discussed here, holds for the upper-lower class as well.

One might expect the same relationship between conjugal role-organization and husbands' desired family sizes. The relationship is in the same direction, but is not statistically significant. The distribution for those with joint role-organizations is the same as for wives, but enough men in medium-segregated relationships want smaller families (usually medium instead of large) than their wives to reduce the difference between the two kinds of conjugal role-organizations to a level just below the 5 per cent significance point. Even so, the difference is fairly large — 58 per cent of those in medium-segregated relationships want four or more children compared to only 29 per cent of those in jointly-organized relationships. Husbands in medium-segregated relationships are perhaps slightly less likely than their wives to see any emotional gain to them from having larger families, or perhaps they are simply more anxious about the financial risks involved.

Presumably women who feel that they have difficulty managing their roles as women — women, that is, who do not find the housewife role as undemanding as Hoffman and Wyatt suggest — will feel less impetus to have more children than women who do not see this as a problem for themselves. An examination of the faults women attribute to themselves in their self-descriptions (when asked specifically to name some of their bad points) shows that this is so. On the other hand, from all we have seen about the meanings of selfishness that attach to a small family, and from the Hoffman-Wyatt model, we would expect that women who are concerned that they are too egocentric or selfish and not giving enough, would be more likely to hold large family preferences. Again, an examination of negative self-descriptions shows that this is the case. Table 6 – 10 presents these data. These descriptions of bad points suggest that women who are concerned about tendencies to be ungiving are much more likely to want large families, and that women who are concerned instead that they

TABLE 6–10:
MIDDLE CLASS WIVES' NEGATIVE SELF-DESCRIPTIONS AND
DESIRED FAMILY SIZE

Wife's main bad point is		Small or Medium Family	Large Family
That she is too egocentric, selfish or stubborn	(20)	35%	65%
That she is too nervous, anxious, depressed, or unenergetic to do her job	(29)	79	21

$X^2 = 7.86$ $T = HO$ $P < .01$

do not have the energy or emotional control to live up to their responsibilities as wives, housewives, and mothers are much more likely to want small families. Looked at the other way, 77 per cent of the women who want small or medium families express the latter concern, and only 23 per cent are concerned about being too narcissistic and egocentric; 66 per cent of the women who want large families are concerned about tendencies toward this kind of self-centeredness, and only 34 per cent are concerned instead about not having enough energy to do their jobs. These findings support the hypothesis that women who want large families are reaching out to embrace an identity in which they are loving and creative persons and to deny or overcome tendencies to seek purely self-centered gratifications. The findings also suggest that those who want small families or stop at the medium-size level are more impressed with the problems of coping with the many demands of their roles. The fact that there are more people of this latter than of the former type suggests that we should not exaggerate the extent to which the housewife's job is so simple and efficient that she is likely to be idle unless she has a large family. A good many middle class women do seem to feel that way, but still more women are concerned about maintaining their equanimity in the emotionally complex setting of the family.

The third trend which Hoffman and Wyatt discuss has to do with "a 'loneliness' and 'alienation' quality" characterizing contemporary American life. They hypothesize that as modern society has become more fragmented, with the individual integrated into fewer primary groups, and as these groups have become increasingly isolated within the society rather than linked together through extended families or such other institutions as religion, one way the individual can compensate for the sense of aloneness that accompanies this isolation is by having a larger family, a ready-made primary group to which he can retreat for meaningful interpersonal relating. They suggest that through the experience of pregnancy and the ties that grow from the mother and child having once seemed as one, women derive a sense of security and warmth absent in their larger interpersonal world. They note also a point made by Ronald Freedman, that this logic applies also to husbands who may find in the family perhaps their only primary group of permanence.

Much that men and women say about their conscious motivations for having a large family fits with this hypothesis—the emphasis on interpersonal gratifications from having a large family, the sense of always having human involvements that are varied but highly meaningful, the sense of personal accomplishment that comes from raising a large family well, all can protect the self against a sense of isolation and of not counting for much. Perhaps also, the fact that large-family wives are not so common among those with joint conjugal relations or those who orient themselves to outside activities or to their husbands as companions could be taken as supporting evidence for the hypothesis. Women, that is, who are able to find meaningful interpersonal anchors in roles other than mothering do not need large families to compensate for isolation or feelings of alienation.

On the other hand, one might hypothesize that couples who feel deeply alone and alienated are more likely to want small families. Since they feel the world is unrewarding they must seek first to take care of an indulge themselves. After all, the greatest impact of *anomie* on Western society came in the period when birth rates were declining rapidly. It might be suggested that it is only those individuals who have some hope about the possibility of creating a more comfortable and congenial world of some permanence who would be likely to compensate for the threat of alienation by having a large family. If the response to the threat is withdrawal and constriction, then the individual is more likely to want a small family and instead to seek his ends in a more blatantly narcissistic way. Perhaps this accounts for one unexpected finding from our data. Table 6–11 indicates that couples where neither partner wants a small family are more likely to place high importance on their sexual relationship than are couples in which one or another member wants a small family. In the main this means that if the wife does not attach high importance to the sexual relationship she is much more likely to want a small family than if she does; but the addition of the few husbands who want a small family although their wives do not, strengthens rather than weakens the observed relationship. In the middle class, at least, women who attach great importance to sex seem overwhelmingly to want a medium-sized or large family while a majority of those who do not, want a small family. These latter are very heavily concerned with outside activities and wish to keep their home life as simple emotionally as possible. Whether their outside interests are a result of an inability to find real gratification in sexual relations or the reverse cannot be discerned in our

TABLE 6–11:
PATTERNS OF SEXUAL RELATIONSHIP IN RELATION TO DESIRED FAMILY SIZE

		One Partner Wants Small Family	Both Want Medium or Large Family
Sexual relations very important to both partners	(27)	18%	82%
Sexual relations not very important to both partners	(24)	58	42

$X^2 = 6.84$ $T = .37$ $P < .01$

data. In either case, having a small family is functional for these women whose concern with a highly self-oriented life style mitigates against interest in a large family. Among the women where a high importance attached to sexual relations is correlated with preferences for a medium-sized or large family, the seeking of similar or compatible gratifications in relating to their husbands and their children is suggested. The fact that those in joint conjugal relationships want medium-sized families rather than large, and that the reverse is true of those in medium-segregated conjugal relationships, suggest that the choice within the range of medium to large is in good part a function of how meaningfully related the husband and wife are to each other in areas other than the sexual.

As a summary for this chapter, let us look at a combination of all of the various factors that have been shown to be associated with preference for a large or small family. Seven factors have been noted; (1) husband-dominated jointly organized conjugal relations, (2) outside interests, and (3) concerns with one's ability to handle housewifely tasks, are associated with preference for smaller family sizes; (4) medium-segregated conjugal relations, (5) orientation to children and home, (6) high importance placed on sexual relations, and (7) concern that one might be too egocentric are associated with larger family preferences. Taken together, a composite index can be made in which each wife receives a score for the frequency with which she gives a small or large family response

TABLE 6–12:
COMPOSITE INDICATORS OF PREFERENCE FOR SMALL OR LARGE FAMILIES

Wife's Preference

		Small Family	Medium Family	Large Family
Preponderance of smaller family indicators	(30)	63%	33%	4%
Preponderance of larger family indicators	(24)	7	23	70

$X^2 = 24.25$, df = 2   T = .56   P < .0005

to the seven items. Table 6–12 presents the results, dichotomized as close to the middle of the distribution of scores as is possible. Overall, 88 per cent of those who prefer small families have a preponderance of scores in that direction, while 92 per cent of those who prefer large families have a preponderance of scores in the other direction. For those with middle-size family preferences the balance is close to 50-50. Actually, no combination of indicators does a better job of discriminating medium-sized from large family preferences than the single factor of jointly-organized versus medium-segregated conjugal role relationships.

7
Family limitation and contraceptive methods

EACH COUPLE is confronted with the twin goals (and necessities) of having "enough" children and not having "too many." In the previous chapters we have examined some of the factors that go into a particular couple's determination of how many children will represent just the right number, and noted how that determination is affected by class status, religion, the quality of the marital relationship, the personal characteristics of the husband and wife, and the norms which people absorb from their social worlds. Now we seek to understand some of the factors involved in the actions people take to insure their success in achieving the family size goals they set for themselves. In this connection we will want to look at the sense of optimism or pessimism people have about achieving their goals, the extent to which family planning is discussed by husband and wife, the knowledge husbands and wives have about contraception, the experience they have had in using one or another method, and (in the next chapter) the determinants of regular use of effective contraceptives versus ineffective family limitation.

200

The expectation of success or failure

At the most general level, we are interested in how husbands and wives approach the issues of family planning and limitation. In listening to what respondents say about their contraceptive histories, about their ideas on the importance of family planning as this has changed over time, about the relative responsibility of husband and wife, etc., one is impressed by the variation in implicit attitude toward the question. Some respondents speak of family planning in a matter-of-fact, cut-and-dried way; family limitation for them is a well-established habit. Others seem less sure of what they are doing, more bothered by the possibllity of accidents, less confident in the method, or they look forward with uncertainty to a time when they will begin using contraception. Finally some respondents are quite passive and fatalistic about family planning; they do nothing because they do not think anything will help, or they go through the motions of using a method in which they have little confidence (and therefore do not use it very consistently).

We will call these three types of responses (1) planful and self-assured, (2) hopeful but unsure, and (3) passive and fatalistic. It is possible to judge each respondent in terms of which of these attitudes his expressions most closely approximate. In Table 7–1 is presented a tabulation of the three

TABLE 7–1:
ATTITUDE TOWARD LIKELIHOOD OF SUCCESS IN LIMITING
FAMILY TO DESIRED SIZE

		Planful and Self-assured	*Hopeful but Unsure*	*Passive and Fatalistic*
Middle Class Protestants	(60)	63%	37%	—
Middle Class Catholics	(51)	23	63	14%
Upper-Lower Class (Whites and Negroes)	(126)	18	58	24
Lower-Lower Class (Whites and Negroes)	(152)	5	32	63

attitudes (for men and women combined, since the differences between them are trivial).

The self-assured attitude — "we know what we want and know how to get it" — is common only among middle class Protestants. They emphasize the necessity of selecting a reliable method, one that both partners find acceptable, so that there will be no "accidents." They are convinced that this is possible, and would regard themselves as at fault were they not able to limit their families successfully. While they may occasionally joke about the child that was a "martini baby," conceived when one partner felt like taking a chance, one gets the impression that the chance was taken in most cases to solve by fiat ambivalence over whether or not to have another child. One upper-middle class woman had been sufficiently persistent to contrive three "accidents" to have the five children she wanted instead of the two her husband wanted. Both partners were quite aware of what had gone on and joked about it.

Although quite a few women in this group begin marriage with only the vague knowledge that there exist reliable methods of limiting and spacing children, they expect to learn, in short order, more precisely what these are. In all classes there seems to be quite a bit of informal discussion of contraception among women (and in the middle class, among men, too). Among middle class Protestants this discussion seems to be quite technical and down-to-earth. Such discussion quickly establishes both which methods are most widely used, and which should be regarded as *the* accepted method (in the middle class this has been the diaphragm; in the future it is likely that it will be the oral pill). Discussion, both within the family and outside, of family planning and methods for it, then, tends to establish in the middle class a very strong expectation that sensible people take family planning for granted and become as competent at it as at other self-care skills.

For middle class Catholics this would be equally so were it not for their sense of conflict between religious beliefs and middle class values. This conflict appears in two ways. First, and probably most important, it involves the belief that a good Catholic has a large family. Thus, interest in family planning is negative and not very rewarding to pursue even when necessary. Consideration of family limitation is, therefore, not as likely to be elaborated technically and less pleasure is taken in discussing it. Secondly, because the rhythm method is the only approved method of family limitation and since few Catholics of any class regard it as a really reliable method, middle class Catholics tend to fall back on a hopeful and optimistic attitude rather than a highly organized, technically sure one. When they are ready to limit their families they "hope for the best" rather than feel sure; similarly, when they wish to space births they are not as sure and insistent about it as are middle class Protestants. Before they begin to limit their families they are also hopeful that either Providence will intervene and stop the pregnancies from occurring or that they will be lucky enough to have rhythm work for them. Those middle class Catholics who decide to use an appliance method, of course, tend to be more planful and self-assured in their orientation to family planning, but in some cases the carry-over of religious concern is still reflected in that there is conflict between husband and wife on whether a method is to be used. The deviation from religious precept is often delegated to the partner more willing to accept the stigma. Thus, in one upper-middle class couple the husband allows his wife to use a diaphragm although he disapproves; in a lower-middle class couple the husband assumes the same function with the condom.

In the upper-lower class the hopeful-but-unsure attitude is the most common among both Protestants and Catholics (whites and Negroes). Here one encounters a belief in the fallibility of all contraceptive methods and a sense that all one can do is try his best to meet the technical requirements of each method. They are usually fairly confident that their efforts will meet with success but they are more likely also to mention condoms that break or diaphragms that do not fit right along with the notion that "rhythm won't work for us because my wife isn't regular enough." In the lower class, women protest very strongly their ignorance of family planning methods at marriage, and, unlike middle class Protestant women, they did not expect to learn very quickly. Often they learned about methods other than the condom only after some years of marriage, and they tend to progress through methods as they go along from the less effective (douche, rhythm, withdrawal) to the more effective ones. Still, as they progress in the experience of having children and become increasingly aware that they want to limit and space births, upper-lower class men and women are more likely to feel confident of their ability to achieve their family size goals than are men and women of the lower-lower class.

Within the lower-lower class, the most common attitude shifts away from hopefulness toward wishfulness. There is less confidence that any one method will be successful and more of a tendency to believe that fate has the first as well as the last word in what happens. Even when quite a few methods are known and tried, the lower-lower class man and woman tend to feel that one can not really count on not having an accident: breakage, poor fit, irregularity of menstruation, an impulsive "taking a chance" as well as "forgetting" are all given a large role in determining how successful a couple will be; planning and well-established habit are relegated to a much smaller role. The extreme of this fatalistic attitude, of course, is found among those couples who say they very much do not want more children but somehow have never gotten around to buying condoms or going to the clinic for a diaphragm; in three or four interviews with lower-lower class Negro women, the respondents commented that although they really would not like to have any more children they just had not gotten around to going across the street (from their housing project) to the Planned Parenthood Clinic they knew was there. In this group, men and women often justify their pessimistic expectations concerning family planning success by pointing to their own poor experience and the lack of success of most of the people they know. In their world, in short, they believe people can not do very well in limiting their families. The example of one's own miserable experience ("I'm a quick breeder") is mirrored by the experience of one's peers.

The expectation of success or failure, and the degree to which one believes one can guarantee success by efforts that are morally acceptable, then, varies within the middle class by religion and within the lower class by status. These expectations grow from the couple's own past experience, but not only from this. Couples who have had none or only one or two children still vary in their attitudes, dependent on their class and religion. To a considerable extent they take their expectations from the world around them — from a generalized faith in planning versus fate, and from observation of how well or poorly their peers seem to do.

Discussion of family planning

To what extent has family planning and limitation been a subject of focused discussion between husband and wife? The interviews reflect a wide range of communication between the marital partners on this subject; in some families it has hardly been discussed, in others the discussion has been fitful and incomplete, in others the couple have talked about what they should do in some detail, either early in their marital history or later. Table 7–2 roughly categorizes the patterns of discussion in our sample. Within the middle class there is a difference between Catholics and non-Catholics; in the lower class there are no religious differences but there are differences between the lower and upper parts of the group.

Among middle class Protestants the dominant pattern involves full attention to the issue early in marriage, usually before the first child is born. This discussion involves a complex of issues — how many children shall we have, when shall we have them, what shall we do to control the timing of and

TABLE 7-2:
EXTENT OF DISCUSSION BETWEEN HUSBAND AND WIFE
ABOUT FAMILY SIZE AND LIMITATION

		Very Little or No Discussion	Casual Discussion Only	Serious Discussion Late in Marriage	Serious Discussion Begun Early in Marriage
Middle Class Protestants	(36)	—	17%	22%	61%
Middle Class Catholics	(25)	8%	44	12	36
Upper-lower class Whites	(57)	19	44	12	25
Upper-lower class Negroes	(23)	12	36	36	8
Lower-lower class Whites	(72)	43	29	26	1
Lower-lower class Negroes	(26)	54	35	8	8

limit conceptions. Because middle class Protestants believe that control of conception is a matter-of-fact, technical issue, well within their competence to achieve, these issues follow logically one upon the other. Where there is uncertainty or an unresolved issue it is more likely to be about the family size goals than about ways of achieving them. That is, middle class Protestants have readily available to them the technical means and psychic skills for family limitation; they sometimes are ambivalent about the goals for which these skills are instrumental.

Among middle class Catholics, as noted, this kind of full attention to the complex of family size goals and family limitation is not common until fairly late in marriage. Early in marriage, and often for a good many years after marriage if regular conceptions do not occur, discussion tends to be at the general level of "we want a large family," or "'we'll just see how many God gives us," and there is only casual mention or bantering about the subject. Later in marriage, when the desire to limit family size becomes strong for one or another partner, the issue is addressed more directly and there may be detailed discussions about how to make the rhythm method work (often it will have been used casually up until that time) or whether or not to try an appliance method. These discussions are more uncomfortable for middle class Catholics than Protestants because of the underlying feeling that family limitation (even by rhythm) is an unfortunate necessity fraught with moral dangers, and because neither partner can be sure how the other feels. Given the hopeful attitude characteristic of this group, the tendency is to postpone such awkward discussions as long as possible. Eventually most middle class Catholics do have to address themselves to this issue seriously, though a good many do not because their large family goals are either not met or just met by the time the wife becomes infertile. When this is not the case, the couple settles down to a careful effort at the rhythm method or, when religius concerns are not strong (and perhaps fortified by the feeling that they have lived up to religious precepts by having a goodly number of children), one or the other partner decides to adopt an appliance method.

In many ways middle class Catholic couples provide a study in the sequential operation of processes of cognitive dissonance. Early in marriage their attitudes are strongly in the direction of large families and against family limitation techniques; as time goes on they feel they must experiment with rhythm to space children or to avoid children at a time of emergency (as when a child is ill and requires sustained care). Attitudes are modified by this behavior in that family limitation is viewed somewhat more positively. At later times, other methods may be taken up in a tentative way; the couple becomes committed to these methods and begins to modify their anti-family limitation attitudes even more.

In the lower class, religion does not seem to be associated with the extent of discussion between husband and wife. To be sure, lower class Catholics have many of the same feelings as middle class Catholics about family limitation (at least in the upper-lower class; lower-lower class Catholics seldom mention religion in their discussion of family size, family planning, or contraception). But lower class Protestants, lacking the more organized approach to planning exhibited by middle class Protestants, behave in similar ways without a religious grounding for their attitudes.

In the upper-lower class, discussions of family planning and limitation tend early in marriage to be rather general and casual, without much attention given to the necessity for communication in developing a plan and a routine for achieving family size goals. As time goes on, fuller discussion develops in the context of the approach of the maximum desired number of children. This movement toward more and more discussion proceeds in step with the trial of different contraceptive methods — moving from "easier" and more "conventional" methods toward those that are less well known and have a "medical" aura. The situation in the lower-lower class is in sharp contrast; here almost half of the couples discuss these issues hardly at all. It is only among them that one encounters with any frequency the statement that "my husband and I have never talked about it," or "she worries about that, I don't know much about what she thinks," or "I tried to bring it up once but he wouldn't talk about it." Thus, it is in the lower-lower class that one finds the dual pattern of low faith in contraception, disinclination to address oneself planfully to the issue, and a concomitant low level of communication between partners about both their goals and the means for achieving them. These two factors, the individual's feeling about the likelihood of success or failure at family planning and the kind of discussion between partners undoubtedly influence each other. It would be hard to argue that one causes the other; rather it seems sensible to regard both as growing out of the life situation of lower-lower class couples, as interrelated and mutually reinforcing expressions of both the separateness of their lives and of a basic sense of futility over guiding one's actions along paths other than those laid down by the nature of life as they perceive it.

Awareness of family limitation methods

Given their overall feelings of confidence about family planning and their discussions between themselves, how aware are couples in different social groups of the methods that can be used to attempt to control conception? Awareness of methods can serve as a general index of the level of knowledge of the technology available for family limitation, although one needs to keep in mind that knowledge of only one effective method, given the willingness to use it, is sufficient to achieve the goal. Tables 7–3 and 7–4 tabulate the methods mentioned spontaneously when respondents were

TABLE 7–3:
MEN'S AWARENESS OF DIFFERENT CONTRACEPTIVE METHODS

	Middle Class		Upper-Lower Class		Lower-lower Class	
	Protestants (34)	Catholics (25)	Whites (38)	Negroes (20)	Whites (44)	Negroes (27)
Method mentioned						
Condom	94%	88%	90%	100%	84%	85%
Diaphragm	82	60	63*	71	41	26
Rhythm	82	92	61†	29	27‡	7
Oral contraceptive	69§	47	32	13	2	4
Jelly or cream	53	12	18	25	18	7
Abstinence	41	24	–	4	2	11
Withdrawal	35	28	11	4	32	18
Douche	21	28	26	17	20	11
Suppository	9	12	5	25	11	22
Other (sterilization, "gold button")	18	12	8	21	7	11
Average number of methods mentioned	5.04	4.13	3.14	3.09	2.44	2.02

*Overall, lower class Protestants 62%, Catholics 40%
†Catholics 70%, Protestants 53%
‡Catholics 47%, Protestants 17%
§Upper middles 76%, Lower middles 58%

TABLE 7–4:
WOMEN'S AWARENESS OF DIFFERENT CONTRACEPTIVE
METHODS

	Middle Class		Upper-Lower Class		Lower-lower Class	
	Protes-tants (34)	Cath-olics (26)	Whites (45)	Negroes (24)	Whites (49)	Negroes (27)
Method Mentioned						
Condom	100%	77%	86%	42%	77%	72%
Diaphragm	97	65	83	83	81	60
Rhythm	85	85	60*	25	41†	20
Oral contra-ceptive	47‡	50‡	32	25	8	16
Jelly or cream	44	4	21	25	13	24
Abstinence	21	12	2	4	2	4
Withdrawal	24	23	16	8	15	–
Douche	24	–	14	38	43	44
Suppository	12	–	19	17	15	32
Other (sterili-zation, "gold button")	12	15	7	4	17	20
Average number of methods mentioned	4.66	3.31	3.20	2.71	3.12	2.92

*Catholics 78%, Protestants 40%
†Catholics 47%, Protestants 37%
‡Upper middles 61%, Lower middles 38%

asked what methods they knew people used to limit family
size. The first fact of importance is that fewer than 1 per cent
of the men and 3 per cent of the women failed to name at
least one method (among lower-lower class Catholic women
the proportion is 15 per cent, in no other group does it rise to
5 per cent). Thus almost all of the people in our sample knew
of some method that one can use to limit family size, a
method which at some time has been used by some couples
with at least moderate success (as with the douche).

The intellectual approach of middle class Protestants
(and, to a lesser extent, Catholics) is suggested by the greater
number of methods they mention—with two exceptions they
mention each method about as often or more often than other

groups. The exceptions are instructive; apparently the suppository is better known among Negroes than among whites, and the douche is more widely known by Negroes and lower-lower class whites. It is also of interest that in the middle class men mention more methods than women, reflecting perhaps a greater curiosity on this subject (since the excess of their references over women's tends to be in the area of the less effective or more drastic [e.g., abstinence] methods). In the lower-lower class the reverse is true; women mention more methods than men, suggesting less interest on the part of men.

Thus, it would seem that very few couples of any class do not know of one or two methods they could use to control the size of their families. At the simplest level of knowledge, even the lower-lower class respondents seem at least as well equipped as were the highest status persons in Europe and England at the time these latter groups began limiting their families; one or the other of the two medically-approved methods of choice, the condom and the diaphragm, come readily to mind for over 80 per cent of the men and women in each subgroup in our sample. It would be difficult to maintain, then, that more than a very few people in our sample fail to limit their families effectively because of lack of knowledge, if knowledge is construed in a purely intellectual sense. If to this is added a social dimension (knowledge that a method exists that other people use routinely and effectively) or a psychological dimension (knowledge that the method one knows about is emotionally acceptable and within one's means to manipulate successfully), then the matter appears in a very different light, as will be discussed below. Construed in this way, however, knowledge is hardly different from motivation and conviction about a method's appropriateness; rational elements take a decided back seat to more emotional and interpersonal factors.

It is in this latter, more complex, sense that people seem to assess their own knowledge when asked how much they knew about contraceptive methods when they were married, and how much they have learned since then. In the lower class, women assess their knowledge of family limitation at marriage as negligible; usually they feel they are only modestly informed now:

> *A white, lower-lower class woman who douches and uses condoms occasionally:*
> I didn't know nothing and I guess my mother didn't either because she was only my age (31) when my father died and she had eight kids; I've learned a little since; one doctor said the only thing was for me to be sterilized. Another one told me about the diaphragm but I never got around to doing anything. It seems like money is so scarce and I didn't have any idea about how much one would cost. One woman told me about suppositories and someone else said some women put salt tablets up in themselves, but I would be afraid to do any of those things unless I talked to a doctor about it.

> *A lower-lower class Negro woman who douches "sometimes"*
> I didn't know nothing (when I got married). I never talked to no one about it. [Not even your mother or girl friends?] No, none of them. Now I've talked around a little bit and I learned about the douche and my husband used a rubber once.

The general tone of the lower-lower class assessment of its present knowledge is well expressed by the thirty-nine-year-old man who said, "I've heard about lots of ways but I don't know if they are any good." In short, although lower-lower class men mention an average of two methods, and women an average of three, they assess this knowledge as a thing by itself, not integrated into either their own sense of available technology or their world's.

Upper-lower class men and women do not seem to have started marriage much better informed than those in the lower-lower class but they feel they have learned more. In a sense, what they have learned, and lower-lower class persons have less often learned, is to accept contraceptive methods as part of their world, and to seek to master the technology that is involved—that is , they have learned more than names and a schematic functional description of the methods they know:

> *An upper-lower class Negro man who plans to start using contraception after the birth of their third child:*
> I didn't know nothing. Wait, I'll take that back, I knew about the boot, you know, the rubber. These things come natural with boys; like an animal, he don't know nothing but how to get more of his kind. It's just nature and the same can be said for people; you might say it just comes natural. [Have you learned more since?] Well, through conversations with the doctor I've learned about the rhythm and diaphragms and jellies. He's well up on that because it's his business. Then, friends talk a lot about it; they always have something to tell you.

> *An upper-lower class white woman who now uses a diaphragm:*
> I didn't know about anything; I guess that's the reason I got pregnant. Since then I've learned from reading books and my mother told me about the diaphragm after our first was born; she's always used one. So I know about rubbers and the diaphragm pretty well because we've used them, and then I read about the vasectomy.

Both of these people, one who has not yet used contraception and one who has, communicate the greater sense of involvement with methods (as more than just names) that is more characteristic of the upper-lower than the lower-lower class. The man suggests something of the meaning of men's greater curiosity—it is part of a "natural" curiosity about all things sexual. He, and most women in this class, try to be interested in what they can learn from their doctors; to the lower-lower class the physician is more often considered to be simply the representative of an alien world. Members of the former group may have difficulty understanding what their doctors tell them and may feel shy or uncertain in relating to them, but they do not experience quite the same gulf between their world and the doctor's. Or if, like the woman quoted above, they feel confident enough about what they have learned from relatives or friends they can simply use the doctor as a technician ("I just told my doctor I wanted to be fitted with a diaphragm; I didn't discuss it with him").

In the middle class, both men and women feel they were reasonably well informed about the existence of contraception at marriage, but that they have had a good deal to learn since then. In the upper-middle class there is often pride in being well-informed and upper-middle class women often mention premarital examinations and discussions with their physicians. The upper-middle class clearly takes a more technical interest in contraception than does the lower-middle class, as is reflected in the fact that its members are more likely to mention the new (at the time of the interviewing) oral method. In any case, middle class couples tend to feel they have learned more than enough about contraception to meet their needs, whether or not in addition they take an intellectual interest in the subject:

> *An upper-middle class Protestant woman:*
> I talked to my doctor about it before I got married and then I talked about it with my girl friends. [With your mother?] No, I didn't talk with her; I learned from reading, too. Then, since we were married I've discussed contraceptives with my doctor several times. I've learned about prophylactics, diaphragms, douche, suppositories, and a way of taking the temperature to determine the period of fertility. Recently I read that they are testing a pill for women.

> *An upper-middle class Protestant man:*
> Well, there's continence and sterilization. Then there's the spurious system of the Catholic Church, the rhythm method. There are mechanical devices; condom, pessary, diaphragm, and chemical devices, like jellies. And now they have female hormones in pills. In certain primitive societies they would make a fistula at the bottom of the penis. Mechanical devices have been in use since the 17th century; at first they used sheep gut, then silk, sometimes lined with natural rubber. I knew all of this except for the oral pills before I was married. I don't know exactly where I learned it, mostly from reading and in the Army.

A lower-middle class Catholic woman:
Well, there's the method advocated by the church, rhythym, it's perfectly fine to use. Then I know about the diaphragm and I've heard some discussion of prophylactics, and then tying the tubes. Before I was married I knew about rhythm from a little booklet, and I knew a young couple and the wife told me the details about using the diaphragm, and I knew about prophylactics from gossip. Since then I learned about a new tape to use to determine the safe period.

Although middle-class Catholics are somewhat less knowledgeable about contraceptive methods than are Protestants, they generally know at least two other methods beside those approved by the Church as the last response above suggests; their intellectual interest in the subject means that they want to know about some methods even though they are not likely to use these methods themselves. This is somewhat less true of women than of men, but the methods not cited by Catholic women are the less common ones (in the middle class) such as the douche, suppositories, and jelly alone.

Use of family limitation techniques

Very few people in our sample, then, do not know about one or more contraceptive techniques. How often do they make use of the methods they know? Table 7–5 gives a picture of how many of the couples in each class and religious group have ever used and are now using a contraceptive

TABLE 7–5:
USE OF FAMILY LIMITATION TECHNIQUES

		Ever Used	Presently Using
Middle Class Protestants	(38)	97%	95%
Middle Class Catholics	(25)	77	69
Lower Class Protestants	(72)	85	78
Lower Class Catholics	(61)	64	56
Upper-lower Class Negroes	(25)	88	72
Lower-lower Class Negroes	(29)	76	59

method (in the next chapter we will consider to what extent the users are using the method regularly). A majority in each group has used a contraceptive method at some time or another; that is, it has made efforts to delay or limit conception by one of the methods discussed above. Almost all middle class Protestants have used and now use a contraceptive method; the proportions are only slightly lower for lower class white Protestants and upper-lower class Negroes, but lower-lower class Negroes are less likely to be using a method at present. At each class level use runs somewhat lower among Catholics than Protestants, a fact that is in line both with the large family size goals of Catholics and their somewhat more tolerant attitude toward having children close in age.

Thus, as with awareness, a very high proportion of couples have had actual experience with a contraceptive method — over three-fourths of each group except the lower class Catholics. Further, among those who have used a method at all, a great many have had experience with more than one method (Table 7–6). Among middle class Protestants, most of these are medically approved appliance methods (principally condom, diaphragm, and pill); as one goes down the class scale this is less true, so that among lower-lower class Catholics and Negroes only about half of the methods used were medically approved appliances.

Fewer than half of the lower-middle class Catholics, but a somewhat higher proportion of the lower class Catholics, have used an appliance method (a finding that parallels that of Freedman, Whelpton, and Campbell, 1959). It is interesting that although lower class Catholics are slightly less likely to have practiced contraception than are middle class Catholics, those that do practice it have used more methods than their middle class confreres; lower class Catholics, when they use a method at all, confine themselves less consistently to the rhythm method.

Upper-middle class Protestants have concentrated heavily on feminine methods (diaphragm, jelly alone, pill) in their

TABLE 7–6:
AVERAGE NUMBER OF CONTRACEPTIVE METHODS EVER
USED

| | Appliances | | | | |
	Feminine	*Condom*	*Rhythm*	*Folk Methods*	*Total*
Upper-Middle Class Protestants (20)	1.05	.45	.15	.05	1.70
Upper-Middle Class Catholics (8)	.25	.37	.37	–	1.00
Lower-Middle Class Protestants (18)	.56	.83	.17	.17	1.73
Lower-Middle Class Catholics (11)	.09	.27	.91	.20	1.47
Upper-Lower Class Protestants (25)	.48	.76	.28	.28	1.80
Upper-Lower Class Catholics (20)	.20	.45	.45	.35	1.45
Upper-Lower Class Negroes (22)	.55	.68	.23	.55	2.11
Lower-Lower Class Protestants (37)	.27	.76	.16	.41	1.60
Lower-Lower Class Catholics (18)	.06	.61	.11	.72	1.50
Lower-Lower Class Negroes (22)	.55	.55	.05	.95	2.10

experimenting with methods, and have had less experience with the condom than have white Protestants and Negroes of lower status. The use of folk methods (douche, withdrawal, suppository) is concentrated among lower-lower class Catholics and Negroes, and close to a majority of upper-lower class Negroes have tried one of them.

In terms of current use, feminine methods continue to dominate in the upper-middle class; use of such methods falls to approximately half this frequency for lower-middle and upper-lower class Protestants and Negroes (Table 7–7). The condom is the main method for all other non-Catholic groups except the lower-lower class Negroes; only 23 per cent of those practicing contraception in this group use the condom. The rhythm method is used by a majority of Catholics only in

TABLE 7–7:
CONTRACEPTIVE METHOD CURRENTLY IN USE

	Appliances			Folk Methods
	Feminine	Condom	Rhythm	Folk Methods
Upper-Middle Class Protestants (20)	70%	20%	10%	—
Upper-Middle Class Catholics (7)	29	29	29	13%
Lower-Middle Class Protestants (18)	28	50	11	11
Lower-Middle Class Catholics (11)	9	9	73	9
Upper-Lower Class Protestants (25)	32	40	16	12
Upper-Lower Class Catholics (20)	10	35	30	25
Upper-Lower Class Negroes (20)	40	40	10	10
Lower-Lower Class Protestants (37)	17	51	11	22
Lower-Lower Class Catholics (15)	—	33	—	67
Lower-Lower Class Negroes (17)	29	23	6	41

the lower-middle class, over two-thirds of other Catholic who practice contraception use other methods, and none of the lower-lower class Catholics is now practicing rhythm. The latter concentrate heavily on douche and withdrawal, and 41 per cent of lower-lower class Negroes use one of these two methods. Fewer than one-quarter of the remaining couples use either of these two methods or suppositories.

Thus in terms of all methods used during marriage and the one method currently in use, there is considerable variation of selection among class, religion, and race groups. Four methods dominate in the choice of contraceptives — rhythm, condom, diaphragm, and the oral contraceptive. In the middle class, and among upper-lower Negroes and white Protestants, these four methods account for 85 per cent of the methods ever used and 88 per cent of the methods currently in use. At the other extreme are lower-lower class Catholics and Negroes; only 51 per cent of methods ever used and 45 per cent of the methods currently in use come from this group of four. In between are the upper-lower class Catholics and lower-lower class white Protestants—68 per cent of the methods ever used and 74 per cent of the methods currently in use are in this group. Thus, although there are ten contraceptive methods couples might use, choice tends to be limited to rhythm when religious sentiment dictates (or when one is not too serious about limiting the family and willing to take a chance that this method will work), and otherwise to condom, diaphragm, or pill.

These use patterns are reflected in the attitudes members of different groups express in discussing each of the contraceptive methods. In the middle class there is the strong assumption that only the condom, diaphragm, and pill are worth considering unless one is Catholic. Other methods are rejected as unreliable, and these three appliance and chemical methods are regarded as highly reliable. In the lower class, the more so as one moves down to the lower-lower group, these sharp differences between "reliable" and "unreliable" methods become less marked. Upper-lower class respondents express doubts about the condom and diaphragm and tell stories of condoms that break or spring a leak, diaphragms that are painful, etc. Lower-lower class respondents add to this a hopeful faith in the pre-appliance standbys of douche and withdrawal. They regard all methods as pretty unreliable, and they give the appliance methods only a slight edge over others. In the abstract, unlike the middle class respondents, they are willing to entertain the idea that withdrawal would be quite effective if one had sufficient self-control, or that the douche would prove reliable and "safe" if the wife were quick enough in going to the bathroom after intercourse. Interestingly, middle class respondents very seldom mention these considerations; they believe withdrawal and douche to be inherently ineffective.

Thus, middle class people think of few reasons to expect

method failures (as opposed to user failures) with condom, diaphragm, or pill, and many reasons for method failures (as well as user failures) with withdrawal and douche. They also have their doubts about jellies alone and suppositories. Lower class people, in contrast, attribute a fairly high method unreliability to condom and diaphragm (they do not yet know enough about the oral contraceptive to have firm views about it) and by contrast to the middle class, express a reasonably accepting attitude toward douche and withdrawal. In addition, some persons in the lower-lower class, particularly Negro men, are frank in saying that they do not care how effective the condom is, they are not willing to use it. Similar views are expressed by lower-lower class women about the diaphragm.

The differences between Catholics and Protestants in attitudes toward different contraceptive methods are most apparent in the middle (and particularly the lower-middle) class. Thus, lower-middle class Catholics are more likely to bring in associations with premarital sexual relations and venereal disease when discussing the condom than are Protestants of the same class. With respect to rhythm, there are, of course, marked differences in attitude. Protestants speak of rhythm as notoriously ineffective; most of them have a vague idea about the principle involved but their interest does not go much further than this. A few have experimented with rhythm early in marriage in hope they would be among the lucky ones for whom it works, and then discontinued it in favor of a method in which they could place more trust.

Middle class Catholics are proud of the morality they display by using this method and foregoing appliance methods, but they are seldom very secure about how effective it will be for them. To some extent, the chance element involved in using rhythm can be assimilated to the idea that in any case God determines the number of children a couple has. Their view is that a sensible couple uses the method in the most developed technical way (that is, by carefully keeping track of the length of cycles and body temperature to determine the time of ovulation), but that in the end, chance or fate plays a large role. During the course of marriage, Catholic couples tend to become more and more technical in their use of rhythm in an effort to limit their families. Early in marriage they follow, as one respondent said, "a sloppy rhythm," because they are not too seriously concerned about spacing and do want more children; with successive pregnancies they seek to increase the effectiveness of their method by more carefully following the necessary record-keeping and temperature-taking routines. Since these routines take time and effort, the couple tends to settle on the minimum amount of this work that seems necessary for them. Some middle class Catholics, both men and women, seem to take pleasure in the relatively complex intellectual exercise that rhythm requires; it is possible that the "rhythm ritual" comes to symbolize their allegiance to the Church, to be a sign of the fact that they are good Catholics. The ritual elements of rhythm may also serve to reduce anxiety about the possibility of failure and to explain failure when it occurs (in the sense that one must have slipped up somewhere in the necessary calculations and measures).

This very complexity, which we hypothesize serves to bind the middle class Catholic to both the method and his Church, makes the rhythm method essentially meaningless for lower class Catholics. The latter do not differ in any essential way from lower class Protestants in their conceptions of rhythm, with the one exception that Catholics are more conscious of the fact that this is the one method which the Church approves. Both Catholics and Protestants often characterize rhythm as a joke, not an effective method. They comment that the wife is not sufficiently regular in her menstrual cycle to be able to use the method, and they tend to generalize this as true of most women. Lower class men and women, Catholics included, tend to think of rhythm in terms of an omnibus rule rather than in terms of charted temperatures or other individualized predictions of day of ovulation. The omnibus rules are often completely turned arund, as these examples (where the reference point is the onset of the menstrual period) indicate: "Nine days before and nine days after is the bad time," "three days before and six days after," "five days before and five days after," "two days before and two days after." Many respondents thus tend to locate the proper time for abstinence as just before and just after the menstrual period, leaving the time of maximum likelihood of ovulation as part of the "safe time" or the "free time." It is not surprising, then, that lower class respondents tend to have unhappy experience with the rhythm method despite its appeal as a simple method (that is, when only an omnibus rule is thought necessary). Given the general hostility many lower class Catholics express toward the Church's policy on contraception as they see it (and often this includes the notion that the Church wants them to have as many children as possible), it is not surprising that they use this poor experience with the method as merely another example of the fact that the Church is not really interested in them and their problems. If the Church were really interested in them, they feel, it would not hinder them in using an effective method; rather it would encourage and help them to limit their families effectively in terms of their economic limitations.

The choice of contraceptive methods by non-Catholics does not have the same constraints as apply to Catholics, even in the attenuated form that seems to characterize the choice of lower class Catholics. What then determines the choices non-Catholics make? In the middle class, as we have noted, the choice is primarily between the condom on the one hand, and the diaphragm or oral contraceptive on the other. In our sample, 70 per cent of the upper-middle class couples are using one of the feminine methods and 20 per cent the condom; in the lower middle class, 56 per cent of the couples are using the condom and only 25 per cent are using a feminine method (all diaphragm). Apparently in the upper-middle class it is more taken for granted that women will take primary responsibility for contraceptions. Furthermore, they rely more on expert medical authority in their dependence on the diaphragm (and more recently the pill, which 30 per cent of them were using in 1961–62; all of the pill users were former diaphragm users). The medical bias in favor of feminine methods fits well with the upper-middle class woman's belief that she should be very much in control of what happens to her, and dependent on no one for her well-being. In the lower-middle class the husband is still regarded as primarily responsible. In their discussions of the condom and diaphragm, it is clear that upper-middle class men and women have adopted the view that while the condom is a highly reliable method, it is not necessary that the husband's pleasure be interfered with by the condom and that acceptable and comfortable feminine methods are available. In contrast, lower-middle class men and women show less interest in and some concern about the diaphragm—they are more likely to feel uncertain that it really works well, to feel a bit suspicious of the method. Lower-middle class husbands speak proudly of their responsibility in using the condom and not taking chances; they don't underplay the idea that the condom detracts from masculine pleasure, but they feel this is a sacrifice they should make for the good of the family.

The diaphragm and condom are rather evenly balanced in terms of the technical involvement required; the decision a couple makes between them has to do with who shall take responsibility and how trusting they are going to be of an appliance that is hidden as opposed to one that can be seen. With the introduction of the oral contraceptive this situation is changed drastically; the choice is between an appliance, the use of which is intimately connected with intercourse and the genitals, and a simple pill-taking routine. Our data suggest that the pill was adopted first by upper-middle class women who are used to taking responsibility for conception, but there is no reason to believe that the method will not diffuse fairly quickly to lower-middle class couples now more frequently using the condom. The husbands will see advantages for themselves (note that in Tables 7–3 and 7–4 fifty-eight per cent of the lower-middle class men and only thirty-eight per cent of the lower-middle class women mention the pill) and wives will be sympathetic to their husbands' desires for greater sexual pleasure so long as this requires so simple a routine for them. In the summer of 1961 our middle class respondents were already fairly well aware that the method existed and were adopting a wait-and-see attitude until the method was "proved effective and not dangerous." Catholics as well as Protestants expressed interest and hoped that the Church would not condemn the method. To their own ways of thinking it seemed not as unnatural as the appliance methods, and they were hoping the Church would see it that way, too.

> It's an oral means whereby it has to be taken with some regularity. It prevents the woman from ovulating. I think it's been tested; I think it could work. It might be an acceptable approach in that it's not an unnatural way. There's no direct instrument being used or no means as we've been talking about where there's a prevention of the seed from entering the vagina and the womb.

The interest in the method that comes automatically from its simplicity and, more importantly, from the fact that the contraceptive measure is totally unconnected with either sexual intercourse or the genitals, is increased by the fact that this method, unlike others, was being given extensive coverage by the mass media, thus giving it both added drama and greater respectability than methods that cannot be talked of in polite company.

There was a sharp drop in the lower class in awareness of the existence of an oral contraceptive; when we asked specifically if respondents had ever heard of "a pill that a women takes every day" there seemed to be not much more knowledge of the method among upper- than among lower-lower class respondents. Those who had heard of the method were intrigued but somewhat mystified. Their attitude can be summed up as "I don't see how a pill would help but they do have pills for almost everything." The pill is probably as appealing to lower class people as it is to the middle class in its simplicity and lack of connection with sexual relations. Some lower class respondents worry about the cost of taking a pill every day, and a few worry about side effects, but it seems likely that they will accept the method if reassured by medical authority that it is safe and effective.

In the non-Catholic lower class we would expect, given the importance of conjugal role segregation in connection with other kinds of family behavior that there might be some association between the role-organization variable and choice for contraceptive method (the same might be hypothesized for the middle class, but no differences are apparent in our data within the upper- and lower-middle groups). Table 7–8 presents data bearing on this hypothesis for three groups of methods: feminine appliances (diaphragm, oral contraceptive, jelly alone), the condom, and folk methods (rhythm, douche, withdrawal, suppositories). The feminine appliance methods are most likely to be used by wives in intermediate relationships; the old-fashioned methods are most likely to be used (and, generally, not to be practiced very regularly) by couples in highly segregated relationships. Compared to the feminine methods, there is a slight tendency for the condom also more often to be adopted by users in highly segregated relationships.

Several factors are probably at work here. First, couples in highly segregated relationships are less likely to be

TABLE 7–8:
CONJUGAL ROLE-ORGANIZATION AND CHOICE OF CONTRA-CEPTIVE METHOD IN THE LOWER CLASS (NON-CATHOLIC)

		Medically Approved Appliance and Chemical Methods		
		Feminine	*Condom**	*Folk Methods**
Joint or Intermediate Role-Organization	(25)	64%	28%	8%
Highly Segregated	(26)	27	35	38

*Combined for analysis $X^2 = 5.60$ $P < .025$ $T = .33$

confident about success in family planning, and therefore are less motivated to adopt one of the more effective methods. Also, the lower class wife who uses a feminine method (principally the diaphragm,) needs a good deal of support from her husband if she is to feel secure about what she is doing; such support is available only to the wife in intermediate relationships. The wife needs such support if she is to cope with commonly held ideas that diaphragms "hurt the insides," "make infections and sores," "cause bleeding." On the other hand, condom, douche, and withdrawal all appeal because they express a sense of sexual separation between husband and wife, as is clear by the choice of synonyms men and women use to denote semen when they talk about how these methods work—"wad," "waste," "germ," "discharge," "urine," "filth." The anxiety lower class men and women express about the condom breaking seems to have to do with a feeling that the penis and the fluid it ejaculates are very powerful; they are anxious that the powerful substance either be prevented from entering the vagina (withdrawal), contained so the woman is not contaminated and injured (condom), or washed out before it does any damage (douche). As will become apparent in the next chapter, there is a progressive increase in the efficiency of contraceptive practice as one moves from couples in more to less segregated conjugal role-relationships involving first their greater use of contraceptive methods, then their more effective use, then the choice of methods that are technically more effective, and finally the centering of responsibility for contraception on the wife, who is more consistently and specifically motivated to limit pregnancies.

8
Effective and ineffective contraceptive practices

WE HAVE TAKEN an inventory of the patterns of use of contraceptive techniques by couples of middle and lower class, and of Catholic and non-Catholic religious persuasion. Even a casual reading of what people say about how they use contraceptive techniques impresses one with the variability among users; some indicate solidly established habits of use, others that their use is sporadic, occasional, not very careful. Therefore it will be useful to inquire into the regularity of use of methods that have a reasonably high degree of effectiveness when used appropriately. We shall call persons who use these methods regularly and consistently *effective* contraceptive practitioners and those who either use no method, or use a method inconsistently and sporadically, *ineffective* contraceptive practitioners.

Overall, as judged from their responses, about half of our sample (heavily weighted toward the lower class as it is) are regular practitioners of contraceptive methods. The ineffective practitioners are divided about evenly between non-users and sporadic users, as is apparent in Table 8–1; however the proportion varies from one group to another. Middle class couples (almost all Catholic) and upper-lower class Catholics in 65 per cent of the cases use no contraception; among the sporadic users, most employ rhythm but without much sense of urgency. Lower-lower class Catholics

227

TABLE 8-1:
FAMILY LIMITATION PRACTICES OF INEFFECTIVE USERS

		Use No Method	Sporadic User
Middle Class, and Upper-Lower Class Catholics	(16)	65%	35%
Lower-Lower Class Catholics	(26)	50	50
Lower-Lower Class Negroes	(22)	43	57
Lower-Class White Protestants and Upper-Lower Class Negroes	(51)	35	65
Total		47	53

and Negroes tend toward sporadic use, as do lower class white Protestants and upper-lower class Negroes.

Most commonly, then, among Catholics, "ineffective" practice is non-practice while among Protestants it is sporadic practice, but there is a sizeable minority in each group for which the reverse is true. The more children an ineffective couple has, however, the more likely are they to be sporadic rather than non-users.

We will examine the distribution of effective and ineffective contraceptive practitioners at two points in the family cycle: first, before the birth of the last child wanted by the wife and second, after the birth of this last wanted child (Table 8-2). Here it is apparent that both before and after the last wanted child there are important differences by both class and religion. Before the last wanted child, middle class Protestants are almost all regular practitioners and so are a majority of our small group of upper-middle class Catholics, but only slightly over one-third of the lower-middle class Catholics and the total group of the upper-lower class are effective practitioners. Finally, only 3 per cent of the lower-lower class in our sample indicate effective practice before this point. Overall, effective contraception up to this point in the family cycle is practiced by only a minority in which middle class Protestants and those Catholics who have a secular orientation stand out.

However, by the time the last child the wife wants is

TABLE 8-2:
EFFECTIVE AND INEFFECTIVE CONTRACEPTIVE PRACTICES

		Effective	*Ineffective*
Before Birth of Last Wanted Child			
Middle Class Protestants	(38)	92%	8%
Upper-Middle Class Catholics	(10)	60	40
Lower-Middle Class Catholics	(13)	38*	62
Upper-Lower Class (White and Negro)	(80)	31*	69
Lower-Lower Class (White and Negro)	(96)	3	97
After Birth of Last Wanted Child†			
Middle Class and Upper Lower Class Protestants	(38)	98%	2%
Middle Class and Upper-Lower Catholics	(33)	73	27
Upper-Lower Class Negroes	(18)	50	50
Lower-Lower Class Protestants	(27)	33	67
Lower-Lower Class Catholics and Negroes	(31)	13	87

*Combined for analysis
$X^2 = 84.31$ df = 3   P < .0005   T = .55
†$X^2 = 66.93$ df = 4   P < .0005   T = .46

born, there is a strong shift. Almost all white Protestants above the lower-lower class level are now regular practitioners, as are 73 per cent of the Catholics above this level. Upper-lower class Negroes seem to have more trouble moving in this direction (often because the husband is not as strongly motivated as the wife to take the actions necessary to limit family size). One-third of lower-lower class Protestants have learned effective contraception by this time, but only 13 per cent of lower-lower class Catholics and Negroes have done so. Although at least two-thirds of these lower-lower class ineffectives are using a contraceptive method, their efforts are not sufficiently organized to insure much success, and, as we have seen, they are more often using methods with which success is doubtful at best. The shift from casual contraception to regular use of an effective method, then, serves to highlight both class and religious differences, but most particularly class difference.

TABLE 8–3:
TIME EFFECTIVE CONTRACEPTION WAS BEGUN

		Before last Wanted Child	Immediately After Birth of Last Wanted Child*	After Birth of Unwanted Child*
Middle Class	(48)	96%	4%	—
Upper-Lower Class (Whites and Negroes)	(40)	62	33	5%
Lower-Lower Class White Protestants*	(19)	16	63	21
Lower-Lower Class Catholics and Negroes*	(9)	—	56	44

*Combined for analysis
$X^2 = 51.55$ df $= 2$ $P < .0005$ T $= .56$

Let us look at the history of those who finally become regular practitioners and ask when they started. (Since fewer than 3 per cent of our sample have been but are now not regular practitioners we will assume that anyone in the sample who is now an effective practitioner will continue to be one). Table 8–3 presents a tabulation of the point at which the respondents became effective practitioners.

Among those who do become regular practitioners, then, middle class people become so before the last wanted child 96 per cent of the time, compared to only 62 per cent of the upper-lower class. The latter, on the other hand, manages to become effective before an unwanted child is born, but the lower-lower class does not so often succeed in this. If our small sample of lower-lower class Catholics and Negroes is at all reliable, the impetus to effective contraception for them is more likely to be the birth of an unwanted child than is the case with other groups.)

The dynamics of ineffective practice

All of these results suggest that ineffective contraceptive practice is a problem largely confined to the lower class, at least in terms of not starting effective practice before the birth of an unwanted child. What might account for ineffective practice within the lower class?

Several studies have suggested that lack of communication between husband and wife may be one important factor. We have seen that in the lower class, discussion about family planning tends to be delayed longer and to be less full than in the middle class. This can be thought of as part of the overall pattern of conjugal role-organization in the lower class. We want to know, therefore, whether effective practitioners have a different pattern of role-organization than ineffective practitioners. Table 8–4 presents a tabulation of effective and ineffective practice by conjugal role-organization for two points in time, before and after the birth of the last child the wife wants. (Although we do not have enough cases to analyze separately the upper- and lower-lower classes, the whites and Negroes, or the Catholics and non-Catholics, the differences in these subgroups are in the same direction as for the combined group, so we feel justified in dealing only with the overall tabulation.) Before the birth of the last wanted child, conjugal role-organization seems but weakly related to effective or ineffective practice; but after the birth of the last wanted child the relationship is stronger—only 26 per cent of those in highly segregated relationships are effective practic-

TABLE 8–4:
CONJUGAL ROLE-ORGANIZATION AND EFFECTIVE CONTRA-
CEPTIVE PRACTICE AMONG LOWER CLASS COUPLES.

		Effective	Ineffective
Before Last Wanted Child			
Joint Role Relationship*	(8)	50%	50%
Intermediate Segregation*	(39)	26	74
Highly Segregated	(51)	6	94
After Birth of Last Wanted Child			
Joint Role Relationship†	(6)	100%	—
Intermediate Segregation†	(30)	60	40
Highly Segregated	(39)	26	74

*Combined for analysis
  $X^2 = 8.39$ $P < .005$ $T = .29$
†Combined for test
  $X^2 = 11.19$ $P < .001$ $T = .39$

tioners, compared to 67 per cent of those in less segregated relationships.

The analysis in chapter 2 leads to the conclusion that couples in the more segregated relationships tend to have less communication with each other, to go their own separate ways more, to have more serious financial and interpersonal problems, and to be generally less family-centered in their conceptions of themselves than couples in less segregated relationships. Both white and Negro husbands in segregated relations were more often seen as disloyal to the family; they spent more time away from home in male-centered activities that made their wives uneasy about the stability of the relationship and about financial security. Negro wives in segregated relationships differed from similarly situated white wives and from less segregated Negro wives in that they more often mentioned outside (church) interests; they apparently find a greater portion of the meaningfulness of their lives in these non-family activities and are less fully bound up in the family. While this could be taken as a motivation for family limitation, it seems more important as an indication of the extreme separateness between husband and wife, and thus of the difficulty the couple has in getting together for concerted action toward family goals. In addition, of course, the fundamentalist religious orientation of these women emphasizes the moral virtue inherent in motherhood, a virtue that is believed to increase as the number of children increases. The family can become a battleground for the struggle between Satan (in the form of male acting-out) and God (in the form of motherly virtue and love).

One of the main differences between white and Negro wives of this class level, then, is that the Negro wives are more organized socially (through the church) to foster their matri-centered family orientations than are white wives, who are more isolated and who have less opportunity for validation and support of their self-conception by similarly situated women. These white wives tend to have less elaborate conceptions of themselves as wives and mothers, to cling to constricted notions of being a "good" person, and to find less gratification in living out moral conceptions of self through performance of interpersonal family roles as opposed to work-oriented ones (cook, housecleaner, etc.).

These characteristics might also be taken as reasons for not having a large family; if these women derive relatively little gratification from being mothers, and little support from their husbands in this demanding task, why are they not more strongly motivated to limit their families? In good part, as we have noted, they are not motivated because they do not believe they have much chance of success; lack of hope reduces the likelihood of making a serious effort, particularly in the context of a marital relationship in which they can not expect close cooperation with their husbands. The end result of such a situation, having children without specifically wanting them, merely confirms the self-conceptions they have developed of being moral, hard-pressed, hapless creatures.

Let us look at several examples of lower-lower class couples in each type of relationship. First, a couple in which the husband, who has a steady but low-paying job, is thirty-eight and the wife is thirty-one. They have been married for thirteen years and have five children. They speak of their relationship as a close and smooth one at present, although some years back the wife left her husband because he drank too much (he promised to reform and she says that he did).

The husband:
   We live from day to day and try to take care of the children, make them as happy as we can. We do what we can afford, we can't afford much. We've had our ups-and-downs with the children; all of them have been in the hospital at one time or another—we had pneumonia and one of them was bit by a black widow spider. [Are there money problems?] Actually, I get along pretty good, as well as the next guy. I stay even, never get ahead, I can buy the groceries, pay the rent and bills, that's about all, I guess. [How are decisions made?] Me and my wife usually discuss things; we think pretty much alike, no bad differences. We make decisions together on what we're going to

buy and about the children. She looks after the house and I pay the bills and take care of the business end of the family. I help some in the house, not as much as I should.

[What is your wife like?] She's a good wife; she looks after the kids good. She don't have any bad faults of any kind. We get along good. She's not interested in any particular thing outside of worrying about the children, taking them out, making life happy for them. We usually do things around the children. [And you?] Well, I'm just an average fellow. Sometimes I'm down in the dumps because of hard going, ups-and-down from everyday living. I don't drink. I'm easy to get along with.

[What do your children think of you?] They're like any other kinds; they think there is no one like their mother and father. We try not to do anything to hurt them and have them change their minds about us.

The wife:
Like all big families with just one working it's hard, but we manage. Nothing spectacular has happened to us, just everyday things. We've had a lotta sickness, everything from a black widow spider bite to getting hit by a car. The children do real well in school; two of 'em got a certificate of merit this year for good grades. We discuss things and do things more or less together. I don't just decide things by myself. We decide things about the kids together like if they want to go places we might not let them go without someone to look after them. We usually go out on Sundays for milk shakes and hamburgers. I do my own washing, ironing, cooking. We both have the duty of the children. He works nights—three to eleven. He helps me shop. He's a good husband; he takes time with the children. He's a good person; he doesn't drink and he doesn't swear and he's kind. I'm a nervous kind of person; sometimes I get irritable but they put up with me. We get along real well; he's affectionate, he cares about me. He's considerate; if I don't feel well, he helps me around the house."

This couple exhibits a closeness and interdependence that is unusual in the lower-lower class. The wife feels she can depend on her husband for more than just financial support, and he takes a good deal more interest in the family than do most of his peers. It is not surprising, then, to find that their discussion of family limitation reflects their close interaction:

> *The husband:*
> A couple should use the right things and know what they are doing when they want to limit their family. They shouldn't use anything harmful. They should both decide between themselves. It's a man's place to keep his wife from getting pregnant.

> *The wife:*
> I didn't do anything about it [contraception] until after the third one. After him I just didn't want any more for awhile. My husband and I talked it over and we decided for me to be fitted for the diaphragm and I went to the doctor and he fitted me, that's all. [Are you still using same diaphragm?] No, after I had it a couple of years I didn't trust it; it was getting old; it's rubber and rubber could burst if its old. We tried rubbers a few times before the third one but I didn't like them and I didn't let him use it. He didn't like them either.

Both husband and wife wanted a large family (the husband feels that in a few years it might be nice to have a sixth — "When you're used to babies underfoot all the time and then there are none you miss them sometimes" — but his wife feels they must "concentrate on doing something for the ones we have". In any case neither became concerned with the issue of family limitation until fairly late in their lives; when they did they discussed it and decided on a method which they felt would be effective, which would not interfere with sexual pleasure, and which places the heaviest demand on the wife, who seems the most strongly motivated to limit the family. The larger marital relationship, in short, was conducive to, rather than an interference in, communication and planning about contraception.

The responses given in discussing family limitation by those in highly segregated relationships reflect the separation between husband and wife. The husbands often accept verbally the idea of their own responsibility, but what they say suggests they are not really very interested. For example in one lower-lower class couple, married for two years and with two children, the husband commented about responsibility for family limitation:

> Both of 'em (husband and wife). More hers than yours really. [What do you do?] Wash and clean up. [You mean your wife?] No, both of us."

And his wife said:

> I think both of them has something to do with it but mainly its on the woman, 'cause he knows he ain't going to get pregnant. [What responsibility does he have?] The man ought to buy her things to keep her from getting pregnant and if she don't use it, it's her fault and he don't care'cause he can't get pregnant.

At another point the husband indicated that he thinks his wife did not get pregnant the second time until she wanted to; she says that she did not want the second child but learned only afterwards about the douche, which she plans to use now to keep from becoming pregnant a third time. In short, the husband at this point has little interest in the question of family limitation; it's his wife's business; for her part she is content to have the responsibility because the one method she now knows is one she can handle on her own.

In other couples the husband interferes directly in what the wife does. Thus in one lower-lower class Negro couple in which the husband and wife have been married for twelve years and have seven children, the husband says:

> I don't think a person should do nothing to keep from having children. It's something that we are blessed with and you ought not to try to stop the blessing. (Do you ever use a contraceptive method?) It don't make sense to do anything like that. It just ain't right. I don't like 'em anyhow. We don't do nothing to keep from having children. Maybe we should but we don't. It takes some of the feeling out of it and it ain't right.

In his discussion of particular methods this man's standards are consistent—if a method "cuts down on the feeling" (condom, withdrawal, and, for no clear reason, suppositories) then it is not a good method; if it does not (diaphragm, rhythm, douche, jelly alone), then he is willing to say it might be all right. His wife, however, sees his attitudes toward contraception as of a piece with his other marital behavior— she complains that he drinks too much and that he teases the children sometimes until they cry. About family limitation she says:

> Well, I was pregnant when we married; that's one reason I got married, I wanted my baby to have a name. I didn't have sense enough to use anything before we was married. We courted for three years. My girl friends told me that when we got through with intercourse to squat down and smash my stomach and try to pee pee. That worked for almost three years but then I got caught. Then I come right back the next year and had another baby. My husband didn't want me to use anything. He says, "We're married now and got nothin' to hide," so I didn't use anything. But after so many I did want to but he didn't. I used things (douche, suppositories) but my husband made me cut it out. I'd slip behind his back but he could always tell. I wanted to get my tubes tied but he said no. I told my husband if we don't want any more he got to help. I tried to myself but he got to help. He got to make up his mind that he don't want no more. If my husband and I would quit [separate] and I married again I wouldn't have no more children.

In her discussion of particular methods it becomes clear that at one time or another this woman has tried condoms, withdrawal, rhythm, the douche, vaseline, and suppositories, but has had failures or embarrassment (vaseline—"It makes me shame, it pops when you have it up in you, when you have your husband it makes a popping noise and I just feel shame") or her husband refuses to co-operate (condom, withdrawal, suppositories). It seems likely that her husband's attitude tends to reinforce her ideas of shame in connection with all contraception. This is not an uncommon attitude among lower-lower class Negro husbands (and to some extent, wives) in our sample. That is, once one is married one no longer has to be ashamed about a woman's becoming pregnant and therefore one does not have to use contraception—to do so seems to be carrying over an attitude of shame from premarital relations. Among whites these attitudes are probably unconsciously present, and sometimes come out into the open in connection with use of the condom, but none of our white respondents make this kind of blanket connection between legitimacy of children in marriage, premarital illigitimacy, and family limitation in general. In this sense, the Negro lower-lower class husband's aversion to family limitation seems to come from a feeling that his wife would be rejecting the marriage tie and her own moral responsibility to have many children and care for them. Among most of these men such attitudes seem to wane as time goes on and the number of children increase, but they do tend to lag behind their wives in developing a clear sense of the desirability of family limitation.

Most of these ineffective lower-lower class couples, at least after several pregnancies, come to recognize that in order to limit their families effectively both husband and wife have to want to do so. Perhaps this is one reason they are not very optimistic about success in family limitation; they have learned that the co-operation which is required is not possible within their kind of marital relationship. Other aspects of marital living are handled by some kind of division of labor and interest, yet here such a division does not seem to work. This, coupled with the strong resistance these men show to the condom, means that no method known to them is both suitable and effective. Even where the wife is willing to try a method like the diaphragm which she can handle reasonably well on her own, requiring of the husband only that he not be importunate in his demands, she feels a need for his moral support in the endeavor. She is sufficiently unsure of the safety and the morality of what she is doing that she cannot function easily with the sole responsibility for contraception.

This is a situation exactly comparable to the wife's problem with respect to sexuality; even though she may be interested in the activity, she needs her husband's support and consideration to feel comfortable about what she does. In some ways it is easier for the woman in this situation to enjoy sexual relations on an autonomous basis than to be effective at contraception, since sexual enjoyment has powerful instinctual forces behind it and proceeds from unconscious sources with less necessity for rational planning and self-direction. Contraception, in contrast, provides no intrinsic reward. Perhaps the main advantage the oral contraceptive has for this group is that because the method has no connection with sexual intercourse the woman is better able emotionally to handle it on her own. Similarly, sterilization often appeals to women who have had the frustrating experience of repeated failures with contraception methods—once she has her "tubes tied" she no longer needs to worry about her husband's understanding or support.

We can hypothesize that there is a relationship between ineffective contraceptive practice and the wife's lack of interest in sexual relations, both being seen as a reflection of the greater emotional distance between husband and wife in highly segregated conjugal role-relationships. Table 8–5 presents for different categories of wife's sexual interest, the distribution of couples who are effective and ineffective users of contraception after the birth of the last child wanted by the wife (there are no differences for the period before the last wanted child). Results are presented separately for whites and Negroes because, as noted in chapter iii, Negro wives seem more often to show mild interest in sexual relations even though they participate in segregated role-relationships. Lower class Catholics are not included in the table because there are no differences between effectives and ineffectives in the wife's level of sexual gratification.

TABLE 8–5:
WIFE'S SEXUAL GRATIFICATION AND EFFECTIVE CONTRA-
CEPTIVE PRACTICE AFTER BIRTH OF LAST WANTED CHILD
IN THE LOWER CLASS

		Effective	Ineffective
White Protestants			
Very positive to sexual relations	(17)*	76%	24%
Positive	(6)*	100	–
Not positive	(17)	41	59
Negroes			
Very positive	(12)	75%	25%
Positive	(10)†	20	80
Not positive	(14)†	36	74

*Combined for analysis
  $X^2 = 5.20$ $P < .025$ $T = .38$
†Combined for analysis
  $X^2 = 5.20$ $P < .025$ $T = .38$

The association between sexual enjoyment on the part of
the wife and effective contraceptive practice is as strong as
that between effectiveness and conjugal role-relationship, but
it is difficult to know how to interpret the association. There
are at least three possibilities: (1) both sexual enjoyment and
effective contraception are expressions of a less segregated
role-relationship; (2) the tension arising from lack of
confidence that she will be able to limit pregnancies interferes
with the wife's sexual enjoyment; or (3) rejection of sexual
relations interferes with the wife's ability to address herself
rationally to effective contraceptive practice. In reading interviews with individual couples, one can see all of these
considerations operating. Some wives discuss specifically the
fact that they can no longer enjoy sexual relations because
they are so concerned about becoming pregnant; others that
they now enjoy sexual relations because they no longer
worry about becoming pregnant. In some couples, the wife
expresses her hostility to sex when she discusses contraception by saying, in effect, that since her husband is the only
one who enjoys sex he should be the one to worry about

contraception; or other wives indicate that they prefer the diaphragm because both they and their husbands enjoy sexual relations more that way than with the condom. Thus, all three directions of causality probably operate here in a system of mutually reinforcing attitudes and behaviors. A highly segregated conjugal relationship makes it difficult for couples to function with the close co-operation required both for mutually gratifying sexual relations and effective contraceptive practice; in this context contraception tends to become a bone of contention in relation to the wife's wish to avoid anything connected with sex, and her aversion to sexual relations is reinforced by her anxiety about becoming pregnant coupled with the difficulty she experiences in doing anything effective to prevent it.

Up to this point, we have not discussed effective and ineffective contraception in the middle class, in large part because few middle class couples seem not to have adopted contraception in a regular way by the time they have their last wanted child, and in part because adoption before that time seems to be heavily conditioned by religion (See Table 8 – 5). We have noted that the conjugal role-relationship does not seem related to the adoption of effective contraception in the middle class. Apparently, in the middle class, the difference in the quality of the marital relationship between joint organization and intermediate segregation does not relate to the ability of the couple to chose a method which they can practice effectively. However, one aspect of the couple's sexual relationship does seem related to whether contraception is adopted before the birth of the last wanted child. Although effective contraception at this point in the family cycle is not significantly related to the level of the husband's or wife's sexual gratification considered separately, there is an important difference when the husband's and wife's levels of gratification are considered together (Table 8 – 6). It is apparent that when there is an equal degree of interest in sexual relations the couple is more likely to adopt

TABLE 8-6:
LEVEL OF SEXUAL INTEREST AND EFFECTIVE CONTRACEP-
TIVE PRACTICE BEFORE BIRTH OF LAST WANTED CHILD IN
THE MIDDLE CLASS

		Effective	*Ineffective*
Equal enjoyment—both very positive	(20)*	90%	10%
Equal enjoyment—but less than very positive	(6)*	83	17
Husband enjoys more than wife	(16)†	56	44
Wife enjoys more than husband	(9)†	33	67

†Combined for test
$X^2 = 8.03$ $P < .005$ $T = .40$

effective contraceptive practice before the birth of the last
wanted child than if either the husband or the wife enjoys
sexual relations more than the other. This relationship is also
apparent (although not significant because of the small numbers involved) when Protestants and Catholics are considered separately.

An examination of Table 8-6 indicates that the great
majority of those couples who have equal enjoyment of
sexual relations (and are effective contraceptors) are very
positive in their interest in marital sexuality, and only a minority are mildly positive. Thus, in most cases, the association of effective contraception with equal enjoyment accompanies very positive interest in sexual relations on the part of
both partners. In contrast, ineffective practice is associated
particularly with a sexual relationship in which the wife enjoys sex more than her husband, or in which he enjoys sex
but she does not exhibit a positive interest in it. Where there
is equal interest in sexual relations the couple is more comfortable about sexual relations and has less anxiety which
might interfere with the adoption of effective contraception. It
is also possible, of course, that among couples who find in
their sexual relationship anxiety rather than a source of security and comfort there may be a tendency to delay effective
contraception in the (unconscious) hope that additional chil-

dren will provide some of this security and comfort. Thus, there would be less emphasis on planning the family and spacing children through effective contraception, even though we know that in the long run couples who are both very interested in sexual relations seldom want small families.

9

Medical assistance
for family limitation

FAMILY LIMITATION and contraception have been at most only partly under formal medical control. For most of the history of this aspect of Western technology, medicine has had relatively little to do with family planning practices; the principal methods responsible for the great decline in births during the 19th century (coitus interruptus and douche) were more or less completely within the area of lay control, and the rise in use of the condom probably had more to do with the public health efforts of the armed services in two world wars than with the prescriptions of individual physicians. However, in the past two or three decades there has been a growth in the social definition of contraception as a medical rather than a purely lay affair, a development finally recognized officially by the American Medical Association in 1937. The development and popularization of methods which require medical assistance, such as the diaphragm, and advice in choosing among the methods available, probably contribute to the growing awareness of contraception as something one should discuss with a physician.

However, it would be incorrect to believe that most couples now rely on their physicians for advice in choosing and using family limitation methods. In Table 9–1 we present the proportions of several social groups who have had one or

TABLE 9-1:
MEDICAL DISCUSSION OF FAMILY LIMITATION

		None	With Physician as Out-Patient	Planned Parent- hood Clinic	Post- partum in hospital
Middle Class Protestants	(34)	6%	88%	12%	—
Middle Class Catholics	(23)	30	59	8	4%
Upper-Lower Class Whites	(26)	39	61	—	4
Upper-Lower Class Negroes	(24)	29	54	17	21
Lower-Lower Class Whites	(24)	46	46	4	12
Lower-Lower Class Negroes	(29)	38	21	14	28

another kind of medical experience concerning family limitation. Among middle class Protestants, almost all wives have had some contact with physicians in which contraception was discussed. (No figures are presented for husbands' contacts since fewer than 5 per cent of men say they have ever talked this over with their doctors; in its medical aspects contraception is very clearly a feminine matter in the eyes of our respondents, and husbands participate at second hand.) Middle class Catholics, of course, have had less contact with physicians both because they delay contraception longer and because they are likely to discuss the rhythm method with a physician only after experimenting with it on their own until there is a failure. Within the lower class, upper-lower class persons are more likely to have had medical contacts than are lower-lower class persons but overall, Negro wives are slightly more likely to have had some medical discussion, in good part because discussion is initiated by medical personnel in hospitals. There is a religious difference in medical contacts only in the middle class; in the lower class Protestants and Catholics are equally likely to have had medical contact.

Table 9-2 reflects the type of medical contact the wife has had for those cases in which there has been some medical

TABLE 9-2:
TYPE AND SITUATION OF MEDICAL DISCUSSION

		Out-Patient of General Physician	Obstetrician- Gynecologist	Planned Parent- hood	Post- partum in Hospital
White					
Middle class	(48)	29%	67%	12%	2%
Upper-lower class	(16)	81	19	—	6
Lower-lower class	(13)	69	15	8	15
Negro					
Upper-lower class	(17)	41	41	24	29
Lower-lower class	(18)	22	11	22	45

discussion. In the middle class (regardless of religion) the practice seems well established that a wife seeks advice from a specialist. Among Protestants the practice of consulting with an OB-Gyn specialist at a premarital examination is quite common; among Catholics this kind of discussion tends to be delayed until later in the marriage when family limitation or spacing become real issues. The attraction of the specialist also accounts for the small number of middle class wives who patronize Planned Parenthood; their comments about the organization clearly indicate that they go there because they want to get the most expert advice available. Lower class whites tend to rely on their "family doctor" for contraceptive advice; about three-quarters of them have discussed family limitation with this source and very few with any other source. Negroes rely much less on the general physician; upper-lower class Negro women are more likely to get the advice of specialists, either at Planned Parenthood or elsewhere. Lower-lower class Negro wives have their medical contacts most often in the hospital; a small minority consult Planned Parenthood or the family doctor, and very few seek out a specialist in any other setting.

Only 10 per cent of lower class whites have discussed contraception with professionals in a hospital, while about 38 per cent of the Negroes have done so. This is partly accountable by the fact that the Negro wives in our sample are likely to have so many children that they are singled out by their hospital physicians as "problem cases", but there is also the distinct possibility that their physicians are more likely to see a problem case where the patient's coloring is dark; that is there is a sense of greater urgency about family limitation for Negroes than for whites. We have no evidence bearing on this point, of course, but this interpretation is consistent with the finding that few of the Negro wives say that they initiated the discussions that took place in the hospital; often they seem slightly intrigued but uneasy about them, and feel they are being "put on the spot".

Are those who have medical discussions more likely to be effective practitioners of contraceptions than those who do not? Tables 9-3 and 9-4 present data on this point. Clearly there is no difference in the effectiveness of those who have and have not had medical discussions. The one exception to the pattern involves Negro effectives, who apparently do more often seek out medical advice on how to effectively limit their families.

When we examine the kind of professional contact these wives have had (Table 9-4), some differences between effectives and ineffectives are apparent for Negroes, though not for whites. The Negro effectives are most likely to have contact with private specialists or with Planned Parenthood; Negro ineffectives are most likely to have had medical discussions in the hospital. It would seem, then, that the post-

TABLE 9-3:
MEDICAL DISCUSSION AND EFFECTIVE CONTRACEPTIVE PRACTICE IN THE LOWER CLASS

		Has Had Discussion	Has Not Had Discussion
Negro effectives	(16)	87%	13%
White effectives	(17)	59	41
All ineffectives who want more children	(21)	57	43
All ineffectives who do not want more children	(42)	60	40

TABLE 9-4:
TYPE OF MEDICAL PROFESSIONAL OR SETTING AND EFFEC-
TIVE CONTRACEPTIVE PRACTICES IN THE LOWER CLASS

| | | Out-Patient of: | | Planned Parent- hood | Post- partum in Hospital |
		General Physician	Obstetrician- Gynechologist		
Whites					
Effectives	(10)	80%	10%	–	20%
Ineffective who want no more children	(10)	70	20	10	10
Negroes					
Effectives	(14)	29	43	36	21
Ineffectives who want no more children	(15)	40	–	13	67
All					
Ineffectives who want more children	(12)	67	42	–	–

partum discussions lower class women have in hospitals are
not particularly useful in directing them toward effective
contraception. This is partly because the discussion tends to
come fairly late in the game, after the wives involved are
pretty well convinced that nothing short of sterilization will
help them, partly because they are uncertain as to whether
to take the advice as constructive or as insulting, and partly
because the communication is, as they remember it, often
quite incomplete. Thus, two Negro women who are ineffective after having had six and seven children respectively,
recounted their hospital experiences (one in Chicago and
the other in Oklahoma City) as follows:

> He just mentioned birth control, but he didn't say what kind.
> The doctor at the [Cook] County [Hospital]. I asked him [about
> birth control] when I had my first. A lot of women are skeptical
> about asking; they wish the doctor would hit on it. If he does,
> then they feel freer to talk about it. [When should he bring it
> up?] With a woman who has had miscarriages, or had babies too
> fast, or it would be bad for her health, or she has just had chil-
> dren and children, too many,

> Yes, the doctor at the hospital told me that as long as it didn't bother me [to have many children] to go ahead but if it bother me he could make me stop. He said he could tell me what to do but he didn't say what. If he thinks she need to stop he needs to tell her; he knows what is best.

It is quite possible that the physicians who initiated the discussions with these two women felt that the women did not seem interested. It is clear from other comments by lower-lower class women that they tend to feel rather distant from the physicians with whom they have contact and that the physicians have to work hard to communicate effectively with this kind of patient. Some of the underlying resistance which these women have, even when they are interested in learning to limit the number of children they have, will be apparent in the sections which follow on general attitudes toward different kinds of family planning advice and programs. All of this is not to say, of course, that advice to women in hospitals is useless—its utility depends on the physician making a real effort, not a hurried one, to consult with the woman and help her understand that there really are available methods that *she* can use effectively. Also, since the method most commonly recommended in these situations, the diaphragm, is probably the most difficult one for lower class women to adopt and use effectively, medical discussion has tended to be fruitless. Now that the much simpler oral contraceptive is available, medical contact in hospitals probably offers more promise of helping at least some women move from ineffective to effective practice.

After asking respondents about their own contacts with physicians, we asked them the following general question about how free a physician should be in initiating advice on contraception:

> Some doctors don't discuss contraception with women unless the woman herself brings it up, even though they feel she needs to learn about it. What do you think of that?

Taking together the women's own experiences and their statements in response to the question above, we gain some insight into different ways of relating to physicians. Within the lower class, upper-lower class women seem to make efforts to relate fairly closely with their physicians, and this probably makes it easier for them to ask for and accept contraceptive advice. Thus, upper-lower class women are more likely to mention the pleasant personal qualities of their family doctors:

A Protestant woman:
The doctor told me about the diaphragm and suppositories. He's a general doctor. After my second baby he told me when I went in for the six weeks check-up. I always feel at ease with him; he's the type that puts you at ease. I always say when I'm going to see him I'm not going to see a doctor; I'm going to see an uncle.

A Catholic woman:
After the second child he said to use rubbers. He was very friendly and nice to talk to. He's just a medical doctor, not a specialist or anything. No one ever told me anything before that. I think they should. A young girl that's married, he should talk that over with her. Some religious person wouldn't believe in anything but the cycle so he wouldn't tell them. So depending on the doctor he could talk — he knows his patient and how the patient feels and can decide whether to tell.

On the other hand, lower-lower class women seldom speak of their physicians in this way — they reflect more distance in their comments, more suspicion and more vulnerability to shame or insult; some women are hopeful that the physician will overcome this barrier and help them, others are more standoffish:

A Negro woman:
I've never talked to him about it. I wouldn't mind discussing it but that's no sign I'd use anything. If he thinks she needs it he

should bring it up cause he's her doctor and most women would be embar.assed to bring up something like that.

A Catholic woman:

After my second child was born I asked the doctor and he told me about the diaphragm and he fitted me. He was a general doctor. The doctor should always mention it. I think there might be other people like me who were ignorant of the fact that there was such a thing.

A Protestant woman:

I talked with him about it two times — when he told me about the diaphragm, that was in 1950, after I had a miscarriage and then after I got pregnant this time was when he told me sterilization was the only answer. I think if people are really interested they will ask the doctor and if they are not interested they wouldn't do anything anyway. I asked him myself when he told me about sterilization.

A Negro woman:

I never talked about it except about the diaphragm with our family doctor and then the doctor at the [Planned Parenthood] Center where I got the diaphragm. As far as I'm concerned I was sort of glad he brought it up because I had thought about it but if a person just brings it up sort of casual like you don't think as much. A doctor can say and you pay attention because you know they know what they're talking about.

We will examine the hopefulness that lower-lower class women express about how a physician might treat them in the next section; at this point we want only to note that many lower-lower class women find their contacts with physicians (as with hospitals) both barren of emotional gratification and not very helpful. Often they do not explicity blame the doctor (they did not expect anything else), but their comments on later questions about how medical people should help them suggest something of what they were wishing for.

Should physicians volunteer advice?

In response to the question quoted above — whether or not a physician should volunteer contraceptive information — men and women mentioned a number of different considerations, though there was considerable agreement that it is the doctor's duty to discuss such matters with his patients. An intriguing minority view is that it is not in the physician's own self-interest to do this, and therefore one cannot count on his doing so:

> *An upper-middle class Protestant woman:*
> I certainly think a woman should be told and that is the advantage of going to a G.P. I think they would be more apt to tell a woman than an O.B.; after all, that's his business.

> *Lower-middle class Catholic man:*
> He probably wouldn't tell her. Why should he knock his own business. A man who sells refrigerators, why should he tell you you don't need it.

> *A lower-lower class Protestant woman:*
> I think the doctor should but they ain't about to. [Why?] If it wasn't for these pregnant women and the men that knock them up, they wouldn't have any business.

It is likely that this suspicion is not unfamiliar to others in our sample, perhaps reinforced by the pro-natal jocularity commonly expressed by physicians to reassure and encourage their pregnant patients

The other extreme in attitude, which asserts the absolute evil of physicians ever offering contraceptive advice, is expressed by the few subfecund Catholics in our sample (and it is important to note the subfecund modifier, since no Catholics in our sample are as vociferous in their endorsement of their Church's position and as critical of those who do not follow it as are upper-lower or lower-middle class subfecund husbands and wives):

> I have no use at all for people, doctors or nurses or anybody else, trying to talk over the size of your family. I think that Sangster [sic] woman ought to be locked up for the rest of her life; I think she's horrible. It's unnatural and should be illegal; I'm against the entire idea. I simply can't tolerate the idea of such presumption. Are they able to play God?

The view offered here is that if the physician brings up the subject of contraception he is meddling in the couple's decision about family size and he has no right to do so. Though the attitude is expressed in extreme form here, we will see that this concern about being dictated to rather than advised by the physician is present among other couples also.

Middle class Protestants take it for granted that one learns best about contraception from one's private physician. Though they thenselves are likely to request such advice when they need it, they are aware that other women may not be comfortable about doing so. Therefore they are almost unanimous in indicating that they feel the physician has a responsibility to "educate" his patients about the necessity for and the methods to be used in family limitation:

> *A man:*
> I think it's wrong for a doctor not to bring it up. It's socially desirable to have fewer children than most ignorant people have.

> *A woman:*
> I think they should bring it up. It should be very matter of fact. Maybe the women are afraid or embarrassed to talk about it and would feel more at ease if the doctor brought it up.

> *A woman:*
> I think a doctor should bring it up. A doctor has an educated opinion; a lot of women are not too well informed. His opinion would make them listen.

A man:

It depends on the stage. On a pre-marital physical he should tell her all he thinks is necessary. I know my wife and the doctor discussed a diaphragm at that time. I'm sure they discussed the other methods. It would depend on the case. If she is Catholic that is something else. If the doctor feels she should know he should tell her.

A woman:

Some women are too bashful to ask and I think they would appreciate their doctors telling them.

A man:

I think the doctor should make a point of discussing it; no reason why he shouldn't. I don't think some women — I think a lot of them run it into the ground having a baby every nine months. If the doctors would make a point of it they would think about it anyway.

A man:

I don't think it would hurt anything — it wouldn't make her mad. Women pay attention to doctors.

A man:

The doctor should bring it up because it is educational and the wife should know about it even though she doesn't want to use it.

As the last quoted man expressed explicitly, the physician should assume the role of *teacher;* he should communicate to the woman the technical knowledge necessary for family limitation so that she may use it when the time comes. These middle class people also hope that physicians can persuade their poorer neighbors to be more sensible, to limit their families in terms of their means, although they themselves are not likely to look favorably on such advice. For themselves they want technical information; for the less fortunate they want education in sensible family living as well.

Protestants, then, are almost unanimous in endorsing a very active role for the physician in teaching about family planning and limitation. Middle class Catholics are more varied in their views. Almost all acknowledge that where the wife's health is involved the physician has a responsibility to discuss family limitation with her; a substantial minority take a more secular attitude and say that he should bring the subject up for whatever reasons he feels are adequate. Mention of the wife's health as a rationale for initiating a discussion of family limitation is frequent only among lower-middle class Catholics, most of whom bring in this aspect of the situation during their discussion of the question:

A lower-middle class Catholic woman:
I think if it were impairing her health he should say something. Otherwise he should leave it up to her to ask him.

A lower-middle class Catholic man:
I don't think the doctor is carrying out his obligation to his patient if he doesn't tell her. If he thinks there's a physical reason and doesn't tell her he's endangering her health. Otherwise he has no business discussing it.

These people, then, make a sharp distinction between the physician as an advisor on illness and health who can legitimately discuss family limitation when these are at stake, and as a teacher concerned with technical knowledge for its own sake or as an authority in counselling on child spacing and optimum family size. They see the latter as an illegitimate exercise of expertness. However, at least a third of the middle class Catholics in our sample express themselves very much along the same lines as the Protestants:

A man:
If in his mind he feels it is a problem he should bring it up. I think all couples should have this discussed with them before marriage. The lower class needs the education more.

A woman:

It's not right for him not to tell. Some women are scared to death to bring it up. It should be up to the medical man to mention it. The woman can use it or not as she wishes.

They feel the physician should be ethically and religiously neutral, volunteering to discuss the question if the patient wishes, but not putting pressure on her to adopt contraception—or only doing so if she is "ignorant" and in need of education to sensible family size values.

In the lower class, Catholics are seldom concerned about the implications for their religion of a physician offering contraceptive advice; they seldom bring religion up at all in discussing what physicians or Planned Parenthood does or might do, and their responses are indistinguishable from those of lower class Protestants. While upper-lower class Catholics seem somewhat more often to concern themselves about Church doctrine in their own decisions about contraception, they do not very often carry this concern over to general statements about where the physician should draw the line in offering contraceptive advice. Lower-lower class Catholics seem quite unconcerned about the religious implications of contraception in general.

A man:

I think it's perfectly disgusting for him not to tell her. He would be withholding vital information that should be told. He should bring it up.

A woman:

I think the doctor should assume the initiative because most women are too shy, even though they would like to discuss it.

A man:

Well, as far as women are concerned I think the doctor or the mother should tell her these things so if she doesn't want any more children she should know how to protect herself.

A man:

The doctor knows and he should tell her. If she needs it for health reasons he really should tell her. I don't see any reason why he shouldn't go into this.

A woman:

I think they should. Some women are bashful, a doctor can tell that and he should come right out and tell them.

A woman:

A doctor should go ahead and say something. A lotta people are backwards and don't want to ask and they're just dumb enough to keep on having children. He should tell them what to do. I believe in birth control. [What about your religion; Catholic, isn't it?] I figure why run into something you can't take care of. They're not going to support my children.

Lower class Catholics, then, say essentially the same things about the physician offering advice that lower class Protestants say. They feel strongly that the physician should be helpful, and they know that they are, or were, ignorant about contraceptive methods, and that most of their peers are. They feel that the physician could easily remedy this if he would only take the trouble.

The majority view in the lower class, then, seems to be that the physician should help his patients to overcome their ignorance and bashfulness by volunteering information on family planning. A good many people recognize either explicitly or implicitly that he will not have outstanding success in doing this, but they feel that he should make the effort. He fulfills his responsibility by making the effort; the woman may or may not fulfill hers by following the advice he gives.

This lower-lower class Protestant woman has five children and has only recently become earnest about family limitation; in part she is making a general statement about women, in part she is saying that she feels no one could have helped her until she decided to help herself. To a considerable extent the very positive attitude lower class respondents express toward the idea of the physician taking the initiative (and toward an active program by Planned Parenthood, as discussed below) is a measure of their own sense of impotence or uncertainty about doing anything effective to limit their families. If only the doctor could take care of it for them, all would be well. It is certainly also true that if the physician is successful in reducing somewhat the social distance between himself and his patient, his encouragement and moral support, as much as his technical advice, gives many of these women the strength to go through the sequence of actions required to limit their families in line with their wishes. A desire that the physician resolve some of the complexities that interfere with effective contraceptions is also reflected in the comment of a Negro wife that

> The doctor should bring it up first and talk with the husband and wife. He should take special pains and talk with these contrary husbands. I think that ought to be their duty.

Lower class women, then, tend to express considerable wishful dependence on the physician. Men, for their part, tend to see the active physician as relieving them somewhat from the responsibility of active involvement in family limitation; it is an issue which the physician and the wife can work out together without bothering the husband too much. Few lower class husbands would be willing to go along with the plan advanced by the woman quoted above; they are willing to acquiesce to plans worked out by others if this involves only a little inconvenience for them.

In summary, a very large majority of our sample believes that it is the physician's responsibility to offer contraceptive advice and information for any reasons he deems sufficient. Only middle class Catholics are inclined to limit the physician to health reasons for offering such advice, and even here a substantial minority do not suggest such limitations. The middle class conception of the physician's role is most clearly that of a teacher who instructs his patients on the techniques and values of family planning long before the fact of immediate need. In the lower class there is probably a stronger sense that the physician should wait until the woman has an immediate need for the information, since she probably won't listen to his advice until she has this need. Most middle class women feel that they do not need this exercise of initiative on the physician's part since they are willing to raise the question themselves; but it is likely that they are reassured when he does take the initiative since they are more bashful about discussing these intimate matters than they like to admit. Lower class women are more likely to admit their bashfulness and ignorance (to some extent it is a sign of their being moral women), and they wish to rely on the doctor to bypass these difficulties and help them understand what to do to limit their families and feel right about doing it. The social distance between physician and patient, however, is a real obstacle to such goals for the lower-lower class women (perhaps even more so for Negroes than whites because of the race as well as class differences between them) and to overcome it probably requires considerable ingenuity on the part of the physician.

Attitudes toward planned parenthood

In our sample, a large majority of the men and women had heard of Planned Parenthood clinics, though often they felt they did not know much more than that such an organization existed. In the middle class, about 90 per cent of the men and women say they have heard of Planned Parenthood; in the lower class, 85 per cent of the women and 60 per cent of the men say they have heard of Planned Parenthood clinics. Among those in the lower class who do say they have heard of the organization, women seem to have somewhat fuller ideas about the organization than men, as would be expected given their greater involvement in the subject. This sex difference is not as apparent in the middle class since middle class respondents tend to think of Planned Parenthood more as a service for the less well-off members of the community or as an ideological bone of contention than as a possible resource for themselves. (This does not apply, of course, to the 10 per cent of our middle class sample who have gone to Planned Parenthood clinics; they are enthusiastic about it on both personal and ideological grounds.)

Respondents were asked the following question to elicit information about attitudes toward Planned Parenthood:

> In most cities there are clinics, the Planned Parenthood clinics, where people can get advice on birth control. Have you ever heard of this and what do you think about these clinics or the idea in general?

Middle class Protestants communicate solid approval of the organization, but they do not evince the same emotional involvement and sense of familiarity in their discussion as they do in talking about how private physicians should behave. Their comments reflect the fact that they believe Planned Parenthood is for other kinds of people.

An upper-middle class man:
I have heard of them and I think the idea should be encouraged. To the end of restricting families to a size that families can support and educate the children properly.

An upper-middle class man:
I have never heard of them but I think the idea is good. Some people might be bashful, but the idea is good. With people without education, some of them might not know—they might know some methods but not all, and it would be good for them.

An upper-middle class woman:
I think it's a very good idea and of course I know about it. I think it's a good idea even for the sake of the middle income as well as the lower income groups. I'm amazed that so many

people know nothing of it. It's amazing how many of the very desperately poor people know nothing of all these free clinics we have here in [Oklahoma City.] So many have never heard of the T.B. Clinic here where they can go for free chest X-rays. There is definitely something wrong someway that these people are not better informed about this.

A lower-middle class man:
I haven't heard of them. I think it would help those people who don't know, who don't have any education about birth control.

A lower-middle class woman:
No, I've never heard of it but I think it would be a very good thing, especially for people with very low incomes.

A lower-middle class woman:
Yes, I've heard of them and I think it's a wonderful thing. The information under those circumstances is sure to be reliable and of course I think all women are entitled to get this kind of information. I feel strongly that families should be planned, that unwanted babies should just never happen.

Planned Parenthood clinics, then, are from the middle class point of view necessary only because some people are not able to learn about family planning in ordinary ways. Middle class Protestants know there are such people and that their needs are real and should be attended to by someone, but they do not personally feel very involved with the subject. A few women (two of whom are quoted above) become quite involved with the issue of really helping people who do not know how to plan their families, but most, while positive, are rather indifferent in their attitudes.

Middle class Catholics have more varied views, and their personal feelings about Planned Parenthood are more ambivalent. A small group of Catholics, somewhat smaller than the group that endorses complete freedom for the physician in deciding whether to discuss family limitation, speaks in the same positive way about the organization as do middle class Protestants, and a similarly small group evinces considerable hostility to the idea.

> *A lower-middle class man:*
> I know of the location of one clinic in the Loop. I don't go along with it; there's too much power in the clinic's hands. It's up to the Good Lord; people take too much into their own hands when they give advice. It's up to the Maker and not to people.

> *A lower-middle class man:*
> I don't agree with them. I think they do harm to people and their morals. People should work out their own problems themselves and not with an organization.

> *A lower-middle class man:*
> Their money could be spent in a better way. Well, they could do the world more good by spending money in better ways than promoting selfishness.

> *A lower-middle class man:*
> I've heard of them, but to me they shouldn't be legal. Everybody that has sex in their lives, they know what it is that makes the babies and if they feel they shouldn't have any more let them lay off sex and settle the matter that way. You can't make it too strong for me that I'm against all this idea.

Those Catholics who express unconditional hostility to the idea of Planned Parenthood clinics seldom relate their attitudes specifically to their own religion; they advance their views as universally valid. It is possible that they have some underlying awareness that to label their position as Catholic would weaken their argument, since those who do introduce Catholicism in their comments do so to point up a pluralistic value system and acknowledge the claims of the other value system for its adherents:

> *A lower-middle class man,* (whose wife says, "I must say I completely disapprove of Planned Parenthood clinics. NO in capital letters."):

They may have a purpose. I understand a lot of people don't have the same outlook as my wife and I do. This is touchy; people should be careful about the Catholic viewpoint and Catholics should be careful about other viewpoints. I don't think the Government should come into it.

A lower-middle class man:
I've heard of them; I don't condone them. I don't believe in Planned Parenthood. For those who don't believe in not controlling birth it's a good idea. I think they should be church or privately supported, but no government backing.

These respondents adopt the more moderate position that Planned Parenthood clinics are all right for non-Catholics, but that the people who believe in such clinics should also respect the Catholic viewpoint. The most direct reference for this argument for mutual tolerance seems to be that clinics should be church or privately supported, and not supported by government funds.

Another kind of Catholic view which involves mixed feelings is on balance more favorable still to Planned Parenthood clinics.

An upper-middle class woman:
I've heard of them. I don't care for the name, especially for Catholics it implies contraception and they would be against it. A better name would be "Family Center." It's very desirable; they do a great deal that needs to be done for poorer people; but with that name I can't even support it when they ask for a donation because it's against my religion.

A lower-middle class man:
Unfortunately, the people I have run into are offensive, bad-breath do-gooders. The ones I have seen were women without children and are offensive in their approach. The ones who do this should be educated and adjusted people.

A lower-middle class man:
I think those clinics are fine if the people are willing to go along. You can't force people to co-operate with them. Such

education seems to be necessary all the time, problems of too many children, families that can't afford them. It's fine to give advice; it's the person's prerogative to use it.

Each of these respondents in his own way seems favorably disposed to the idea of family planning, both for himself and others. The first woman uses the diaphragm, and the man quoted second uses the condom, but all are aware of the religious contentions about birth control and they do not take the existence of these clinics as much for granted as do Protestants. The first woman makes especially clear the social awkwardness for Catholics of taking a stance on Planned Parenthood—she believes in family planning, has used a diaphragm for many years, but because contraception is opposed by her religion (but not against her personal beliefs) she feels she cannot become personally involved.

Thus, except for those few Catholics who maintain consistent hostility to the idea of anyone or any organization fostering contraceptive practice, the position of the middle class Catholic is complex and uneasy, though uneasiness comes to the fore only when there is some public discussion of family limitation, as when pressure is brought to establish family planning clinics in publicly supported hospitals, or to provide this kind of medical service to welfare recipients.

As with attitudes toward how physicians should deal with issues of family limitation, lower class Catholics and Protestants have quite similar views. Thus, the following excerpted comments of lower class Catholics are essentially the same as those made by lower class Protestants.

Man:

I think it's a good thing. Too many people are in the dark and need to be enlightened. They'll get a better viewpoint on sex; knowing would help.

Man:

I never knew they existed, however, I certainly think they are a good idea especially for people who have children out of ignorance.

Man:

I've never heard of them but I think it's a good idea. There are these teenagers that don't know what they are doing and they get married and have child after child. I think if there was a clinic like that there would be less of these teenage marriages.

Woman:

I just heard about it, read about it in the paper. I think if anybody needs help they are very good as a lot of girls don't know where to turn. I don't believe in having a lot of children and having them run around naked and no one to bother to see if they are fed properly or dressed.

Woman:

I would be very much in favor of it; it might help women to learn things they wouldn't have a chance to learn about how to keep from having more children than they can afford.

Woman:

I know how the Church feels about them but I still think it's all right for people to get this kind of information. There would be a lot of happier homes if women could have something to say about when they wanted a baby. And lots of good Catholic parents can't afford to send their kids to parochial school if they get too many; the priests ought to think about that.

Catholics and Protestants in the lower class seem to agree that it is a good idea that there should be a place where one can go for help in limiting the number of children one has. However, we know that fewer than 4 per cent of the whites and only about 15 per cent of the Negroes have ever had contact with Planned Parenthood. In part, of course, this is because the more highly motivated couples have either independently learned to use one of the methods that do not require medical assistance or have consulted a private physician. However, a considerable number of lower class wives have not consulted a physician, or are dissatisfied with their experience when they have, and yet know that a Planned Parenthood clinic could give them the assistance they need. Several attitudes that come up in the interviews seem to mitigate against recourse to Planned Parenthood in this situation.

The most general formulation of these attitudes which discourage attendance at Planned Parenthood clinics is that the people who express them believe the organization is mainly for special, "problem" cases and are reluctant to define themselves in this way. For example, one lower-lower class Negro woman believes Planned Parenthood makes its services available only to those who have a large family, five or six children. Another believes that only women who are desperate go there because the method (diaphragm) the clinic offers hurts a great deal and would only be used by a woman who had no other choice. And, given the fact that so many people say the clinics are for ignorant, immature, or poverty-stricken people, the helpfulness attributed to the clinic loses some of its appeal. To need the service is in some sense to define oneself as not able to manage as well as an adult should; to go for contraceptive advice to a clinic which has this as its only business is to confirm this definition publicly. Most of these people would feel more comfortable about getting family limitation advice in a general medical setting in which less attention would be called to the specific ignorance and failure they feel are reflected by their need for contraceptive advice.

Attitudes toward a door-to-door family planning service

A more active method of teaching family planning attitudes and techniques involves sending the clinic workers out into the community, directly to their prospective clients, rather than waiting for the clients to come to them. Such methods have been tried on an experimental basis in this country and in many underdeveloped parts of the world (India, Ceylon, Japan, Puerto Rico, and Jamaica, for example.) What are community attitudes toward such a program? After discussing attitudes toward how the private physician should handle contraceptive advice and toward Planned Parenthood clinics, we asked our respondents:

> Some people say that for those who don't know about methods of limiting their families, and therefore have more children than they want or can afford, a health agency like Planned Parenthood should have a program of sending a medical worker into poorer neighborhoods and go door-to-door to talk to women about this problem, and help them to find a method for limiting their families if they want. What do you think of that?

This question was purposely biased in a positive direction (by emphasizing "health" agency, "medical" worker and the need of the prospective clients) because we believed a negative response would be quite common and we wanted to probe behind it. As the material presented below indicates, however, negative responses were quite infrequent, and we would perhaps have been better off if the question had been more neutral and thus maximized the chance that negative attitudes would be expressed and developed.

The discussion elicited by this question closely parallels what men and women said when we asked them about Planned Parenthood clinics. They seem to regard a door-to-door approach as a logical next step in encouraging the adoption of family limitation by those who by common consensus need it most. In general, middle class Protestants are strongly in favor of the idea, although one or two interesting reservations crop up.

An upper-middle class man:
I think if you can afford the right kind of people to do it, it's a splendid idea. If a private agency can raise funds and get good people to do this it's an important social good. I suspect that there are a lot of people in social work who, if they went into neighborhoods where this is needed, they would just have no impact.

A upper-middle class man:

I would think a better approach might be—that approach might be a little too abrupt. Perhaps sending the information through the mail, or dropping it off at the house, and if they are interested, they could come into the office. It's too delicate a subject to discuss at the door.

An upper-middle class woman:

I think every family should be given this information and especially the low income groups. It has always seemed they are the ones who have the most children and need it the most. I even think Catholic women should be told.

An upper middle class woman:

Oh yes, I think they should tell these poor women, not only about limiting their families but about other things they should know. [What things?] Well, for one thing, about "tampax," if they could afford them; I wouldn't ever go back to using a sanitary napkin since I've used tampax.

A lower-middle class woman:

I think that's a wonderful idea. I think they'd probably get three-quarters of the people to listen and they haven't had the opportunity to learn previous to their coming. They may not realize what caused it every nine months. I don't think these clinics would be very useful unless they did send people out. If people had to come to them they wouldn't take advantage of it.

A lower-middle class man:

I think it would be good. But, I think if they are dumb enough to have all those children they are too dumb to listen. There might be some response. Actually I was poor all my life; but those who stay there are never going to do anything right or get anything right. They don't have enough education to overcome it. Oh, they may be smart enough but they are too lazy. There are plenty of guys on skid row right now who could really be something if they could get up off their tail. I believe a man is what he makes himself, no matter how poor he is to start with. He has to strive and have ambition.

A lower-middle class woman:
  I think it is a very good idea providing that it is a well-trained medical worker. I think they would have to be special trained to get the message over to these people.

A lower-middle class woman:
  It's a good idea to find out if they are intrested although it is still their business. Some people would get mad, but most people would use it.

A lower-middle class woman:
  I think it is a very good idea. A lot of these women are ignorant of these things and their husbands, too, and they need somebody to explain it to them.

Positive attitudes toward the door-to-door approach involve the belief that there is a group of women in great need of family limitation advice who know too little to seek out the advice and who should be helped in every way possible. Reservations are of two kinds. Some respondents look down on anyone so ignorant that they cannot develop contraceptive competence on their own or by actively seeking out the services required; people who express this view believe that lower class people are simply lazy and that even the direct approach is not likely to get far. They tend to be unsympathetic to the plight of lower class people who have too many children. The second reservation has more to do with propriety, and a middle class sense of privacy is projected onto the proposed recipients of this door-to-door service. Here the respondents are reluctant to have medical workers initiate on the doorstep a discussion of this subject. These respondents are willing to go so far as to have leaflets and signs announcing the availability of a family planning service, but they are uneasy about a direct and personal approach. It is interesting, however, that the latter objection comes up only infrequently; apparently most middle class people are willing to see the subject of family limitation and contraception dealt with quite openly, at least in situations where the need is great and justifies this breach of propriety.

The views of middle class Catholics are distributed in much the same way as are their views about Planned Parenthood clinics; some are violently opposed, some affirmitive as long as Catholic sensibilities are not violated (e.g., by government support of such a program,), and others positive without reservation. The main fact of interest is that those who have religious concerns are not more negative and hostile to the idea of an active door-to-door program than they are to the more passive program of maintaining clinics. In some ways, because our initial statement of the idea specified poorer neighborhoods and women in real need, the middle class Catholic attitude becomes slightly more favorable.

An upper-middle class woman:
It's fine. It has practical limitations, though; it's hard to go door-to-door and would they know who to see. People should have sense enough to go to them if they need help and their whereabouts should be known to these people.

A lower-middle class man:
Yes, I think it would be a very good idea because people could be educated and not put out too much effort to seek out the agency. I think we should be able to spend government funds on it.

A lower-middle class woman:
It would be better arranged if a place was open and let them come. Let them know, put a sign in the window or neighborhood paper. [How would a medical worker be received?] Maybe they might like it. Some people don't like to help themselves; sometimes they're too lazy. I'd go find out for myself. What about pamphlets, flyers, or leaflets dropped under the door— "For further information call us." Maybe if something is put in front of them they might read it and go.

A lower-middle class man:
Provided these people were not supported by government funds, there's nothing wrong with it. Provided they gave advice on all types of prevention [i.e. including rhythm].

A lower-middle class man:

I think it's an insult to walk into a house and even intimate that one should not have children. I think she [the medical worker] better be careful she doesn't get her head knocked off.

A lower-middle class man:

In the poorer neighborhoods that would be a good idea. I don't think you would find many going to Planned Parenthood from there, and you would have more success this way. [Would there be any objections?] Well, religion, a person's beliefs in religion, it would have a tendency to draw them away from their beliefs.

A lower-middle class woman:

I would be against it. It would be an invasion of privacy. The people on ADC are terrific. [What do you mean?] It's ridiculous for them to have eight or ten children and be supported for it. I don't approve of someone pushing birth control. I think sending a person door-to-door would be absolutely wrong. If a woman wants to know about such things she can go and find out. I think the whole thing is wrong and should be stopped.

It is apparent both Protestants and Catholics of the middle class are not very deeply involved with this issue; they believe it has to do with people quite unlike themselves, people who do not have their advantages or do not know how to live a sensible life. If they feel sympathetic and concerned about how poorer people fare in life they think the program is a good idea; if they are denigrating in their attitude toward such people, they tend to feel the program would be a waste of time and money; finally, if they feel protective of Catholic views, they feel such a program would be immoral.

As before, Catholic and Protestant attitudes do not differ in any important way within the lower class. In the great majority of these cases, Catholics do not refer to religion at all in their discussion, but orient themselves instead to the need they feel there is for this kind of service:

An upper-lower class woman:

It's a wonderful idea; you would accept it because they would know about it and you could learn. Where else can you hear about it?

An upper-lower class man:

I think that's a good idea because, well, the poor families they have no car to go out anyplace, no TV maybe, so eventually he turns to the wife to keep himself occupied. It's a good idea to keep from having large families but it should be with the father and the mother to tell them what they're depriving their family of—better neighborhood, better education for their children and their children's children.

An upper-lower class woman:

I think that would be a good idea; I myself wouldn't know where to get help if I wanted it. Poor people don't have phones. They don't see anything but their children and their crummy neighborhoods, and they learn from mouth-to-mouth and that would be a very good thing.

A lower-lower class woman:

If you don't want to talk to her you don't have to let her come in; maybe a lot of people would like to learn something but don't know how to go about it.

A lower-lower class woman:

Maybe some people would say they're nosey; they just don't want anybody in to tell them how many children to have. Some people might like it. They may be bashful and glad to have somebody to help them. I wouldn't mind it; I'd like to hear how to stop having them so close together.

A lower-lower class woman:

That's a good idea. Help people to support their kids if they didn't have so many. The state shouldn't have to pay [for support]; every man can work. The medical worker should tell the women; the welfare should too. Especially for people with too many kids. A woman with five kids and is pregnant she goes to welfare and collects—where's the husband?"

A lower-lower class woman:
I think maybe the majority of people that live in poorer neighborhoods are people that have lived with this all their lives and just accept it and may not even be interested in a change. There may be others like me who live here through forced poverty and would like to know these things. I certainly would have welcomed a woman a couple of years ago. I would have been glad to get the advice and be more careful not to get pregnant so I wouldn't have had two more children.

The comments of white Protestants and Negroes present essentially the same picture.

An upper-lower class woman:
I would be in favor of it. So many women in the poorer families would not know about it unless someone did come and tell them and I think they would be glad to have someone do this.

An upper-lower class woman:
I think it's a very good idea; it's more or less educational for them. It's just like a missionary taking Christianity; something they don't know about that can be helpful and useful to them. The only thing bad about it I can think of is that people might turn them down but they can try again.

A lower-lower class woman:
I think that would be OK 'cause how are they going to know unless someone comes and tells them. I think it would be a real good idea if it was a woman. Of course, if a man said things like that I'd hit him over the head with my broom or my mop.

A lower-lower class woman:
A lot of people would appreciate the advice because before they learned it they thought the clinic was an expensive thing and they couldn't afford it.

A lower-lower class Protestant woman:
I wouldn't like that. I don't think people are so ignorant they need somebody coming around to their doors. Not if they have clinics and doctors to go to. They're liable to get doors slammed in their faces.

An upper-lower class Negro man:
Anyway I could get the information would be good, I don't care how they send them out.

An upper-lower class Negro woman:
I don't think it's a bad idea. It would help a lot of folks. Where some won't go to a doctor they could get information at home.

An upper-lower class Negro man:
I think it's a good idea because too many people lie down and have kids one after another without thinking. It's pretty bad to bring a child into the world and can't afford them.

A lower-lower class Negro woman:
Yes sir, it would be a good idea! Those that don't need them always have the most. I look at some of these girls in the neighborhood, now they is too young to have so many and they husbands don't provide.

A lower-lower class Negro woman:
I think this is a good idea. Some people just don't know. I wish I knew a sure way or could go through the change.

A lower-lower class Protestant woman:
I think it would be real helpful, especially if it's a woman that comes. Some of 'em around here won't go to a clinic but they would talk to someone if she came around house-to-house. Most of 'em are real backwards unless they are at home. If someone came around they would talk to 'em. A lot of these people are real backward; they wouldn't go to a clinic if you payed their busfare but they would think and talk about it if they were at home with a nurse.

The discussions of this matter by lower class respondents were in many ways more informative than those offered by middle class men and women. The lower class respondents live with the problem—they feel themselves unsure about family limitation, or at least they know the problem of unwanted large families is common in the world around them. They are hopeful about any program which might make it easier to learn what to do and which demonstrates that others want to help them. The idea that it would would be easier to learn in the comfort and security of one's own home is noted by several respondents. Apparently, if instruction comes in the home women feel less intimidated by the foreign, middle class world of the clinic and are less likely to feel that they stigmatize themselves as special "problem" cases. The door-to-door method is seen as having the advantage of bringing family planning into the real world in which the woman lives, rather than requiring her to go into the unreal world of the clinic or the private physician's office. That she will deal with a woman (explicitly or implicitly assumed by the respondents) cuts down on embarassment; that the woman comes to her probably also symbolizes a providential act of Fate and helps her feel more optimistic about the outcome of any action she may take.

The main obstacle our respondents pose in their comments about the door-to-door approach has to do with the possibility of defining the medical worker as "nosey," as forcing her own opinions and values on an unwilling subject. It is really surprising that so few of our respondents even hint at this definition of the medical worker, although perhaps understandable in terms of the majority's strongly felt wish that they not have more children than they can afford. In any case, these few respondents do highlight the fact that a door-to-door worker would have to be very careful not to seem either overly curious about how poor people live their lives or dictatorial about what decisions they should make about family size.

10
Conclusions

THIS BOOK has traced out in considerable detail the influence of social class sub-cultures on family size preferences and on family limitation behavior. As stated in the beginning, the research has been exploratory, extending an earlier exploration which concentrated exclusively on the white lower class. Whereas the first study was directed primarily at family planning practitioners and only incidentally at social scientists interested in research on this topic, the second study has been much more self-consciously directed at laying out hypotheses about family size and family limitation, indicating the evidence from these exploratory studies that tends to support the hypotheses, and suggesting fruitful lines for further investigation by family planning researchers, both with regard to American behavior and behavior in other cultures.

It is unfortunate that family planning research has been defined primarily as an applied branch of demography, since the concepts of primary usefulness in this field lie not so much within the typical area of interest and technical competence of demographers as within the range of techniques and interests of family sociologists and social psychologists. The very success of demography in specifying the independent and dependent variables with which it typically deals has perhaps tended to encourage overly ambitious standards of certainty in the family planning studies that have issued from

276

this tradition, beginning with the Indianapolis fertility studies and continuing through the Princeton studies. It is not so much that these studies were failures — by the standards of the great majority of social psychological research they were distinct successes — but rather that their areas of both failure and success tend to discourage sponsoring agencies and investigators from pursuing other lines of inquiry and to project an overly narrow pattern on the kind of research that is thought of as appropriate for this field.

This study will have achieved its goal if it contributes in a small way to cracking the overly quantitative mold into which those studies seem to have cast our conceptualization of the process by which families come to prefer a particular number of children and are successful in achieving the goals they set for themselves.

Social class and family role-organization

This study traces out in detail one major subcultural variable, that of social class, and deals also with one other extremely important variable, religion, as a control variable. The reader will have noted that there are many cases which Catholics and non-Catholics within a given social class do not differ, just as there are many in which they do (cf. Lenski, 1961: 324–25). Further, social class is seen as exercising its influence primarily through two characteristics of the family as a social system which vary from one class subculture to the other: first, the conjugal role-organization, values, and practices that are characteristic of different social classes, and second, the particular role concepts and the values and practices attendant on them that are deemed appropriate for men and women in different social classes. The first category has to do particularly with the kind of separateness and connectedness, the division of labor, that is characteristic of marital relations; the second has to do with the various non-familial role behaviors that are to be expected of men and women.

Any study that proceeds past the demographic level of analysis (in which variations by socio-economic status are demonstrated) must make use of some set of intervening variables such as these, since class per se does not influence behavior of any kind. It is only the culture and social system within each class subgroup which differentially influences behavior. The intervening variables, then, provide something of the "why" for the demographic facts of variation by social class groups. The influence of social class subcultures conceived in this way is traced out here in connection first with sexual relations in marriage, then with family size preferences and motives, and finally with respect to family limitation behavior in terms both of types of methods used and relative success with each method.

Role-organization

A high degree of conjugal role segregation is found most commonly in the lower class, with intermediate degrees of segregation in the upper-lower and lower-middle class and an emphasis on joint role-organization in the upper-middle class. Along with this go typical concepts of how the husband and wife act in their roles. In the higher status groups there is heavy emphasis on outside activities, on involvements that can be viewed as bringing resources into the family (intellectual and artistic interests, social activity, etc.). This emphasis is relatively infrequent at the lower-middle class level and still less frequent at the upper-lower class level. Emphasis on outside activity, at least by the husband, is apparent at the lower class level but here these activities are viewed as potentially dangerous to the family, either from waste of income or because they are regarded as precursors of indiscretion by the husband.

All of this adds up to a strong emphasis in the middle class, and also among those of the upper-lower class who participate in the pattern of intermediate segregation, on the resolution of family difficulties by discussion, compromise and mutual accommodation. In contrast, relatively few lower class husbands and wives use such techniques. They accommodate instead to a pattern of a high degree of segregation and often to a pattern in which there is a good deal of dissatisfaction with the marriage on the part of both partners.

Sexual relations in marriage

We have tried to examine here some aspects of patterns of sexual gratification in marriage. Our goal has had to be modest because this was only one of many subjects in which we were interested and also because we were dealing with an area that can be probed only superficially unless a particular kind of rapport is developed in which the respondent becomes motivated to search his own feelings and memory with frankness and accuracy. (Kinsey and his collaborators seemed to achieve this rapport, although unfortunately they used their opportunity more to count than to understand.) However, given the relative paucity of non-clinical information on sexual relationships in marriage, we believe our data have considerable value and allow for a somewhat more dynamic understanding of marital sexuality than previous studies permit.

Respondents were given an opportunity to express their feelings about their sexual relationship in response to several different kinds of questions and they were encouraged to speak as freely and in as much detail as they wished. From the open-ended material which resulted, assessments were made of the level of sexual gratification that respondents seem to find in their marital relationship or at least to seek in it; also, certain specific attitudes and views about the relationship were noted. From this analysis it appears that the degree of sexual gratification varies quite markedly by social class, and in the lower class also by type of conjugal role-organization. Both men and women, but particularly women, more frequently find gratification in sexual relations in the middle class than in the lower class, and within the lower class, in relationships characterized by less segregated role-organizations. It also becomes apparent that in the less segregated relationships the husbands are more likely to know how their wives feel about sexual relationship, whether they find sex gratifying or not. Going along with this, wives in highly segregated relationships are much more likely to think of their husbands as inconsiderate of their feelings in connection with sex than are others.

Similarly, there is greater emphasis on purely "physical" gratifications in the lower class and among highly segregated couples and more emphasis on social-emotional gratifications in the middle class and among less segregated couples. There is some evidence that within the middle class the highest degree of interest in and value placed on sexual relationships occurs in families where there is also a high degree of emphasis on togetherness and a family-centered focus of activities. The more individualistically oriented upper-middle class couples seem much more concerned about placing sex "in perspective" with other meaningful activities.

Family size — preferences, norms and motives

Studies of ideal family size conducted over the past twenty-five years document an increasing focus on a moderate ideal of two to four children. As Ronald Freedman (1962) notes, the important question for research on family size becomes whether or not we can "explain the variations within this range by reference to a combination of social and psychological variables." While from the broad macroscopic focus of the demographer the concentration of over 90 per cent of choices for ideal family in the two-to-four-child range suggests a homogeneity of preference, the differentiation within that range suggests to the family sociologist important questions for research.*

In our sample there is a tendency for middle class Protestants and Catholics to offer smaller ideal family sizes than their lower class co-religionists; while there is some tendency for these same differentials to apply to the number of children the couples themselves want, the tendency is not nearly so strong. When people are asked whether they believe that there is a trend toward larger or smaller families, the reverse obtains. That is, middle class people tend to see a trend toward larger families while lower class people see a trend toward smaller families. This suggests that a good many lower class people are saying that what they want are small families within the range they believe to have been common in their group, while for middle class people, the ideal numbers are those that represent relatively larger families within the range they believe to have been characteristic of their group. The lower class respondents are suggesting greater prudence in the ideals they offer while the middle class respondents are suggesting greater affluence.

When one examines the rationales offered by respondents for large and small families it is possible to abstract one central norm about family size: *one should not have more chil-*

---

*As a methodological aside, it should be noted that the common practice of presenting family size data in the form of averages ("3.2 children") tends to obscure the fact that we are dealing with a very short scale of three numbers. For most purposes it probably makes more sense to treat this as a set of qualitative categories than as a continuous range. For example, to specify the increase in ideal size as from 3.0 in 1941 to 3.4 in 1955 obscures the fact that during that time the proportion of persons preferring four children doubled, the proportion preferring two children was halved, and the proportion preferring three children changed not at all. While an average takes less space on a page, this economy is hardly sufficient compensation for the relative paucity of information it carries. This is not simply a methodological issue. When one examines the way couples talk about the different sizes of families, one becomes aware that psychologically this is not a continuous distribution but a highly discontinuous one.

dren than one can support, but one should have as many children as one can afford. "Afford" is the operative term here, and men and women recognize that families vary in the number of children they can truly afford. While there is no hard and fast norm in our society which says that we should have two or three or four children, this should not be taken to mean that in this situation sanctions are not exercised by significant others or that internalized sanctions are not significant. Rather, the way people talk about their own family size and the family sizes of others suggests clearly that the thinking of husbands and wives about the number of children they should have is strongly influenced (albeit selectively) by normative considerations they have internalized as participants in the larger society.

Thus, there seems to be general agreement that to have fewer children than one can afford is an expression of selfishness, ill health, or neurotic weakness; to have more is an expression of poor judgement or lack of discipline. Implicit in the comments of the great majority of respondents is the idea that when people are able to have a large family, they want a large family. The good person does this. The person with moral failings stops short of the number he can afford in order to have something extra for himself or for his fewer children, and these extras connote selfishness in the parent and cause it in the child. The child gains from being a member of a larger family by being less spoiled, less selfish, more co-operative in giving, and he has more fun. The parent of a larger family gains from a greater chance to love and be loved, and he lives in a happier milieu. The "stingy" parent instead, lives with his small family according to a life plan that emphasizes goods for himself and his children, time and freedom for outside interests, and education.

Having a larger family, then, becomes a way of resisting materialism, a way of spreading the wealth and thus avoiding some of the evils people believe inhere in materialistic self-indulgence. Affording a given size of family is therefore only superficially conceptualized as an economic matter. Nonetheless, this is the most acceptable reason for not having more children, and people believe it is the major legitimate factor behind variations in preferred family size. Parents vary in the extent to which they perceive the question of "affording" in terms of short-term or long-term economic issues, the major long-term concern being that of the cost of educating children. It is interesting that there is not a larger class variation in this as a rationale for smaller families; the knowledge that the demand for educated workers is increasing seems very widespread, and at each class level the necessity for children staying in school longer tends to be picked up by people as an important rationale for desiring a smaller family.

A central problem for any given couple in arriving at an optimum family size is that of selfishness versus responsibility. It is interesting that having a large family is often described as a manifestation of irresponsibility. There is implicit here the notion that larger families can be very enjoyable but this is an enjoyment one cannot afford. However, less clearly verbalized than relatively straightforward financial concern are concerns about the psychic costs of having a large family. These tend to be poorly formulated; to admit that one could not handle a larger family tends to be taken as an admission of weakness, and to want only two children for this reason is thought to represent a kind of psychosocial hypochondriasis. There seems to be little clearly formulated conception of what children might gain in non-financial ways from growing up in a smaller family. It is the parents who gain in this area by having greater freedom to pursue their own interests, and this is in sharp contrast to the belief that both parents and children gain from the luxury of interpersonal pleasures and growth in a large family.

There seems to be a fairly widespread pattern of active discussion of family size, both in general and specifically in terms of one's own needs and desires. Only a small minority of those in our sample deny ever having discussed family size with anyone. The kinds of people with whom family size is discussed varies by social class; in somewhat simplified form, the following pattern emerges: At the lowest status level, the wife's mother and sometimes other females in her family form the core of those concerned with how many children the couple has, and the subject is casually discussed with relatively few others. At higher status levels, the members of the husband's family become more involved, and also friends outside the family are more often included in these discussions. Thus considerations of family size are interpersonally more complexly conditioned at higher than at lower status levels. Although the data in this study contain only very tentative leads to this process of interpersonal influence on testing and evaluating decisions concerning family size, the kinds of comments and justifications people offer for their own particular decisions suggest strongly that decisions about family size are not immune to the influence of both the extended family and the peer group.

We can make much more sense out of the functions of large and small families for middle class couples than we can for lower class couples because the former are more likely actually to have the number of the children they desire and no more. Thus, it is possible to compare with some confidence the manifest reasons these couples offer for their preferences, and to probe some of the deeper motivations involved by comparing these groups in terms of certain background social psychological characteristics. From the previous discussion of rationales offered for different family sizes, it should not come as a surprise that middle class couples who prefer larger families tend to be those who indicate a greater need to deny selfishness and to validate and symbolize their identity as larger and more moral persons. These people tend to see most clearly the interpersonal gains they can offer their children by providing them with a larger family and also to perceive for themselves the gains of enhanced self-esteem that come from thus denying themselves in order to be good parents. This is particularly true of men; the more manifest level of the functions of small and large families do not seem to differentiate the family size preferences of middle class women.

The functions of a small family are also more obvious at the manifest level for men than for women. Middle class men who want a smaller family seem to find gratification in thereby confirming their identities as sensible persons, as men who understand well the long-range interests of their children. At the same time, middle class men who want smaller families do not seem really to have much understanding of why other men might want larger families. In general, both men and women who want smaller families seem less involved with the whole question of family size; they are less likely to discuss questions of family size widely with others, either relatives or friends. Perhaps they feel somewhat out of step with the rest of the society, and try to minimize the divergence between their own minority views and those of the larger middle class world in which they live.

At the deeper lever of motives, our data provide some support for the hypotheses outlined by Hoffman and Wyatt (1960) concerning factors which differentiate couples preferring large and small families. The first of these hypotheses states that larger families are functional for resolving housewives' conflict over whether or not, and how, to be active in the world outside the home, either through a job or through other kinds of outside activities. Women who seek and find gratifying outside activities which are not anxiety producing tend to prefer smaller families, and those who do not find such activities tend to prefer larger ones. Conversely, women who find their homemaking responsibilities demanding and/or providing opportunities for creativity will tend to prefer smaller families. The second hypothesis has to do with the parent role. Here Hoffman and Wyatt note that an emphasis on the parent role can function to make up for a sense of lack of involvement in the homemaking role; activity as a parent can make up for the declining creativity that is provided by the homemaker role as housekeeping becomes more mechanized and prepackaged. By increasing the number of children they have, couples can feel they have an opportunity to practice both more fully and for a longer period of time a set of interpersonal skills which have become highly valued in our increasingly child-centered society. The anxiety which tends to accompany parental functioning may also tend to encourage larger families, since parents will seek to assuage their guilt over not doing a good job by having more children and hopefully doing a better job with the younger ones. Also, involvement with the very demanding routine of young children may serve to distract and to justify difficulties parents have in measuring up to their ideals of parental care and guidance for their older children.

We have seen that parents who want large families tend to emphasize the gains that children have by virtue of their contact with other children. Thus it would seem that one way of coping with the increased emphasis on good child-rearing practices is to see in the large family a child rearing gain per se; that is, to emphasize that each additional child contributes to the socialization of the others by helping to create an atmosphere that at once builds character and makes for fewer demands on the parents (since the children can make demands on each other). The large family serves to moderate the intensity with which parents take their child-rearing responsibilities by spreading it over more individuals. Parents are able to verbalize their belief that having a large number of children both increases the individuality of each child and brings about a desirable lower emotional involvement of the parent in the individual child.

The data in our study which seem to provide a test of these related hypotheses are of several kinds. First, we find that, as one would predict from the Hoffman-Wyatt hypothesis, middle class wives who describe themselves primarily in terms of their orientation to outside social and intellectual interests, or to their husbands as companions, tend overwhelmingly to prefer a small family, whereas those who describe themselves solely as orientated to their children tend

overwhelmingly to prefer large families. Those who emphasize both outside and home orientations most frequently
prefer medium families and next most frequently, large families. (This cannot be accounted for simply by differences in
family size at the time of the interview.) Similarly, one could
hypothesize that in the families in which there is emphasis on
joint role-organization the wife will tend not to orient herself
to a large family, whereas in those characterized by a relationship of intermediate segregation the wife will tend to look
to her children for a sense of deeper interpersonal involvement. This holds true in our data: wives who are in relationships of intermediate segregation overwhelmingly prefer
larger families, and those in joint relationships tend to prefer
small or medium sized families.

The Hoffman and Wyatt hypothesis suggests that women
who are particularly concerned with their responsibilities as
homemakers and parents will tend to prefer smaller families,
whereas those women who are particularly concerned about
their possible self-definition as egocentric or selfish will tend
on a compensatory basis to prefer large families. In our data,
a majority of those who think of their main "bad point" as
involving an inability to stand up to the pressures of their
roles (too nervous, anxious, depressed, or unenergetic) overwhelmingly prefer small or medium sized families, whereas
those who think of their main bad points as involving egocentricity, selfishness, and stubbornness tend to prefer larger
families. The fact that the majority are concerned with an
inability to measure up to the demands of their family roles
suggests that one should not overemphasize the extent to
which wives feel that their homemaking functions do not fully
involve them.

Third, Hoffman and Wyatt hypothesize that as more and
more individuals in modern society are characterized by
aloneness and alienation, one compensatory mechanism
adopted by couples has been that of having larger families,
thus providing themselves with a ready made primary group
to which husband and wife can retreat for meaningful inter-

personal relating. We have less relevant data here. While our data clearly indicate that Americans see the family as offering these possibilities, we are not able to test in any systematic way the extent to which those husbands and wives who prefer large families are particularly characterized by a tendency to be alienated. That is, we can say that compensation for alienation is a function which larger families serve for those who have them, but we cannot say that this is a differential motivation for desiring larger families. It may simply be a secondary gain.

Further, we can hypothesize a kind of curvilinear influence of alienation on fertility preferences. It would seem equally reasonable to believe that to the extent to which individuals become sharply alienated from the representations of value in their society, as they feel more isolated and cut off from a meaningful identity with the collectivity of which they are a part, they will be less interested in having children (indeed, perhaps less interested in marriage). As persons become more isolated, one would expect that they would also become more narcissistic and self-involved and less willing to cope with demanding interpersonal relationships. Perhaps the relationship between alienation and family size desires is curvilinear, in that individuals who are highly alienated will not want to become responsible for large families nor will individuals who are deeply integrated into a large network of significance. On the other hand, individuals who feel threatened by a tendency toward aloneness and alienation, but who are still hopeful about the possibilities of avoiding the pain of that state, may seek to do so by creating a meaningful primary group with a larger number of children. One finding in our data seems to bear on this point. We find that among a majority of couples for whom sexual relations are not very important to either partner, at least one partner wants a small family, whereas an overwhelming proportion of couples for whom sexual relations are very important to both partners want a medium sized or large family. We take this as confirmatory of the hypothesis about extreme alienation, since we believe that highly alienated individuals will not be able to establish marital sexual relations in which both partners attach a great deal of importance to these relations.

Contraception and family limitation

We have discussed contraceptive behavior in terms of generalized attitudes toward the possibility of planning a family, the discussions husband and wife have of this subject, the kinds of methods known and used and the effectiveness with which they are used, and finally, the attitudes which couples express toward different kinds of medical and family planning clinic approaches to contraceptive advice and prescription.

Several different approaches to the whole question of how one might plan a family and limit the number of children one has were evident in our data. Some couples approach this subject in a very planful and taken-for-granted way. They are interested in the technical aspects of contraception. They expect to be able to plan their families and they feel that they have developed routines that make it possible for them to do so. Other couples are hopeful on this score, but uncertain. They are not sure that what they are doing will work and their general attitude is one of involved and optimistic uncertainty—somewhat like the feelings the typical suburbanite often has about his lawn. Finally, there is an attitude that can be summarized as fatalistic—an attitude of relatively low optimism, a sense of (at most) going through the motions of family planning with a rather low confidence that one's abilities will suffice to achieve the desired goal and a tendency therefore, not to be particularly involved in the mechanisms of family planning. The first attitude, the planful one, seems by far the most common among middle class couples, particularly Protestants, and much less common among lower class couples, particularly those at the very bottom level. Whatever their particular knowledge of contraceptive methods or the strength of their personal desires to limit family size, couples at the lowest class level seem to show relatively little confidence that they will be able to make successful use of the methods known to them.

These patterns of attitude toward family planning in general, tend to go along with particular patterns of husband-wife discussion of contraception and family limitation. By and large, there was full discussion early in marriage among middle class Protestants. This was somewhat less characteristic of middle class Catholics, who tended to have only casual discussion of the subject, particularly since they expected to have large families and did not think it necessary to concern themselves with the problem of family planning and limitation until fairly far along in their child-bearing history. At this later phase, however, most middle class Catholics did begin to discuss family planning fully and seriously and to bring this subject more centrally into their marital planning. Within the lower class there was a strong tendency among Protestants and Catholics, Negroes and whites alike, to postpone full discussion of this as a marital task until fairly late in the couple's life together. It was much more common among lower-lower class couples not to discuss the subject more than casually, even after having had more children than either partner wished. As other researchers have noted (particularly Hill, Stycos, and Back, 1959) the resources for communication and co-operative decision-making in lower class families are often not up to the task of making and carrying out sensible decisions about contraception even when there is a desire for family limitation on the part of both partners.

Our data indicate a widespread knowledge of the existance of different contraceptive methods among all groups in the sample. Only among lower-lower class Catholic women are there more than 4 per cent of the respondents who are not able to name at least one contraceptive method. Although the number of methods of which individuals are aware varies rather markedly by social class, with middle class people able to name more methods than lower class people, it also seems

clear that even at the lower class level there exists the knowledge of one or two methods which have the capacity of
limiting conceptions. At the simplest level of knowledge,
then, even lower-lower class couples seem at least as well
equipped as were the higher status persons in Europe and
England at the time these latter groups began limiting their
families. One or the other of the two medically approved
methods of choice, the condom or the diaphragm, come
readily to mind for over 80 per cent of the men and women in
each of the subgroups in our sample.

It would be difficult to maintain, then, that anyone in our
sample does not effectively limit his family because of lack of
knowledge, if knowledge is construed in a purely intellectual
sense. If to this is added a social dimension (knowledge that
a method exists that other people use routinely and effectively, and in which, therefore, one may some confidence) or
a psychological dimension (knowledge that the method which
one knows to exist is emotionally acceptable and is in one's
means to manipulate successfully), then the matter appears in
a very different light. Construed in this way, however,
"knowledge" is hardly different from motivation and conviction about a method's appropriateness, and rational elements
take a decided back seat to more emotional and interpersonal
factors.

It is in this sense that people seem to assess their own
knowledge when asked how much they knew about contraception when they were married and how much they have
learned since. Middle class women are more likely to assess
their knowledge as adequate at marriage and to feel that they
have learned a good deal since, so that now they know a great
deal more about contraception and family limitation than they
need to know. The same is true of middle class men. In
sharp contrast, lower class women very often assess their
knowledge of contraception at marriage as low and they tend
to feel that they are only modestly well-informed even at
present. There is a strong tendency on the part of lower-lower
class respondents to assess their knowledge of methods as

something by itself, as not integrated either into their own sense of available technology or into their worlds. They know about methods but do not understand them, they seem to be saying. Their lack of understanding is not simply technical; it extends to the whole social process of planning a family with contraceptive methods. Upper-lower class men and women do not say they started marriage much better informed than men and women in the lower-lower class, but they feel they have learned more, even when this means only that they have learned a sense of *really* knowing something about the same methods whose names they knew earlier in marriage. The main thing they seem to have learned is to accept contraceptive methods as part of their world and to seek to master the technology that is involved.

Knowledge of contraceptive methods in the middle class, particularly among Protestants, seems to be pursued not only in terms of direct functions for the couple but also as a matter of interest. Thus middle class men and women are much more likely to learn about new methods that come on the market, even though they do not immediately adopt them. They seem also to be oriented toward trying to select the "best" method from among those available, rather than simply settling on an acceptable method. Thus, women who for many years have used and apparently been satisfied with the diaphragm shift to oral pills as they begin to get the idea that this is now the best method.

Middle and lower class people differ in the ways they think about the effectiveness of family planning. Middle class people tend to have high confidnece in some methods (condom, diaphragm, pills) and to have a low expectation of method failure. They seem to believe that most people have accidents either because they are too ignorant to use effective methods or because they do not use effective methods correctly. In other words, middle class people tend to differentiate methods rather sharply in terms of effectiveness and to differentiate users in terms of competence. In the lower class these distinctions are very much blurred. There is a greater tendency to see the more effective methods as subject to failure, and also a greater tendency to see the less effective ones as perhaps proving adequate "if you're lucky." There is a similar tendency not to see competence in using contraceptive methods as paying off, but rather to feel that one is always at the mercy of the method's inherent shortcomings. Thus lower class people are much more likely to blame the method, much less likely to blame the user. This is particularly true of the lower-lower class.

Within the lower class the choice of methods seems to some extent determined by the kind of conjugal role-relationship the couple has. Those in joint or intermediate relationships are much more likely to choose one of the effective feminine methods (diaphragm, pill, cream, or jelly alone) and those in highly segregated relationships are more likely to use one of the "folk methods" (douche, withdrawal, rhythm incorrectly understood). Approximately equal proportions of the two groups use the condom. Several factors seem to operate here. Couples in less segregated relationships are more confident about the success of family planning and therefore more likely to use an effective method. The choice of a feminine method (principally diaphragm) needs a good deal of support from the husband if the wife is to feel secure about what she is doing, and such support is available only to the wife in the less segregated relationship. She needs support to cope with the fears that she often has about the diaphragm and its mysterious functioning.

Effective contraceptive practice

The couples in our sample were categorized as either effective or ineffective contraceptive practitioners on the basis of their descriptions of the methods they used and the ways they used them. While this is a rough categorization, it does represent the typical practice of couples in the sample as they were able to report it to us. The reader should understand that some of the effective practitioners may on occasion "take a chance" but do not report this to us, instead indicating that they try to be regular about their use of a method. Ineffective practitioners on the other hand either use methods in ways that minimize their effectiveness (as with many of the lower class rhythm users), use no method at all, or indicate that their use of effective methods is sporadic. Overall, about half of the ineffectives in our sample use no method and the other half use a method but not in such a way that it is likely to prove effective. The latter is much more true of the lower class respondents in our sample; the former is primarily true of the middle class and of Catholics in all classes. Ineffective practice varies quite strikingly by social class, both before and after the birth of the last wanted child. In the latter case, 98 per cent of middle and upper-lower class Protestants are classified as effective as are 73 per cent of the comparable Catholics. At the other extreme only 13 per cent of lower-lower class Catholics and Negroes and 33 per cent of lower-lower class Protestants are classified as effectives. Among those who finally do become effective contracetptive pactitioners, there are systematic variations as to timing, with 96 per cent of the middle class becoming effective before the birth of the last wanted child and 44 per cent of lower-lower class Catholics and Negroes becoming effective only after the birth of an unwanted child.

We hypothesized that effective practice would be positively related to lesser segregation in the conjugal role-relationship, and this proves to be true, both before and after the birth of the last wanted child but particularly in the latter case. We take this relationship to indicate the importance of communication between the husband and wife and involvement by the husband in family issues. In the more segregated relationships it is much more common for the husband to regard the whole question of family planning as mainly his wife's business. While most of Stycos' (1962) argument about the shortcomings of the feminist and medical biases of traditional Planned Parenthood and Public Health approaches to family planning is convincing and solidly based in available evidence, his argument at times seems to substitute an equally unreasonable masculine bias. It seems likely that there are many areas of the world in which lower class sub-cultures are characterized by a low operating commitment by the husband to what goes on in his household, whatever formal norms of masculine-dominance may obtain. It would seem most useful to encourage family planning workers to tailor their approach to the particular patterns of conjugal role definition that exist in the groups they seek to serve, rather than to encourage on a blanket basis either a feminine or masculine emphasis.

We find also a positive relationship between effectiveness at contraception and the extent to which the wife indicates that she finds sexual relations with her husband gratifying. This relationship does not hold for Catholics but only for lower class white Protestants and Negroes. The relationship between sexual gratification and contraceptive effectiveness is a complex one and seems also related to the nature of the conjugal role-relationship. A highly segregated conjugal rela-tionship makes it difficult for couples to function in the close co-operation required both for mutually gratifying sexual relations and effective contraceptive practice. In this context, contraception tends to become a bone of contention in rela-tion to the wife's wish to avoid anything connected with sex, and her aversion to sexual relations is reinforced by her anx-iety about becoming pregnant coupled with the difficulties she experiences in doing anything effective to prevent it.

Correlations with effective and ineffective contracep-tive practice within the middle class are not easy to come by. First of all, both before and after the birth of the last wanted child, well over 90 per cent of the middle class Protestant couples were effective practitioners. This is not to say that these people may not have accidental pregnancies, but our method was not sufficiently refined to investigate accidents as opposed to the generalized habit of ineffective contraceptive practice. It would be interesting to study the kinds of couples who have accidents, particularly ones which result in more children than one or both partners wanted. A minority of middle class Catholics do continue ineffective contraceptive practice past the birth of the last wanted child, but we have not been able to determine what the difference is between those Catholics who do this and those who instead become regular practitioners of an effective method (including rhythm).

However, while the major variable of importance within the lower class — the conjugal role-relationship — does not seem to be related in the middle class to effective versus ineffective contraceptive practice, a variable concerning the sexual relationship of a couple is related to effective practice before the birth of the last wanted child for both Catholics and Protestants. Among couples in which husband and wife indicate equal levels of enjoyment of the sexual relationship, almost 90 per cent of the couples were also effective contraceptive practitioners, whereas among those couples in which one partner enjoyed sexual relations more than his spouse only about half of the couples were effective contraceptors. It seems possible that in relationships of unequal enjoyment there is a tension which reprercusses on contraceptive practice, either by affecting the kind of method which is acceptable to the couple, or by affecting the regularity of use. The latter seems the stronger possibility since the relationship holds for both Catholics and Protestants and therefore across a number of methods, including most particularly diaphragm, condom, and rhythm. It is also possible, of course, that among couples who find anxiety in their sexual relationship rather than security and comfort there may be a tendency to delay effective contraception in the unconscious hope that additional children will improve the relationship. Thus, there would be less emphasis on family planning and spacing of children through effective contraception.

Medical assistance for family limitation

For the greater part of history, family limitation and contraception have been only partly under the control of medicine. It is only in the past thirty or forty years that many couples have turned to physicians as the primary source for learning about contraceptive methods. With the development of the diaphragm, chemical methods of contraception, and lately the pill, the expertise of the physician has come to seem necessary if one is to have the most effective method available. We were interested, then, to see to what extent couples of different classes had availed themselves of medical counsel in connection with contraception. Almost all of the middle class Protestants had done so, but a third, or slightly more, of all the other groups had never discussed contraception with a physician. The use of Ob-Gyn specialists was concentrated in the middle class. Lower class whites were much more likely to use a general physician when they sought such advice, and lower-lower class Negroes were relatively more likely to receive such advice post-partum in a hospital. Within the lower class, Negro in the upper-lower class were most likely to use Ob-Gyn specialists. Planned Parenthood was most often used by Negroes, perhaps as a function of the location of clinics in Chicago where the majority of Negroes in the sample lived. The availability of medical counsel does not seem by itself strongly related to effectiveness of contraception practice, a finding which is not surprising considering that the condom is well known and available to anyone who wants to use it.

Among lower class whites the type of medical contact does not seem related to whether or not a couple is effective or ineffective. But among lower-lower class Negroes there is much more likelihood that effectives have sought out advice on an out-patient basis or gone to Planned Parenthood; ineffectives are much more likely to have been the more passive recipients of advice when the wife is in the hospital after the birth of a child. Our results suggest that this kind of post-partum advice, at least as it is given to Negroes in Cook County Hospital, has not been particularly useful. When lower class women discuss the medical contacts they have had with respect to contraception, it is obvious that the physician has a difficult problem with which to deal. The hurried advice that these lower-lower class Negro women say they received in the hospitals often was not sufficient to enable them to go further in adopting an effective method.

Since one or another kind of more assertive program for making contraception available to couples seems necessary, we sought to tap attitudes toward three different kinds of assertive family planning programs: (1) a greater assertiveness on the part of physicians in bringing up the subject with their women patients, (2) Planned Parenthood clinics, and (3) door-to-door family planning programs. In general the response to all three programs was quite positive. Middle and lower class, Protestant and Catholic, men and women seemed to be more favorably disposed toward medical assertiveness in this area than one might have thought.

Protestants almost unanimously agree that the physician should volunteer advice to his patients about family planning and limitation. This applies across class lines, but seems to be particularly important for lower class patients who more often indicate that they are too embarrassed to bring up the subject themselves and wish the physician would. In the lower class, Catholics do not differ from Protestants in their positive attitudes on this score, but among middle class Catholics views are more varied; almost all acknowledge that where the wife's health is involved the physician has a responsibility to discuss family limitation with her, and a substantial minority takes a more secular attitude and says that he should bring the subject up for whatever reasons he feels are adequate.

Most respondents indicate a positive but rather distant attitude toward the value of Planned Parenthood clinics. Middle class Protestants think they are a very good idea, but of course, not for them, since they have their own physicians.

A few middle class Catholics expressed strong hostility toward the idea of Planned Parenthood, and a similar number endorse the idea of the clinics heartily. The majority of Catholics indicate a conditional acceptance of the idea based on the notion that someone should help poor people plan their families, usually saying that such clinics are all right for people who have no religious objections to the idea of family limitation.

Within the lower class there are, then, very favorable attitudes toward the idea of Planned Parenthood clinics. Yet we know that few of the respondents have ever used these clinics. The particular conception that these lower class respondents have of the clinics seems to mitigate against their using them more fully. The most general formulation of these attitudes is that these people believe the organization is mainly for special problem cases, and they are reluctant to define themselves in this way. They believe that Planned Parenthood is for the very, very poor, or for those with very large families, or for people who are too ignorant to be able to figure things out on their own. The woman who has these feelings is reluctant to define herself in this way by going to the clinic.

Responses to the idea of a door-to-door family planning program were considerably more positive than had been expected. Middle class people generally thought that such a program would be useful since they believe that there are many women who need to limit their families and want to, but do not know how to do so. The responses on this score closely parallel those for attitudes toward Planned Parenthood except that, surprisingly, middle class Catholics are more often favorably disposed to the idea of a door-to-door program than they are to Planned Parenthood clincs. Apparently they feel more comfortable about a program which does not carry the "controversial" Planned Parenthood name. Lower class respondents indicate few misgivings about the door-to-door approach as prying or an invasion of privacy. Instead they suggest that women would feel more comfortable all the way around about learning about family planning in their homes rather than in the alien atmosphere of a clinic. We are not, of course, evaluating the effectiveness of a door-to-door program here; but our data do suggest that there would be little direct rejection of family planning workers who go into the community to seek clients.

Appendix A:
Role concepts and role difficulties

Chapter 2 concentrates on the patterns of family organization characteristic of each social class, and particularly on the degree of separateness in the ways husbands and wives go about conducting family business and enjoying their leisure time. Closely related to these aspects of the family as a social system (indeed, separable only for analytical purposes) are the conceptions that husbands and wives have of themselves as persons and as actors in their assigned family roles. Following Hess and Handel (1959:6–7), we consider the "images" each family member holds of himself and of others in the family as of central importance in understanding the ways in which they behave toward each other and the goals they seek to realize in family interaction:

> Living together, the individuals in a family each develop an image of what the other members are like. This image comprises the emotional meaning and significance which the other has for the member holding it. The concept of image is a mediating concept. Its reference extends into the personality and out into the interpersonal relationship. Referring to one person's emotionalized conception of another, an image is shaped by the personality both of the holder and of the object. The image emerges from the holder's past and bears the imprint of his experience, delimiting what versions of others are possible for him. It says something about him as a person. But it is also a cast into the future, providing the holder with direction in relating to and interacting with the object. While it represents the holder's needs and wishes, it also represents the object as a source of fulfilment.
>
> Each family member has some kind of image of every other member and of himself in relation to them. This image is compounded of realistic and idealized components in various proportions, and it may derive from the personalities of its holder

and its object also in various proportions. It draws from cultural values, role expectations, and the residue of the parents' experiences in their families of origin. One's image of another is the product of one's direct experience with the other and of evaluations of the other by third parties. From this experience, from evaluations of it and elaborations on it in fantasy, a conception of another person is developed, a conception which serves to direct and shape one's action to the other and which becomes a defining element of the interpersonal relationship. *An image of a person is one's definition of him as an object of one's own action or potential action.*

Social class and role concepts

Much of what husbands and wives think of themselves and their spouses has been implicit in the discussion of role-relationships in Chapter 2. That discussion, however, was necessarily rather abstract. We want to consider here the question of how men and women of each social class think about themselves and the others with whom they are in intimate contact. As has been apparent in the long interview excerpts given in Chapter 2, each respondent was asked to describe himself and his spouse "as a person" and to tell what sorts of things he was interested in, what his good and bad points were. The tables which follow present the kinds of appelations most often used by men and women in each social class. Tables A–1 and A–2 present data for the characterizations made of husbands, and Tables A–3 and A–4 for those made of wives.

We will discuss these tabulations in terms of three major areas that seem common to the characterizations men and women make, characterizations (1) as a spouse or parent, (2) as a particular kind of person apart from familial roles, and (3) in terms of possible shortcomings. Then we will examine in more detail that pattern characteristic of each social class.

CONCEPTION OF THE HUSBAND

Familial roles.—When asked how they view themselves as persons, men of all classes most commonly characterize themselves in terms of their family roles, although white lower-lower class men are less likely to do so than others. Mainly this means that men characterize themselves as "good fathers," as interested in their children, and somewhat less, as "good spouses." The same pattern appears when their wives speak of them, except that white lower-lower class wives seldom mention their husbands' parental role in describing them as persons (as would be expected, given the greater frequency of segregated role-relationships in this group). In general, wives more often than husbands describe the husband as a good spouse, suggesting the greater importance of this to the wife than to her husband; we will see that the same pattern appears when the wife is described. It should be noted that only one white lower-lower class wife characterized her husband in terms of how well he fulfills the role of spouse, as distinct from father.

Personal qualities.—The three characterizations of personal qualities tabulated in Table A–1—constructive, intellectual, and socially active—are those most commonly used to describe upper-middle class husbands and least commonly used to characterize white lower-lower class husbands. Upper-middle class men are most likely to call themselves constructive in their interpersonal relationships (understanding, considerate, helpful, trustworthy); white lower-lower class men are least likely to do so. When wives characterize their husbands, however, those in the white lower-lower class are joined by both lower classes of Negroes in their rare use of this designation. Just as wives are generally more likely than their spouses to say that the husband is a good spouse, they are more likely to say that he is a constructive person; This suggests that both of these characterizations are simply ways of saying that they are reasonably well-satisfied with the

TABLE A–1:
SOCIAL CLASS AND HUSBAND'S "GOOD POINTS"

| | White | | | | Negro | |
	UM	LM	UL	LL	UL	LL
Husband's conception of himself						
As a good family man	42%	57%	48%	30%	50%	44%
Specifically, as a husband	4	21	19	17	4	4
Specifically, as a father	42	50	48	26	50	44
As a constructive person	42	29	24	9	29	36
(understanding, considerate, kind, helpful, trustworthy)						
As intellectual	27	18	9	4	4	4
(artistic, cultured, interested in ideas)						
As socially active	31	18	10	4	17	8
(interested in people, active in groups, interested in parties, entertaining, etc.)						
Specifically, interested in people	23	11	5	4	17	4
Specifically, active in social affairs	4	4	–	–	4	4
Specifically, active only in PTA or church	4	7	5	–	–	–
N =	26	28	21	23	24	25
Wife's conception of her husband						
As a good family man	50%	64%	62%	21%	56%	47%
Specifically, as a husband	23	36	31	4	28	25
Specifically, as a father	42	46	62	21	44	39
As a constructive person	84	82	88	58	32	39
As intellectual	39	7	–	–	8	4
As socially active	23	39	4	4	4	7
Specifically, interested in people	15	32	4	4	–	–
Specifically, active in social affairs	12	7	–	–	–	–
Specifically, active only in PTA or church	4	7	–	–	4	7
N =	26	28	26	24	25	28

husband, that he is a "good man." Qualitatively, in the lower class "a constructive husband" seems most often to connote one that is not too demanding; less often implies a more active constructiveness.

Two kinds of descriptions seem characteristic of the middle class, particularly the upper-middle class: husbands are more often seen as having intellectual interests (reading, interests in art, in ideas, etc.) and as being active socially, in either formal or informal (recreational) groups. Lower-middle class wives seem most often to stress the husband's interest in people.

A comparison of the proportions of men characterizing themselves in terms of family roles and in terms of other personal qualities suggests that in the highest status group, family roles are less complete in defining the husband than in lower status groups. Within the middle class, particularly, this seems to distinguish the upper- from the lower-middle class husband. In contrast to both, white lower-lower class husbands are more likely to characterize themselves in negative terms only.

These results suggest that in the lower class the model of positive qualities for the husband is that he be a good family man (mainly a good parent) and that he be reasonably easy to get along with, not aggressive in his relationships to those with whom he lives. In the middle class, this model is also important, but in addition a man is also expected to show interests, intellectual or social or both, in the outside world, which will enrich the social and psychological resources for his family. Overall, the husband is characterized, by himself or his wife, as having intellectual or social interests in 73 per cent of the upper-middle class couples and 57 per cent of the lower-middle class couples.

Shortcomings.—The shortcomings shown in Table A–2 represent those mentioned by respondents which permit differentiation between classes; one other shortcoming, being critical and argumentative, is mentioned fairly often in all

TABLE A-2:
SOCIAL CLASS AND HUSBAND'S SHORTCOMINGS

	White				Negro	
	UM	LM	UL	LL	UL	LL
Husband's conception of himself						
Can not take pressure (gets depressed, lazy, nervous, uneasy, insecure, jumpy with spouse or children)*	35%	29%	5%	4%	25%	12%
Egocentric (selfish, stubborn, not properly attentive to others)†	39	46	14	26	13	—
Disloyal to family (stays away from home, drinks, gambles, chases women)‡	—	7	33	39	25	56
No bad points	19	29	29	35	33	32
N =	26	28	21	35	24	25
Wife's conception of her husband						
Can't take pressure§	23%	25%	15%	—	16%	7%
Egocentric ‖	42	43	19	13%	20	7
Disloyal to family#	—	7	8	29	12	32
No bad points**	19	11	39	33	40	46
N =	26	28	26	24	25	28
Husband or wife mentions that *husband is disloyal to the family*	—	11%	27%	62%	32%	61%

*MC *vs.* LC X² = 7.29   T = .22   P < . 01
†MC *vs.* LC X² = 14.83   T = .32   P < .0005
‡MC *vs.* LC X² = 20.18   T = .37   P < .0005
§MC *vs.* UL *vs.* LL X² = 7.15   df = 2   T = .18   P < .05
‖ MC *vs.* LC   X² = 13.89   T = .30 P < .005
#MC *vs.* UL *vs.* LL X² = 14.36   T = .30 P < .0005
**MC *vs.* LC   X² = 9.08   T = .24 P < .005

classes. Two kinds of shortcomings seem to stand out at the higher status levels and one in the lower-lower class.

In describing middle class husbands, husbands and wives agree that they often becoming disturbed over the pressure of responsibilities and the demands of others; they are moody, or lazy, or lack enough energy to do the things they should. Middle class husbands are also often described as egocentric (selfish, stubborn, and self-absorbed). In both cases, the middle class husbands and wives express their sensitivity to anything that disturbs the closeness of their conjugal relationship and emphasize the value they place on co-operation and willingness to meet each other's needs.

Lower class men and women are less sensitive to these failings in marital relations, perhaps because they do not involve the same threat in their more segregated conjugal relationships. In fact, many lower class men and women mention no husbandly shortcomings at all; this is especially true of the lower class wives and appears far more frequently than in our interviews with middle class couples. Whereas the latter are apparently quite sensitive to the threat of interpersonal difficulties, lower class women, except for the more extreme shortcomings discussed below, seem to feel that they have little to complain about (or little right to complain?).

Lower class men and their wives do however show considerable concern about the direct threat to the family which comes from behavior that keeps the husband away from home a great deal (a more direct kind of egocentricity than that which disturbs the middle class). Most commonly, the problem is that the husband not only goes out but drinks more than he, or his wife, feels he should. Much less often he is said to gamble or to chase women, although fear of the latter is probably in the back of the minds of a good many of the wives who complain. Curiously, not as many wives as husbands mention these shortcomings. Where the husband but not the wife mentions them, he seems to be trying to remind himself of his potential for disrupting family life; often he says that he tries to keep such behavior to a minimum. In some lower-lower class families, the separateness of husband and wife is such that the wife has given up worrying about such behavior as long as the husband does not bring his misbehavior into the home; he, on the other hand, still feels guilty about it. When either the husband's or the wife's mention of such behavior is considered, we see that this kind of shortcoming is mentioned by over 60 per cent of the lower-

lower class whites and Negroes, by about 30 per cent of those in the upper-lower class and by less than 10 per cent of the middle class couples. There is, of course, a wide range in the seriousness with which this behavior is regarded by husbands and wives, and in its frequency. In some cases the shortcoming is that of an occasional "bender" or a little too frequent "night out with the boys," in others the problem is of a more recurrent nature. In either case, these results point up the sense of basic threat to conjugal solidarity that permeates lower class marital life, though most wives resolve to stick it out unless the situation is intolerable (cf. Rainwater, Coleman, and Handel, 1959: 72–74); and most husbands resolve to hold such behavior to the minimum to which they feel their hard work and everyday frustrations entitle them.

In summary, then, the assets and liabilities ascribed to husbands suggest the following: upper-middle class husbands are seen as significantly involved in the outside world of ideas and people, and as struggling to have enough energy and resistance to narcissistic demands to function well in their jointly organized conjugal roles; lower-middle class husbands are seen in much the same light, but as more narrowly focused on family life; upper-lower class husbands are seen to be even more heavily weighted in terms of their familial function and their general willingness to be easy-going and unaggressive; lower-lower class husbands are more often seen in a negative light, less often as functioning well in a familial role or as constructive in their orientations to others.

CONCEPTION OF THE WIFE

Familial roles. — Wives are seen primarily in terms of their familial roles, more so than husbands, and generally among all classes. However, upper-middle and white lower-lower class wives deviate from this pattern. The latter are much less likely than other groups to characterize themselves positively; they say fewer and more varied things about themselves, reflecting less consensus in their conceptions of themselves.

Upper-middle class women, in contrast, de-emphasize their familial functions but reflect a good deal of similarity in the other things they say about themselves. The conception of the wife as mother is most striking among whites in the lower-middle class, where there is high consensus between husbands and wives. Among lower-lower class Negroes, there is similar consensus on the wife as "mother," but the emphasis on the husband as "father" is not as strong. These results suggest that lower-lower class Negroes see their lives, in spite of segregated role-relationships, as pivoting more on a mother-dominated home than do whites of the same class. However lower-lower class Negro and white women do not differ in ignoring almost completely the role of wife in characterizing themselves.

Personal qualities. — The most striking difference in the conceptions men and women hold of wives has to do with social activities outside the home. Upper-middle class women are seen, both by themselves and their husbands, as very interested in social contacts outside the home, most particularly in formal and informal social gatherings (clubs, parties, organizations, etc.). Thus, in 70 per cent of the upper-middle class couples one partner or the other mentions the wife's interests in such gatherings, compared to only 25 per cent of the lower-middle class couples. The difference between classes is characterizing the wife as having intellectual interests is not as large; the comparable figures are 70 per cent and 53 per cent. Middle class women stand out, then, as viewing themselves, and being viewed by their husbands, as intrested in the world beyond the family more often than are lower class woman. The major difference between the upper- and lower-middle class wife lies in the former's more active penetration into the outside world; lower-middle class wives express such interests by passive consumption of intellectual materials at home.

Lower-lower class Negro wives are also actively involved outside the home; in about 40 per cent of the couples either the husband or the wife comments on her activity in her church, compared to about 20 per cent of Negro upper-lower

TABLE A-3:
SOCIAL CLASS AND WIFE'S "GOOD POINTS"

	White				Negro	
	UM	LM	UL	LL	UL	LL
Wife's conception of herself						
As a good family person	39%	75%	54%	33%	56%	68%
Specifically, as a wife	19	14	19	4	16	7
Specifically, as a mother	39	71	54	33	52	64
As a constructive person	42	43	23	21	24	29
As an intellectual	42	29	8	4	8	8
As socially active	75	43	12	4	12	43
Specifically, interested in people	35	39	8	4	4	14
Specifically, active in social affairs	42	11	—	—	—	—
Specifically, active only in PTA or church	8	11	4	—	8	29
N =	26	28	26	24	25	28
Husband's conception of his wife						
As a good family person	69%	75%	62%	74%	75%	76%
Specifically, as a wife	54	47	33	44	29	16
Specifically, as a mother	69	68	52	70	67	76
As a constructive person	46	46	38	39	50	48
As an intellectual	58	36	—	4	4	—
As socially active	46	22	19	13	25	24
Specifically, interested in people	23	18	14	9	8	—
Specifically, active in social affairs	39	4	—	—	4	—
Specifically, active only in PTA or church	—	—	5	4	13	24
N =	26	28	21	23	24	25

class couples and less than 10 per cent of the four white groups. In the context of a segregated role-relationship this means that the wife seeks on her own the gratifications which the church provides.

Shortcomings. — Wives' shortcomings seem much the same as husbands', except that wives are not criticized, by themselves or by their husbands, for the kind of disloyal behavior so common among lower class husbands. (Again,

Table A–4 does not present the shortcomings which do not differentiate among classes; principally these describe the wife as unnecessarily critical, argumentative, or aggressive.) We note that in the middle class two kinds of shortcomings are common: (1) the wife has difficulty living up to the demands of her role and reacts by feeling depressed, unenergetic or nervous, and (2) she is sometimes too concerned with her own needs and wishes to be properly attentive to the others in the family. By and large, lower class husbands and wives do not worry about these shortcomings. As noted for the husbands, both of these concerns reflect the greater sensitivity of middle class persons involved in less segregated role-relationships to interpersonal threats to conjugal closeness. It is interesting in this connection that the proportion of lower-lower class Negroes who describe no shortcomings is very high, as if to indicate that if nothing is radically wrong in the wife's role-performance, there is no reason to complain.

In summary, the positive and negative qualities attributed to wives suggest the following overall pattern of class dif-

TABLE A–4:
SOCIAL CLASS AND WIFE'S SHORTCOMINGS

	White				Negro	
	UM	LM	UL	LL	UL	LL
Wife's conception of herself						
Can't take pressure*	27%	29%	23%	8%	20%	4%
Egocentric†	23	36	8	4	8	–
No bad points	12	7	19	21	28	57
N =	26	28	26	24	25	28
Husband's conception of his wife						
Can not take pressure‡	31%	32%	10%	9%	21%	8%
Egocentric§	19	36	4	4	25	4
No bad points	31	25	33	39	25	68
N =	26	28	21	23	24	25

*$X^2 = 7.63$ T = .22   P < .01   (MC and UL *vs.* LL)
†$X^2 = 16.79$ T = .33   P < .0005   (MC *vs.* LC)
‡$X^2 = 7.28$ T = .22   P < .01   (MC *vs.* LC)
§$X^2 = 6.97$ T = .22   P < .01   (MC *vs.* LC)

ferences. The upper-middle class wife likes to think of herself as a person with wider horizons than "just a housewife"; her husband shares these values but emphasizes her role as wife and mother much more strongly than she does (or than she emphasizes his roles as husband and father). Although the lower-middle class wife has similar interests, she and her husband emphasize her family roles more than is true for the upper-middle class wife; values of intellectuality and social activity take a subordinate place in the conception of the wife's role. Both middle class groups are concerned about the threats to the martial relationship posed by difficulty in meeting complex responsibilities and becoming self-involved. The lower class wife is seen as even more confined to family roles. The white lower-lower class wife has relatively little to say about herself and does not seem as proud of herself as a mother as do other lower class women. Lower-lower class Negro wives are more often seen, by themselves and by their husbands, as busy in church activities, which provide them an opportunity for valuable involvement that does not seem as available to their white lower-lower class counterparts. Lower class wives are relatively more preoccupied (in the sense that other shortcomings do not occur to them) with aggressiveness and "shrewishness" in their relations with the family, and their husbands share this perception when they offer any criticisms at all.

Conjugal role-organization and role concepts

We have found that within each class couples differ in the degree to which their role activities and the values that go with them are handled separately or jointly. It should follow, then, that couples with similar patterns of role-organization will have similar self-concepts and concepts of spouse, and that these concepts will differ from those held by couples having other patterns of role-organization. Ideally, we would like to examine such differences with each class, but our sample is not large enough to allow this. Therefore, we will deal separately only with the middle class as a whole and the lower class as a whole.

ROLE CONCEPTS IN THE MIDDLE CLASS

Slightly over 60 per cent of the middle class couples were judged to be characterized by jointly organized role-relationships, and the remainder by relationships of inter-mediate segregation. Almost all of the upper-middle class couples show the former pattern; the lower-middle class shows a slight preponderance of the latter pattern. The differences to be discussed below (Tables A – 5 and A – 6) are derived from the total middle class sample, but in all cases jointly or-ganized lower-middle class couples show almost identical pat-terns with those for the upper-middle class, indicating that the results are not materially affected by the differences between the two classes in distribution of role-relationship types.

From Table A – 5 it is apparent that couples in joint role-relationships think of themselves and their spouses more often as interested in the world outside the family than do those in relationships of intermediate segregation. This means, for one thing, that the differences noted in the previous section of this chapter between upper-middle and lower-middle class couples in the frequency with which such in-terests are mentioned are due to the fact that in the latter group there are more couples in intermediate relationships; lower-middle class couples in jointly organized relationships are equally interested in social activities and intellectual pur-suits. This does not mean that couples in jointly organized relationships do not mention family roles when they describe themselves, but that they add to such roles activities and interests in the outside world as well.

It may seem strange that the jointly organized, presuma-bly were closely-knit, couples emphasize outside roles and activities more than the couples with relationships of inter-mediate segregation. Such interests tend to have a centrifugal

TABLE A–5:
CONJUGAL ROLE-ORGANIZATION AND CONCEPT OF HUS-
BAND AND WIFE: MIDDLE CLASS COUPLES

	Social, Career, or Intellectual Interests Only	Both Family and other Interest	Family Interests Only	Constructive Personal Qualities Only
Conception of husband				
By husband				
Joint relationship (35)	43%	34%	23%	—
Intermediate relationship (18)*	28	22	50	—
By His Wife				
Joint relationship (35)	23	37	20	20%
Intermediate relationship (19)	5	11	47	37
Conception of wife				
By Wife				
Joint relationship (32)*	34	50	16	—
Intermediate relationship (16)	25	19	56	—
By Husband				
Joint relationship (35)	37	43	20	—
Intermediate relationship (19)	16	31	53	—

*Total N is 35 for joint relationships and 19 for intermediate relationships; smaller numbers due to no responses.

First two and last two columns combined for each chi-square test.
Conception of husband—by husband: $X^2 = 4.61$ $T = .29$ $P < .05$
                        by wife: $X^2 = 7.90$ $T = .38$ $P < .01$
Conception of wife—by wife: $X^2 = 6.56$ $T = .37$ $P < .025$
                        by husband: $X^2 = 4.61$ $T = .29$ $P < .05$

influence on the couple's relationship since their interests may not be the same – the wife in club activities, the husband in political or sports activities, etc. However, even if couples in joint role-relationships do not participate jointly in outside activities, they expect each to listen to the other with interest and sympathy. In so far as separate interests are incorporated in group activities, each partner is expected to treat the other's friends (and their spouses) as his friends.

Couples in intermediate relationships more often adhere to the heavily familial model outlined for the lower-middle class in the previous section. This is particularly apparent with regard to whether the wife is active socially in formal or informal groups. In almost 60 per cent of the jointly organized couples, either the husband or the wife mentions that the latter is socially active in this way,compared to only 21 per cent of the couples with relationships of intermediate segregation. For such families, social activities, if pursued with real interest, are probably regarded as a threat to the family, since the couple does not expect to share outside experiences and integrate them into the relationship between husband and wife. For these couples, outside interests can be regarded as a foreign body introduced into the family-centered relationship; in the jointly organized families they occur in the context of a more adult-centered relationship.

The shortcomings characteristic of each role-relationship type are consonant with the differences in the more positive qualities ascribed to each spouse. The problems described by husbands and wives in joint relationships have to do with living up to the demands of their particular kind of relationship. Those mentioned by individuals in relationships of intermediate segregation are concerned with centrifugal tendencies in the relationship.

In each case, however, the problems of the husband and wife are somewhat different. In Table A–6 we see that over 80 per cent of the men in joint relationships are concerned that they may be too aggressive and demanding in their relations with their families; those in intermediate relationships are mainly concerned about their tendencies to withdraw from the family through activities of personal interest only, to deny the legitimacy of the family's demands ("selfishness"), or to be passively self-absorbed, hence unresponsive to the demands of wife or children ("laziness"). The former tendencies have to do with overactive participation in family life; the latter have to do instead with an inability to live up to familistic participation values. As noted in the previous sec-

TABLE A–6:
CONJUGAL ROLE-SEGREGATION AND SHORTCOMINGS OF
HUSBAND AND WIFE: MIDDLE CLASS COUPLES

	Joint Relationship *(35)*	*Intermediate Relationship* *(19)*
Husband's Conception of Self		
Problems of assertiveness in relations with family	58%	27%
Problems of retreat and self-involvement *vis a vis* family	19	60
Both	23	13
Number mentioning shortcomings	(26)	(15)
Wife's Conception of Self		
Cannot take pressure does not have enough energy	56%	18%
Egocentric and demanding	31	64
Both	13	18
Number mentioning shortcomings	(32)	(17)

tion, the more highly segregated pattern of staying away from home is morally unacceptable to middle class couples; hence the husband's withdrawal tends to be within the home (TV, "naps," hobbies) rather than outside it.

Wives in jointly organized relationships are concerned about the difficulty of coping with the complexities of their role activities; they complain that they become nervous, depressed, anxious or insecure. Sometimes they refer to uncertainties about themselves in their socially active roles ("I feel insecure when I don't know people well"), more often they react to the complex demands of husband, children, and valued non-family interests. Wives in intermediate relationships less often complain about these things and more often reproach themselves for resistance to living up to the legitimate demands of the family, for wanting their own way too often, for "selfishness." Thus, both husbands and wives in these intermediate relationships are concerned about the threat that egocentricity poses to the relationship, but the wives more often attribute an aggressive quality to this (they do not want to feel they "hen-peck" their husbands) and the husbands more often attribute a passive, withdrawn quality to their resistance. The wives' responses suggest they are aware of their central — perhaps superior — position in the family organization, and are concerned that they not take advantage of it to the detriment of family "democracy."

In the jointly organized relationships the wife's concern seems not that she will be too authoritative but that she will not be able to integrate her own individualistic interests with the assertive participation of the husband in the family, as well as with the complex demands of the children. Another way of interpreting this pattern of shortcomings is to say that the husbands are concerned about being too roughly "masculine" and the wives about being too weakly "feminine." Both tend to underemphasize sex differences in this kind of relationship, but they cannot avoid the reality of a sexual identity that has more to it than the conjugal ideology of equality. Furthermore, the husbands must be assertive and authoritative in their work if they are to maintain their status; they probably do not find it easy not to behave similarly at home.

In summary: Within the middle class, jointly organized couples tend to emphasize as positive attributes outside interests for both husbands and wives. Husbands are concerned that they may be too assertive and authoritative in their relations with their families, and wives are concerned that they cannot integrate the complex demands imposed by their roles in the family and their activities as individualistically-oriented modern women. Couples in intermediate relationships tend to concentrate on family role activities as descriptive of their positive attributes. The shortcomings husbands in this group perceive have to do with tendencies to behave narcissistically or to withdraw from the family; their wives are also concerned about egocentricity, but in addition, are concerned that they may be too aggressive or dominant in the relationship and thus deny the husband the proper exercise of his voice in family life.

ROLE CONCEPTS IN THE LOWER CLASS

In the lower class there are sharp differences in the ways couples in intermediate and in segregated role-relationships describe the husband, but differences in the wife's self-concept are less clearcut, and there are few differences in the descriptions husbands give of their wives.

In couples with segregated relationships, both husband and wife often describe the husband as oriented away from the family, most often by staying away from home, or drinking, gambling, or "playing around" (Table A-7). Sometimes the husband is also "interested in the family,"often he is not. In contrast, the couples in intermediate relationships most often either mention only family interests on the part of the husband (this is true of 72 per cent of the women) or, while not mentioning family characteristics, describe the husband as a self-controlled, constructive-minded person. These tendencies are present in both the upper-lower and lower-lower class, and to about the same degrees. Whites in segregated relationships are less likely than are Negroes to ascribe to the husband any family interests (even in combination with disloyalty), but in both groups there is a difference between the two role-organization types in the frequency with which family interests are attributed to the husband. As we have noted before, there is a sense of harshness about the separation between husbands and wives among lower class whites in segregated relationships that is not so prevalent among similarly situated Negroes.

White and Negro wives of the two role-organization types, describe themselves differently. The Negro wives are more likely to mention outside interests (principally their church activities) in segregated than in intermediate relationshps. The result is that in intermediate relationships there is more exclusive emphasis on the family functions of wives, a pattern comparable to that for husbands. Among white wives, outside interests are seldom mentioned. Instead, wives in intermediate relationships tend to emphasize their concern

TABLE A–7:
CONJUGAL ROLE-ORGANIZATION AND CONCEPT OF SELF AND SPOUSE:
LOWER CLASS WHITES AND NEGROES

	Spouse Making Characterization			
	Husband's Concept		*Wife's Concept*	
Spouse Being Characterized	*Intermediate Relationship* (42)	*Segregated Relationship* (51)	*Intermediate Relationship* (49)	*Segregated Relationship* (51)
Husband				
Disloyal to family	21%*	55%	14%*	57%
Not disloyal, outside interests, other	10*	20	14*	20
	48†	17	72	23
Interested in family only	21†	8	–	–
Self-controlled and moral only	(X^2 = 15.81 T = .41		(X^2 = 21.23 T = .46	
	P < .0005)		P < .0005)	
Wife				
Positive characteristics of white wife			N = (25)	N = (25)
Interested in children			48%	16%
Other home interests only			28*	48
Non-family qualities only			24*	36
			(X^2 = 4.50 T = .30	
			P < .05)	
Positive characteristics of Negro wife			N = (25)	N = (29)
Outside interests			16%	62%
Family interest only	NO Significant Differences		60*	28
Other constructive qualities			24*	10
			(X^2 = 10.21 T = .43	
			P < .005)	
Shortcomings of white wife			N = (25)	N = (25)
Has difficulties doing her job			30	52
Is too assertive			40%*	12%
Both			20*	12
No shortcomings			16	24
			(X^2 [without NR] = 4.91	
			T = .31 P < .05)	

*, †Combined for analysis.

with children and "family" generally, and wives in segregated relationships tend to emphasize instead either homemaking ("I'm a good cook," "I keep my house clean," "I sew well") or non-family qualities that suggest, sometimes defensively, that they are "good persons" ("I try to get along with people," "I mind my own business," "I don't drink or smoke"). The family-centered quality of the self-descriptions of wives in intermediate relationships is, thus, clear for both whites and Negroes; white women in this group talk about their children and the more segregated wives do not; Negro wives in this group speak only of family activities and the more segregated wives add personal interests in church and other outside activities.

With respect to shortcomings, white wives in intermediate relationships are rather like their lower-middle class counterparts in their concern about their assertiveness in relating to their families. They believe they become angry too quickly, are too strict, want things too much their own way, etc. Wives in more segregated relationships are concerned more about failure in their roles than about aggressiveness. This superficially resembles the attitude of middle class wives in jointly organized families, but these lower class wives emphasize more specifically their failings as homemakers than their difficulties in integrating the demands of others with their own wishes and desires. The lower class women worry about their failure to measure up to the minimum standards of the housewife's job rather than to the more varied standards that preoccupy the middle class housewife. Their sense of depression or lack of energy seems to have to do more with a feeling of pointlessness and barrenness in life than with a feeling of inadequecy about fulfilling the complex role-ideal which preoccupies the middle class woman in joint relationship.

In summary, lower class husbands and wives in intermediate relationships describe themselves and each other as more family-centered than do couples with segregated relationships. The separateness of the latter is particularly apparent in the frequent characterization of the husband as either being disloyal to the family or having many legitimate outside interests. Negro wives also speak of outside activities, especially the church; among white wives the emphasis shifts to more impersonal homemaking chores or to a description of the self as well-meaning without specific reference to family.

Marital difficulties

What kind of difficulties do couples in different social classes feel they have had to cope with in maintaining their families? Respondents were asked to discuss the problems and difficulties of their marriages and how they had felt about and coped with these problems. The responses are helpful both in understanding the challenges couples in different social classes have to deal with as they act out their instrumental and expressive family roles and in throwing light on the concerns and anxieties which preoccupy these groups.

The marriage problems described can be fairly readily categorized. Table A-8 presents a tabulation of the main types of problems mentioned by the men and women in our sample. Two common types have to do with (1) conflict of one kind or another between the husband and wife and (2) financial difficulties. It is apparent that women generally are more likely to mention husband-wife difficulties and men somewhat more likely to mention financial problems. The proportion of men mentioning difficulties with their wives varies from class to class; lower-middle class whites and upper-lower class Negroes mention such difficulties most often. Among men, financial problems are more likely to be mentioned the lower the man's social status, but among women, Negroes are less likely to mention such problems than their white lower class counterparts, suggesting that Negro women take such difficulties more for granted.

In-law problems (usually in the early period of marriage)

TABLE A-8:
SOCIAL CLASS AND FAMILY PROBLEMS

	White				Negro	
	UM	LM	UL	LL	UL	LL
Men N =	30	30	38	47	24	27
Interpersonal problems						
Husband-wife	33%	57%	29%	30%	58%	22%
In-law difficulties	20	13	16	15	4	—
Family size problems	3	3	—	4	4	—
Other problems						
Money and job instability	20	40	58	66	54	59
Illnesses	20	10	18	30	8	7
Husband's slow-starting career	13	17	—	2	—	4
None	23	13	8	13	8	29
Women N =	30	29	46	48	24	28
Interpersonal problems						
Husband-wife difficulties	57%	52%	37%	50%	63%	47%
In-law difficulties	20	21	17	13	—	11
Family size problems	7	3	2	15	8	11
Other problems						
Money and job instability	33	38	65	56	42	43
Illnesses	17	17	20	28	4	8
None	13	10	11	8	13	18

seem equally prevalent among whites of all classes, but Negroes almost never mention them. Family size problems (too many children, too close together, etc.) are not often mentioned, but over 10 per cent of the lower-lower class women do refer to them. Illnesses in the family come up in all classes, although slightly more often in the white lower-lower group. References to illness often involve the costs of medical care more than the threat of the illness itself. This is especially true in the lower class.

One type of marital difficulty occurs only for the middle class. About 15 per cent of the men refer to the problem of getting started in their careers. They speak of marriage before finishing school or when just getting started in work, as making their relationships with their wives more complicated and difficult than they would otherwise have been.

The two main types of problem, husband-wife and financial, can both be subdivided into two major subcategories. In each case, some of the problems are regarded as common, to be expected, readily surmounted with sense and good will; others are regarded as threatening to the integrity of the marriage, as leading toward breakup or serious deprivation. Table A-9 presents the division into "more" and "less serious" problems for the husband-wife difficulties that men and women mention.

Into the less serious category go those problems which in-

TABLE A-9:
SOCIAL CLASS AND HUSBAND-WIFE DIFFICULTIES MENTIONED AS PROBLEMS IN MARRIAGE

		Problems of Adjusting to Each Other	Disruptive Problems Leading to Separateness	No such Problems Mentioned
Men				
White				
Upper-middle	(30)	33%	—	67%
Lower-middle	(30)	47	10%	43
Upper-lower	(38)	16	13	71
Lower-lower	(47)	9	21	70
Negro				
Upper-lower	(24)	42	17	41
Lower-lower	(27)	7	15	78
Women				
White				
Upper-middle	(30)	57%	—	43%
Lower-middle	(29)	45	7%	48
Upper-lower	(46)	30	7	63
Lower-lower	(48)	13	38	49
Negro				
Upper-lower	(24)	42	21	37
Lower-lower	(28)	18	29	53

Men: $X^2 = 25.61$ df = 10   T = .20   P < .005
Women: $X^2 = 34.45$ df = 10   T = .23   P < .005

volve the difficulties husbands and wives experience in adjusting to each other, learning to understand each other, coming to a consensus on family tasks like child-rearing, the wife's working, sexual relations, etc. These are problems, in short, of getting together.

The more serious problems have to do with a centrifugal tendency in the relationship, problems of incompatibility ("we just don't seem to have anything in common any more") or, more commonly, of the husband's tendency to disregard his marital responsibilities by staying away from home, gambling, drinking heavily, or (infrequently mentioned) being unfaithful. These problems are more disruptive since they increase separateness in the relationship. They are, in short, problems of drifting apart.

Both men and women in the middle class are more likely to mention problems of "getting together" and less likely to mention more serious interpersonal stresses in their relationships. This is in keeping with the emphasis middle class couples place on the importance of getting along well, of coming to common understanding, of sharing, etc. This is not to say that lower class couples do not have similar problems, but they are less sensitized to such concerns because their value system does not place the same emphasis on the importance of coming to rational, commonly understood, mutually acceptable ways of dealing with life together. Upper-lower class Negroes seem in this respect to have more in common with lower-middle than with upper-lower class whites. We will note at other points that Negro upper-lower class couples seem in some ways more interpersonally oriented than comparable whites.

The other type of serious problem, in which the husband is regarded as "disloyal" to the family or the partners are drifting apart, is more common at the lower, particularly the lower-lower, class level and women are more likely to mention this than are men. Although lower-lower class men are more likely to mention "disloyal" behavior when asked about their "bad points" than their wives are to characterize their husbands in this way, the wives seem more often to take such behavior as a real threat to the family than do the husbands. In this respect, lower class men (with the exception of Negro men in the upper-lower class) seem least sensitive to interpersonal issues in their relations with their wives; they tend, instead, to concentrate on financial and job problems as threats.

The problems of income can also be subdivided into those of managing an adequate income and those where either there is a sense of real deprivation or, more commonly, where income is uncertain and inadequate because of lack of continuity in the husband's work. Table A – 10 presents this breakdown for men and women in the various social classes.

TABLE A – 10:
SOCIAL CLASS AND FINANCIAL DIFFICULTIES MENTIONED
AS PROBLEMS IN MARRIAGE

		Problems of Living on Income, Managing a Budget	Serious Financial Problems, Job Instability, Unemployment	No Such Problems Mentioned
Men				
White				
Upper-middle	(30)	17%	3%	80%
Lower-middle	(30)	33	7	60
Upper-lower	(38)	24	37	39
Lower-lower	(47)	21	45	34
Negro				
Upper-lower	(24)	42	13	45
Lower-lower	(27)	22	37	41
Women				
White				
Upper-middle	(30)	33%	–	67%
Lower-middle	(29)	31	7%	62
Upper-lower	(46)	39	26	35
Lower-lower	(48)	22	33	44
Negro				
Upper-lower	(24)	29	13	58
Lower-lower	(27)	21	21	58

Men: $X^2 = 29.51$ df $= 10$ T $= .21$ P $< .005$
Women: $X^2 = 18.70$ df (MC combined) $= 8$ T $= .18$ P $< .025$

Generally, middle class people are less likely to mention such problems than are those in the lower classes, as would be expected, and when they do refer to them, their emphasis is on the problem of not being able to have all the things one wants rather than on economic insecurity. Apparently very few middle class couples have ever experienced anything they regarded as a serious economic threat to the integrity of their marriage (and, rather curiously, they are joined in this by the upper-lower class Negroes who seem to often have trouble making ends meet but do not feel seriously threatened). Lower-lower class people, particularly the husbands, have frequently felt buffetted by the labor market or seriously deprived by incomes that cannot be stretched to provide what they regard as the minimum amenities of life. Sometimes this experience has come only once; the couple speaks of concern lest it happen again and with relief that "things are better now." But for a good many of the lower-lower class there is a sense of constant deprivation, of things not being likely to get better or quite likely to get worse. As was apparent in chapters 4 and 5 in connection with reasons offered for why couples might want small families, such feelings of economic vulnerability are often strongly preoccupying when lower-lower class people think about their responsibilities and their future. It is interesting, on the other hand, that so few lower-lower class Negro women mention such problems, since many in our sample have husbands whose earning power is very low and uncertain and others are living on public assistance payments that seem inadequate for their large families. These women seem to take their poverty for granted; they feel they do the best they can under the circumstances and seem unaware of the possibility of a better life — an awareness that is necessary if they are to see their situation as a "problem" rather than as "the way life is."

In the lower, but not the middle, class the degree of seriousness of any given problem is related to the degree of conjugal role-segregation that characterizes the couple. Table A–11 presents this tabulation on the basis of problems men-

TABLE A–11:
CONJUGAL ROLE-ORGANIZATION AND FAMILY PROBLEMS:
LOWER, CLASS COUPLES

	Joint and Intermediate Organization (44)	Highly Segregated (54)
Husband-Wife		
Interpersonal problems*		
Problems of adjustment	46%	13%
Disruptive problems	11	41
No such problems	43	46
Money or job problems†		
Living on income,		
managing a budget	43%	20%
Serious financial		
difficulty, job insta-		
bility, unemployment	27	56
No such problems	30	24

*$X^2 = 14.71$ $df = 2$ $T = .33$ $P < .001$
†$X^2 = 7.29$ $df = 2$ $T = .23$ $P < .05$

tioned by either husband or wife. A detailed examination of the data indicates that in each class and race group (upper-lower whites and Negroes, lower-lower whites and Negroes) the more serious problems are manifested more frequently in those couples with segregated role-relationships.

Those in less segregated role-relationships are most likely to mention problems of adjustment to each other; those in segregated relationships are most likely to mention disruptive behavior in marital relations. As has been noted above, one of the difficulties in segregated relationships is that husband and wife may become increasingly separate in their lives to the point that one (usually the wife) feels that the relationship itself is threatened by the other placing outside interests above those of the family as a whole. Sometimes this is a current problem for the family, with the husband creating anxiety by spending time away from home; the wife often is more concerned about the money he spends than about his absence per se. In other cases, the problem is believed to have been solved; the husband stays home now, does not drink and run around, but the wife still expresses concern that he may backslide if things do not go to his liking at home or if things go badly with his employment.

The fact that those in less segregated relationships are more likely to emphasize problems of interpersonal adjustment is to be expected. These problems arise because of an effort to make the marital tie closer and more solid. The couples recognize that this is not easy, that there must be give-and-take, and that in the process there is likely to be some disturbance. Often these problems are said to have been already solved by good will, understanding, and tolerance on both sides. The husband or wife will express pride that together they were able to achieve a mutually satisfactory resolution; they view their success in weathering these storms as proof of the strength of their relationship and of their love for each other. The problem was not only a problem but also an opportunity to reinforce their relationship by working through their disagreements or difficulties.

While different kinds of marital problems can be regarded as expressions of (and as defining) the kind of role-relationship a couple has, the different kinds of economic problems characteristic of the two polar role-organization types can be a cause or an effect or both. In any case, it is clear that couples in the more segregated relationships are more likely to have serious problems of economic insecurity and instability, and not only because such couples are more often of the lower-lower class. To some extent, these problems are an expression of the life style characteristic of the group; that is, both segregated role-organization and econimic insecurity are part of the lower class life situation. But in addition, some financial problems arise out of the segregated relationship; husband and wife do not consult each other and plan together; each acts separately, and they overspend and accumulate debts, which, in turn, can lead to loss of the husband's job when his employer is asked to garnishee his wages. More commonly, poverty and economic insecurity deepen the separation of husband and wife by lessening the respect of the wife for her husband and encouraging the husband to pursue his own interests as compensation for his sad lot in life and as a way of defending himself against feelings of impotence as a man and as provider for his family. (cf., Davis, 1946:84 – 106).

Appendix B
Interview Guide

Date: _____ City: _____
Interviewer: _____ R.'s Name: _____
                                              White: _____
Time began: _____ Age: ____ RL: _____ Negro: _____
Time ended: _____ SC: _____
Write-up: _____ COMMENTS ON INTERVIEW SITUATION:

BOTH FORMS:

a. Last grade completed in school? _____ (IF COLLEGE, NAME): _____ Field studied in college, degrees? _____

b. Describe your job for me, what do you do, what is the job called, where is it, what kind of a business, what's it like, etc.?

c. Does your income come from an hourly wage, a salary, fees, profits, or what?

d. Father's occupation and education? _____

e. What clubs and organizations, church groups or get-together groups do you belong to, how active are you in them, what do those groups do?

f. (What is respondent's religious background in childhood and present affiliation and participation in church?)

g. What about family background—where grew up, parent's background, how many generations in this country, where immigrant ancestors come from?

h. What is the family's total income? How much from husband, how much from wife? From children? Is it better or worse than it has been in the past?

i. How many rooms in home? _____ What are they? _____

Describe the block R. lives on, or the area if not block. What are the houses and apartment buildings like, what feelings does the block give, you, what kinds of people live on the block, etc.?

Describe the exterior of the home — what is it, what does it look like, what kind of feeling does it give you, how old does it look, what is the yard, if any, like?

What about the interior of the home? Describe the living room, or other rooms if you didn't see it — what does it look like, what is the furniture like, describe any pictures, what is the window treatment, the floor, etc.?

Briefly describe the physical appearance of the respondent, the way he was dressed, his manner, appearance — add anything you feel might help in adding to our picture of R.

What was his approach to the interview? Describe how he acted.

WIFE'S FORM:

1. When were you married (month and year)? _____
   Is this your first marriage? _____ (IF NOT): When did your first marriage begin? _____ When did it end? _____
   How did it end (death or divorce)? _____ Were any children born in that marriage, and if so, how many? _____

2. How many children have you had (in this marriage)? _____
   FOR EACH CHILD ASK THE QUESTIONS BELOW AND INDICATE THE ANSWERS IN THE COLUMN FOR EACH CHILD. PUT THE NAME AT THE TOP OF THE COLUMN STARTING ON THE LEFT WITH THE FIRST CHILD. (BE SURE RESPONDENT INCLUDES CHILDREN BORN BUT NOW DECEASED, AND IN THE PROPER ORDER OF BIRTH. IF RESPONDENT HAS HAD MORE THAN SIX CHILDREN, CONTINUE ON OTHER SIDE OF PAGE.) [See form on p. 332.]

HUSBAND'S FORM:

First, let's get some of the main facts about your family:

1. On your job, do you work during the daytime, at night; does your work take you away from home often, etc.? (THAT IS, PROBE FOR DEVIATIONS FROM CONVENTIONAL 9 TO 5 WORK PATTERN.)

2. When were you married (month and year)? _____ Is this your first marriage? _____ (IF NOT) When did your first

Name	First	Second	Third	Fourth	Fifth	Sixth
Month and year of birth						
Sex (M or F)						
Now living with couple (yes/no)						
Date of death if deceased						
DO NOT WRITE HERE						

marriage begin? _____ When did it end? _____
How did it end (death or divorce)? _____ Were any
children born in that marriage, and if so, how many? _____

BOTH FORMS:

1. Do you expect to have more children?_____ (IF YES)
   How many do you think you might have?_____

   Is wife pregnant now? _____

2. (IF ANSWER TO Q. 1 IS "NO", OR "UNCERTAIN", OR
   "YES, IF WE CAN" OR IF R. SAYS A CHILD MAY BE
   ADOPTED, ASK: Do you have any reason to believe that you
   and your wife could not have another child if you wanted? _____
   (IF YES): PROBE FOR DISCUSSION AS TO WHY R.
   BELIEVES THEY CANNOT HAVE MORE CHILDREN.
   RECORD ANSWERS BELOW. THEN IF R. SEEMS CER-
   TAIN THEY CANNOT HAVE CHILDREN AND SAYS A
   PHYSICIAN HAS VERIFIED THAT THERE IS SOME
   PHYSICAL INCAPACITY, DISCONTINUE THE INTER-
   VIEW, AND *DO NOT* INTERVIEW THE SPOUSE.

3. Would you like to have a child within the next year? (IF WIFE IS PREGNANT, ASK): Would you like to have a child within 18 months of the birth of this child? _____

4. Now, we've got the main facts about your marriage and your children; let's talk more generally. Tell me something about your family, about the important things in your married life since you were married, and so on. (PROBE FOR FULL DISCUSSION, INDICATE PROBES.)

5. How are the decisions made in your family? Who makes what kinds of decisions? (PROBE FOR WHO IS THE MAIN DECISION-MAKER, WHO MAKES THE DECISIONS IN THE AREA OF MONEY, OF THE CHILDREN, OF RECREATION, ETC.)

6. And what are the main duties you have as a husband/wife, and the one's your husband/wife, has as a husband/wife? (PROBE FOR DISCUSSION OF THIS PARTICULAR COUPLE'S DIFFERENT DUTIES.)

7. Tell me something about your husband/wife, (WAIT FOR RESPONSE BEFORE PROBING.) How would you describe him/her as a person? What sorts of things is he/she interested in? What are his/her good points? What are *his/her bad points*?

8. And what about yourself? (WAIT FOR RESPONSE BEFORE PROBING.) What are you like, what are you interested in, what do you do, what are your good points, what are your bad points?

9. How do you think your husband/wife feels about you and how you behave in the family?

10. (WHERE APPROPRIATE): And what about your child/children, what do you think are the main ideas he/she/they have about you? (PROBE FOR DETAILS.)

11. Every family has some problems and difficulties. Tell me about some that you had early in your married life? (PROBE FOR WHAT HAPPENED, WHY IT HAPPENED, AND HOW IT ALL CAME OUT.)

And what about some problems or difficulties you've had later in your married life? (AGAIN, PROBE FOR WHAT HAP-

PENED, WHY IT HAPPENED, AND HOW IT ALL CAME OUT.)

12. Now, let's change the subject a little. What do you think is the ideal number of children for the average American family? _____ Why that number?

    (IF R. SAYS *3* IS IDEAL, ASK): Suppose you had to choose between *two* and *four* as the ideal number, which would it be? ___

13. Early in your married life, did you think about how many children you might have? (DISCUSS)

14. How many children did you think you would like to have then? _____. Did you and your husband/wife talk about that much then? (DISCUSS)

15. What about now, how many children do you want? Why do you think that is a good number, why not fewer, why not more? (DISCUSS)

16. What about your husband/wife, how does he/she feel about the number of children you might have? Do you discuss this much between you, or is it something you never talk about? (PROBE FOR GOOD DISCUSSION.)

17. Many people say that the amount of income you have is important in determining the number of children. But, families with much the same income want different numbers of children—some want one, some two, some three, some four, some five or six. Why do you suppose that families with the same income may still have different ideas about the desirable number of children? (PROBE FOR GOOD DISCUSSION.)

18. What are the main things about your children in the way you feel about them, the pleasure and difficulties of having them and so on. (PROBE FOR DISCUSSION.)

19. And how would this be different if you end up with more children, say two more, than the _____ (NUMBER FROM Q. 14) that you want?

20. And how would it be different if you ended up with fewer children than the _____ (NUMBER FROM Q. 14) that you want?

21. Who besides you and your husband/wife are interested enough and close enough to you to be concerned about how many children you have? How would they feel if you had fewer children? If you had more children than _____?

22. With whom have you discussed the question of the number of children a couple has, and how many is enough or too many? What sorts of ideas do these others have and why do you suppose they feel that way?

23. From your own feelings, and from what you've heard other people say about having children, what do you think are the main reasons a man/woman wants more than one or two children, what are the main satisfactions he/she gets from a larger family?

24. People's preferences for a particular number of children may change from time to time. How do you think most people's preferences have changed in the last 25 years, do people want larger or smaller families than then, and why do you suppose that is so? (PROBE FOR GOOD DISCUSSION.)

25. We've talked quite a bit about the number of children people want, what about the time between them? How important do you think it is to plan the spacing between children—what length of time do you think is best, and how much should parents try to make sure that there is that much time between children? (DISCUSS WELL.)

26. Now, what about the different ways people can use to keep from getting pregnant—what methods do you know of? (PROBE FOR RECALL OF AS MANY METHODS AS POSSIBLE, LIST IN ORDER OF MENTION AND *INDICATE YOUR PROBES.*)

27. How much did you know about this when you first got married? Where had you learned what you knew? (PROBE WELL.)

28. And how have you learned the things about how people keep from getting pregnant that you have found out since your marriage? (PROBE FOR WHEN, WHO, WHAT.)

29. Now, can you tell me as fully as possible what your understanding is of how a woman gets pregnant? (PROBE FOR UNDER-

STANDING OF BIOLOGY OF REPRODUCTION AND INDICATE YOUR PROBES–BE SURE TO USE R.'S EXACT WORDS.)

30. What do you think are the main things a couple needs to think about when they consider doing something to keep the wife from getting pregnant?

31. After your marriage, but before you had your first child, did you do anything to keep from having a baby? _____. (IF YES): What and what were your experiences with the method(s); (IF NO): Why not, was it considered and how did both partners feel about this. (*BE SURE TO GET NAME OF METHOD(S)*.)

32. After your first child, but before your second, did you do anything? (PROBE AS ABOVE FOR EITHER *YES* OR *NO* ANSWERS–IF R. ONLY HAS ONE CHILD, SIMPLY CONTINUE TO PROBE FOR FULLER DISCUSSION OF THE COUPLE'S EXPERIENCE, OR LACK OF IT, WITH CONTRACETPION.)

33. And how about since your second child? (AGAIN, PROBE FOR FULL DISCUSSION OF THE COUPLE'S EXPER-IENCE WITH AND FEELINGS ABOUT CONTRACEP-TIVE METHODS. BE SURE TO FIND OUT IF ANY METHODS WERE USED BETWEEN EACH PREG-NANCY, FOR HOW LONG, AND HOW THE COUPLE FELT ABOUT IT.)

34. In general, who do you think should have the main respon-sibility for seeing to it that something is done to keep the wife from getting pregnant? _____. How is it with you and your husband/wife? Why do you feel it's his/her/both's responsibility?

35. INTERVIEWER: BELOW ARE LISTED MOST OF THE CONTRACEPTIVE METHODS IN USE TODAY. FOR EACH ONE THAT THE RESPONDENT HAS MEN-TIONED, EITHER AS HAVING HEARD OF OR USED, ASK ABOUT R.'S UNDERSTANDING ABOUT HOW IT WORKS, WHAT MAKES IT EFFECTIVE OR NOT, AND HOW R. WOULD FEEL ABOUT USING THAT METHOD. IF R. HAS NOT MENTIONED THE METHOD, ASK IF HE/SHE HAS EVER HEARD OF IT. IF SO, INQUIRE AS

ABOVE: IF NOT, ASK WHAT R. THINKS THE METHOD
MIGHT BE LIKE. INDICATE BY AN *X* WHICH CATE-
GORY OF KNOWLEDGE R. FALLS IN.

			prompted	never
CONDOM OR RUBBER:	heard__	used__	recall____	heard__
			prompted	never
DIAPHRAGM WITH			prompted	never
JELLY:	heard__	used__	recall____	heard__
WITHDRAWAL (OR			prompted	never
"PULLING IT OUT"):	heard__	used__	recall____	heard__
RHYTHM METHOD			prompted	never
(OR SAFE PERIOD):	heard__	used__	recall____	heard__
			prompted	never
DOUCHE:	heard__	used__	recall____	heard__
JELLY OR CREAM WITH-			prompted	never
OUT DIAPHRAGM:	heard__	used__	recall____	heard__
			prompted	never
SUPPOSITORIES:	heard__	used__	recall____	heard__
PILL THE WOMAN TAKES			prompted	never
ORALLY 24 DAYS A				
MONTH	heard__	used__	recall____	heard__

36. Have you ever discussed with a doctor any of these methods to
keep from getting pregnant? (IF YES, PROBE FOR A RE-
PORT ON WHEN, WHERE, HOW OF THE DISCUSSION
AND BE SURE TO GET WHAT KIND OF AN MD – GP,
OBSTETRICIAN, GYNECOLOGIST, ETC. IF NO, PROBE
FOR WHY NOT AND HOW R. WOULD FEEL ABOUT
THE DISCUSSION.)

37. When you've been in the hospital with a baby, has anyone ever
discussed this with you, a nurse or someone like that? (PROBE
FOR DETAILS.)

38. Some doctors don't discuss contraception with women unless
the woman herself brings it up, even though they feel she needs
to learn about it. What do you think of that? (PROBE FOR
PROS AND CONS OF THIS ATTITUDE AND FOR THE
OTHER – THAT IS, THAT THE MD SHOULD BRING
UP THE SUBJECT.)

39. In most cities there are clinics, the Planned Parenthood clinics, where people can get advice on birth control. Have you ever heard of these, and what do you think about these clinics, or the idea in general? (PROBE)

40. Some people say that for those who don't know about methods of limiting their families, and therefore have more children than they want or can afford, a health agency like Planned Parenthood should have a program of sending a medical worker into poorer neighborhoods and go door-to-door to talk to women about this problem, and help them to find a method for limiting their families if they want. What do you think of that? (DISCUSS)

41. It is difficult for doctors and medical workers to understand all they need to know about family planning and birth control without knowing more about people's sexual knowledge and experience. So, can you tell me about what you knew about sexual relations when you got married? Where did you learn this (parents, friends, reading material, etc.)? How did you feel about this part of marriage then?

42. And how was it just after you got married, how were your sexual relations then, and how did you feel about it? (PROBE FOR SATISFACTIONS, PROBLEMS, CHANGES IN ATTITUDE, ETC.)

43. What have been the main changes in your sexual relations since that time? (PROBE FOR DISCUSSION.)

44. About how often do you and your husband/wife have sexual relations? _____ (IF R. SAYS 3 TIMES A WEEK, SAY): Well, it's probably not exactly 3 times a week, would you say that you average slightly fewer or slightly more than than 3 times a week? _____.

45. Would you like to have intercourse more often or less often? And how about your husband/wife _____? Tell me more about that (PROBE FOR DISCUSSION AROUND THE TWO ANSWERS.)

46. How would you compare your and your husband/wife's feelings about your sexual relations? (PROBE FOR SIMILARITIES AND DIFFERENCES.)

47. What would you say are the main satisfactions you get from sexual relations? (PROBE FOR POSITIVES AND NEGATIVES, IF R. SAYS SHE GETS NO SATISFACTION.)

48. And what about your husband/wife, what are the main satisfactions he/she gets from sexual relations? (AGAIN, PROBE POSITIVES AND NEGATIVES.)

49. When you have intercourse, do you (does your wife) always or sometimes or never have an orgasm ("come")? (PROBE FOR DISCUSSION OF THIS, TRYING TO GET SOME NOTION OF FREQUENCY AND OF WHAT A WOMAN'S ORGASM MEANS TO THEM.)

50. How about your husband (you) does he (do you) always have the same kind of satisfaction, or does it change from time-to-time? (PROBE FOR HOW AND WHY OF VARIATION.)

51. Overall, how important would you say sexual relations are for your marriage, how important to you, how important to your husband/wife? (PROBE FOR DISCUSSION.)

References Cited

Banks, Joseph A.
1954. *Prosperity and Parenthood: A Study of Family Planning among the Victorian Middle Classes.* London: Routledge & Kegan Paul, Ltd.

Bell, Norman W., and Ezra F. Vogel
1960. *A Modern Introduction to the Family.* New York: Free Press.

Blake, Judith
1961. *Family Structure in Jamacia: The social context of reproduction.* New York: The Free Press of Glencoe, Inc.

Blood, Robert O., Jr.
1960. *Husbands and Wives: The Dynamics of Married Living.* New York: Free Press.

Bogue, Donald J.
1962. "Some Tentative Recommendations for a 'Sociologically Correct' Family Planning Communication and Motivation Program in India," in Clyde V. Kiser, *Research in Family Planning.* Princeton: Princeton University Press.

Bossard, J. H. S.
1956. *The Large Family System.* Philadelphia: University of Pennsylvania Press.

Bott, Elizabeth
1957. *Family and Social Network.* London: Tavistock Publications.

Coolidge, Susannah
1960. "Population vs. People," *Population Bulletin*, October.

Davis, Allison
1946. "The motivations of the under-privileged worker," in William D. Whyte (ed.), *Industry and Society.* New York: McGraw-Hill Book Company, Inc.

Davis, Allison, Burleigh B. Gardner and Mary R. Gardner
1941. *Deep South: A Social Anthropological Study of Caste and Class.* Chicago: University of Chicago Press.

Davis, Kingsley, and Judith Blake
1956. "Social structure and fertility, an Analytic Framework," *Economic Development and Cultural Change*, Vol. 4, No. 3, pp. 211–35.

Freedman, Deborah S., Ronald Freedman, and P. K. Whelpton
1960. "Size of Family and Preference for Children of Each Sex," *American Journal of Sociology*, LXVI, No. 2, pp. 141–46.

Freedman, Ronald, G. Baumert, and M. Bolte
1959. "Expected Family Size and Family Size Values in West Germany," *Population Studies*, November, pp. 136–50.

Freedman, Ronald, P. K. Whelpton, and Arthur A. Campbell
1959. *Family Planning, Sterility and Population Growth.* New York: McGraw-Hill Book Company, Inc.

Gans, Herbert J.
  1962. *Urban Villagers.* New York: The Free Press of Glencoe, Inc.
Glass, D. V.
  1962. "Family Limitation in Europe: A Survey of Recent Studies," in Clyde V. Kiser, *Research in Family Planning.* Princeton: Princeton University Press.
Goffman, Erving
  1961. *Encounters: Two Studies in the Sociology of Interaction.* Indianapolis: Bobbs-Merrill Company, Inc.
Hagood, Margaret J.
  1941. *Statistics for Sociologists.* New York: Henry Holt.
Handel, Gerald, and Lee Rainwater
  1964. "Persistence and Change in Workingclass Life Style," in Arthur B. Shostak and William Gomberg (eds.), *Blue-Collar World.* New Jersey: Prentice-Hall, Inc.
Hess, Robert D., and Gerald Handel
  Family Worlds. Chicago: The University of Chicago Press.
Hill, Rueben, J. M. Stycos, and Kurt Back
  1959 *The Family and Population Control.* Chapel Hill: University of North Carolina Press.
Hoffman, Lois W., and Frederick Wyatt
  1960. "Social Change and Motivations for Having Larger Families: Some Theoretical Considerations," *Merrill-Palmer Quarterly,* Vol. 6, pp. 235–44.
Kiser, Clyde V.
  1962. "The Indianapolis Study of Social and Psychological Factors Affecting Fertility," in Clyde V. Kiser (ed.), *Research in Family Planning.* Princeton: Princeton University Press.
Lenski, Gerhard
  1961. *The Religious Factor.* New York: Doubleday & Co.
Pearson, E. S., and H. O. Hartley
  1958. *Biometrika Tables for Statisticians:* Vol. I Cambridge University Press.
Population Reference Bulletin
  1960. October.
Rainwater, Lee
  1960. *And The Poor Get Children,* Chicago: Quadrangle Books.
Rainwater, Lee, and Gerald Handel
  1964. "Changing Family Roles in the Working Class." in Arthur B. Shostak and William Gomberg (eds.), *Blue-Collar World.* New Jersey: Prentice-Hall, Inc.
Rainwater, Lee, Gerald Handel, and Richard P. Colemen
  1959. *Workingman's Wife: Her Personality, World and Life Style.* New York: Oceana Publications.

Tabah, Leon, and Raul Samuel
  1962. "Preliminary Findings of a Survey on Fertility and Attitudes toward Family Formation in Santiago, Chile," in Clyde V. Kiser (ed.), *Research in Family Planning*. Princeton: Princeton University Press.
Westoff, Charles F. *et al.*
  1961. *Family Growth in Metropolitan America*. Princeton: Princeton University Press.
Yaukey, David
  1961. *Fertility Differences in a Modernizing Country*. Princeton: Princeton University Press.

Index

"Accidents," as factor in determining family size; *see* Fate
American Medical Association, 244

Back, Kurt, 120, 290, 341
Banks, Joseph A., 25, 340
Baumert, G., 120, 340
Bell, Norman W., 29, 340
Birth control; *see* Contraception, Family limitation
Blake, Judith, 25, 118, 120, 340
Blood, Robert O., Jr., 41n., 45n., 46, 340
Bogue, Donald J., 120, 340
Bolte, M., 120, 340
Bossard, J. H. S., 340
Bott, Elizabeth, 29, 46–47, 340

Campbell, Arthur A., 118–20, 162, 216, 340
Children, ideal number of; *see* Family size, ideals; Family size, norms; Family size, preference
Coitus interruptus; *see* Contraception, methods of, withdrawal
Coleman, Richard P., 41, 308, 341
Condom; *see* Contraception, methods of
Conjugal role organization, by social class, 278–79
Conjugal role relationship
   definition of
      intermediate, 31
      joint, 30
      segregated, 30
Contraception
   attitudes toward, 219–24, 289–90
      by religion, 220–22, 290
      by social class, 219, 225, 289–90
   and attitudes toward sexual relations, 16, 223, 226, 239–43
   choice of, and conjugal role organization, 225–26, 293
   effectiveness of, 227, 293–300